MW01295144

"Revival—or even more, the longing for revival—has been central throughout American Christian history. But what is meant by revival? Robert Caldwell's well-researched and exceedingly evenhanded book explains clearly what leaders of the American First and Second Great Awakenings taught concerning conversion, free will, the Holy Spirit, and how to interpret Scripture. He also explores with rare sensitivity what they assumed in their revival theologies. The result is a book rich in historical insight but also practical in guiding believers today in thinking about this vitally important matter."

Mark Noll, author of *The Rise of Evangelicalism*

"*Theologies of the American Revivalists* should be a valuable resource for scholars, evangelists, and laypeople. It provides clear accounts of the various understandings of evangelical conversion from the days when proponents of revival thought carefully about and debated such matters."

George M. Marsden, author of *Jonathan Edwards: A Life* and *C. S. Lewis's Mere Christianity*

"How can we explain the transformation of American revivalism between Edwards and Finney? Why did Americans move from eighteenth-century convictions about the bondage of the will to nineteenth-century confidence in the will's freedom? What drove the transformation of American theology from systematic constructs to common-sense approaches? Caldwell's study provides new answers to these important questions. It is an immensely helpful work of historical theology that is well researched and clearly written. Recommended for all students of American religion and theology."

Gerald R. McDermott, Beeson Divinity School

"Conversion experiences and narratives have long been central to evangelical identity, but the doctrines undergirding them are seldom understood with much clarity by their subjects, let alone most others. In this evenhanded history of theologies of revival from the time of George Whitefield to that of Charles Grandison Finney, Robert Caldwell helps us out. He supplies what we need to understand our own experiences, those of converts in churches with different doctrinal perspectives, and the engine of the evangelical movement itself. Everyone interested in American church history, evangelicalism, or the history of revival and evangelistic methods will want to read this reliable, comprehensive, and fair-minded book."

Douglas A. Sweeney, Trinity Evangelical Divinity School

"Since it entered the English language in 1820, the term *revivalist* has come to be used generically. Like a one-size-fits-all shoe, the designation has been deemed equally applicable to every evangelistic preacher from Whitefield to Moody, from Edwards to Graham. But these awakeners were not just so many duplicates. The strength of Robert Caldwell's *Theologies of the American Revivalists* is that it helps us see that there were distinguishable ideas of Christian revival in circulation prior to the Great Awakening, that the Great Awakening immediately spawned competing theologies of revival, and that the early nineteenth century's Second Awakening spawned still more. This is now the go-to volume for those wanting to trace these developments and to understand their bearing on our time."

Kenneth Stewart, professor of theological studies, Covenant College, Lookout Mountain, GA, author of *Ten Myths About Calvinism*

"Robert W. Caldwell's *Theologies of the American Revivalists* offers an illuminating and authoritative review of how leading American revivalists, from Jonathan Edwards to Charles Finney, grappled with issues such as the nature of gospel preaching, conversion, and sanctification. I recommend it highly."

Thomas S. Kidd, distinguished professor of history, Baylor University

"In this one volume, Robert Caldwell has carefully traced the fascinating story of revival through an event-filled century of change. Dependent on primary sources and freshly locating figures from Fuller to Finney, this is important theology presented by an even-handed guide."

Mark Dever, pastor of Capitol Hill Baptist Church, president of 9Marks.org

"Robert Caldwell offers a sophisticated and thought-provoking analysis of revivalist theology, rooted in the peculiarities of Jonathan Edwards's Reformed and evangelical theology, but developing and bearing fruit in ways that at times were flatly contradictory to Reformed doctrine. Linking Finney to post-Edwardsean theologians like Hopkins, Caldwell's monograph will stimulate scholarly discussion on a topic important both for the history of theology and the practice of the modern church."

Joel R. Beeke, president of Puritan Reformed Theological Seminary, Grand Rapids, Michigan

THEOLOGIES

OF THE

AMERICAN

REVIVALISTS

From **WHITEFIELD** *to* **FINNEY**

ROBERT W. CALDWELL III

IVP Academic

An imprint of InterVarsity Press
Downers Grove, Illinois

InterVarsity Press
P.O. Box 1400, Downers Grove, IL 60515-1426
ivpress.com
email@ivpress.com

InterVarsity Press® is the book-publishing division of InterVarsity Christian Fellowship/USA®, a movement of students and faculty active on campus at hundreds of universities, colleges, and schools of nursing in the United States of America, and a member movement of the International Fellowship of Evangelical Students. For information about local and regional activities, visit intervarsity.org.

All Scripture quotations, unless otherwise indicated, are taken from the King James Version, KJV.

Cover design: David Fassett
Interior design: Daniel van Loon
Images: Hugh Bridport / Kennedy & Lucas Lithography / Library of Congress

ISBN 978-0-8308-5164-5 (print)
ISBN 978-0-8308-9178-8 (digital)

Printed in the United States of America ∞

Library of Congress Cataloging-in-Publication Data
A catalog record for this book is available from the Library of Congress.

P 25 24 23 22 21 20 19 18 17 16 15 14 13 12 11 10 9 8 7 6 5 4 3 2 1

Y 38 37 36 35 34 33 32 31 30 29 28 27 26 25 24 23 22 21 20 19 18 17

Lovingly dedicated to my two daughters,

Audrey Grace Caldwell and Natalie Ann Caldwell

3 John 4

CONTENTS

ABBREVIATIONS

CEM   *The Connecticut Evangelical Magazine*

MMM   *Massachusetts Missionary Magazine*

WJE   Works of Jonathan Edwards

INTRODUCTION

IN SPRING 1806, sixteen-year-old Ann Hasseltine found herself in the midst of spiritual turmoil. "I often used to weep, when hearing the minister, and others, press the importance of improving the present favorable season, to obtain an interest in Christ, lest we should have to say, *The harvest is past, the summer is ended, and we are not saved.*" Her town of Bradford, Massachusetts, a small rural village north of Boston, was experiencing a revival, and Ann greatly desired to be found among the converted. Having spent several years in worldly pursuits ("balls," "parties of pleasure," "innocent amusements") interspersed with halfhearted religious concern, she was now ready to give serious attention to Christianity. "The Spirit of God was now evidently operating in my mind; I lost all relish for amusements; felt melancholy and dejected; and the solemn truth, that I must obtain a new heart, or perish forever, lay with weight on my mind." The spiritual counsel of others only intensified her desire to seek reconciliation with God. Her aunt assured her that the concerns she entertained were indeed the work of the Holy Spirit and that she should take care not to lose her spiritual impressions lest "hardness of heart and blindness of mind" settle in, after which it would "be forever too late." Her minister urged her to "pray for mercy . . . and submit to God" and gave her evangelical literature that narrated others' dramatic conversions. With that, Ann set her sights on finding a new heart. "[I] spent my days in reading and crying for mercy."[1]

Yet mercy came slowly and only after an unexpected turn. After "two or three weeks" her anxiety only increased when she caught a glimpse of the wickedness of her heart. "My heart began to rise in rebellion against God," she noted. Complaints

---

[1] James D. Knowles, *Memoir of Mrs. Ann H. Judson, Late Missionary to Burmah*, 3rd ed. (Boston: Lincoln & Edmands, 1829), 15-17. The memoir pieces together selections from her journal and an autobiographical narrative of her conversion, which was written after the event.

arose in her mind regarding God's injustice: he took no notice of her prayers for mercy; he had no "right to call one [to salvation] and leave another to perish"; he is "cruel" to send any to hell for disobedience. Most of all she noted her "aversion and hatred" toward God's holiness: "I felt, that if admitted into heaven, with the feeling I then had, I should be as miserable as I could be in hell. In this state I longed for annihilation."[2]

It was only at this point that a calm island appeared in the midst of her spiritual storm. "I began to discover a beauty in the way of salvation by Christ. He appeared to be just such a Saviour as I needed." She notes that in the midst of entertaining these new views of Christ that she did not give much thought to her own spiritual status but was solely preoccupied with the person and work of Christ: "I did not think I had obtained the new heart, which I had been seeking, but felt happy in contemplating the character of Christ."[3] From this point on the narrative reveals a growing awareness of the wonders of the Christian gospel and an increase in evangelical patterns of piety. In the following months she filled her time with reading Scripture, praying, attending religious worship, and making resolutions for moral and spiritual reformation. Others were undergoing similar experiences. "Five new members were added to the church," she notes on April 12, 1807. During this time she grew nearer to God: "I had a sweet communion with the blessed God, from day to day; my heart was drawn out in love to Christians of whatever denomination; the sacred Scriptures were sweet to my taste; and such was my thirst for religious knowledge, that I frequently spent a great part of the night in reading religious books."[4] Books specifically mentioned include Joseph Bellamy's *True Religion Delineated*, the recently published biography of Samuel Hopkins, and works by the authors Philip Doddridge and Jonathan Edwards.[5] Intertwined with these spiritual discoveries are pointed theological statements on God's moral perfections, his benevolent disposition "to the good of beings in general," Christ's atonement, and the justice of God.[6] "I felt that if Christ had not

---

[2]Ibid., 17.
[3]Ibid.
[4]Ibid., 18.
[5]Ibid., 17, 29, 20. Joseph Bellamy, *True Religion Delineated; Or, Experimental Religion, as Distinguished from Formality on the One Hand, and Enthusiasm on the Other, Set in a Scriptural and Rational Light*, in *The Works of Joseph Bellamy, D.D.* (Boston: Doctrinal Tract and Book Society, 1853), 1:3-361; Samuel Hopkins, *Sketches of the Life of the Late Rev. Samuel Hopkins, D.D., Pastor of the First Congregational Church in Newport* (Hartford, CT: Hudson and Goodwin, 1805).
[6]Knowles, *Memoir of Mrs. Ann H. Judson*, 17-18, 30.

died, to make an atonement for sin, I could not ask God to dishonor his holy government so far as to save so polluted a creature, and that should he even now condemn me to suffer eternal punishment, it would be so just that my mouth would be stopped."[7]

During these months her "many doubts" about her spiritual state gradually subsided as an assurance of salvation took root in her soul. A year after her first religious impressions, she recorded these last words in her regular journal:

> But though my heart is treacherous, I trust that I have some evidence of being a true Christian; for when contemplating the moral perfections of God, my heart is pleased with, and approves of, just such a Being. His law, which once appeared unjust and severe, now appears to be holy, just, and good. His justice appears equally glorious as his mercy, and illustrative of the same love to universal happiness. The way of salvation by Christ appears glorious, because herein God can be just, and yet display his mercy to the penitent sinner.[8]

Confident in God and certain of her salvation, she no longer required a journal to test her religious experiences and could turn her energies to a life of radical Christian service. Several years later Ann married Adoniram Judson, a recent graduate of Andover Seminary, and in time the two would serve a remarkable tenure as missionaries in Burma, becoming America's first well-known missionary couple.

For centuries conversion experiences like Ann Hasseltine's have been a central feature of the evangelical movement, especially during seasons of revival.[9] As the entryway into the kingdom of God, evangelicals held that the conversion experience served as *the* crucial divide in an individual's biography: it spiritually united them to Christ, sociologically set them apart from the "world," and vocationally molded them into men and women who eagerly sought to advance God's kingdom on earth.

Often overlooked, however, are the numerous theological assumptions that undergird these conversion narratives. Hasseltine's journal brims with assumptions that were shaped by her church, her denomination, and her revival tradition. For instance, we can discern several assumptions regarding *the proper expectations of a*

---

[7]Ibid., 18.

[8]Ibid., 30.

[9]For English evangelical conversion narratives, see D. Bruce Hindmarsh, *The Evangelical Conversion Narrative: Spiritual Autobiography in Early Modern England* (New York: Oxford University Press, 2008).

true conversion: the length of her conversion was not sudden but drawn out over a period of weeks, even months; her religious anxiety at the beginning of the process was identified as being a work of the Holy Spirit, which could be lost "forever" if she were not careful to preserve it and allow the Spirit to complete his work; and the goal of her search for spiritual resolution was not merely the desire to follow Christ, but the genuine identification of a converted heart, one that prized divine holiness. Similarly, after entertaining new "views" of God, the accent of her account reveals more theological assumptions *about the nature of God, salvation, and sanctification*: a joy in contemplating God's "moral attributes" (his holiness, love, and justice); a wonder at the atoning work of Christ that underscores how God can both uphold his "holy government" and justify sinners at the same time; and a gradual growth in assurance that slowly dissipated her doubts over the course of a year. Standing behind these statements lie long-established theological positions that cohere with an identifiable tradition of revival theology, the New Divinity theological tradition. The pages that follow seek to identify and explore not only this tradition but also other traditions of revival theology that informed the conversions of countless evangelicals in the century after the First Great Awakening.

WHAT IS "REVIVAL THEOLOGY"?

In the period of 1740–1840, American evangelicals thought deeply about conversion and the nature of religious revivals. The great prominence of revivals in the landscape of North American Protestantism compelled evangelical theologians to address a host of issues associated with them: the theological and experiential nature of human redemption, the proper balance of divine and human activity in the conversion process, the analysis and authentication of true religious experience, and the ways in which a preacher calls individuals to Christ. Consequently, they published hundreds of works investigating these subjects, from shorter works, such as Albert Barnes's sermon "The Way of Salvation," to lengthy manifestoes, such as Jonathan Edwards's *Religious Affections*. These theological writings form a prominent subgenre in evangelical literature from the First Great Awakening to the Civil War that contains what we might call the numerous "revival theologies" of the American revivalists.

Revival theology is more than just the theoretical foundations that undergirded the preaching of salvation by early American revivalists. To be sure, a revivalist's *soteriology*, or doctrine of salvation, did color how ministers presented the gospel to sinners during awakenings.[10] Thus in the pages to come we will become acquainted with the major theological systems that animated the revivals of the First and Second Great Awakenings, such as traditional Calvinism, Wesleyan Arminianism, and Edwardsean Calvinism. Yet there were other, more practical elements that factored prominently into their revival theologies, elements that were intimately tied to their soteriologies. Two of them stand out.

First, there were issues related to what ministers are to do while preaching the gospel. Numerous questions surfaced here:

- Is preaching *the moral law* (the Ten Commandments) a necessary prelude to preaching the gospel?

- Are ministers to direct sinners to use the *means of grace* (such as praying, reading the Scriptures, attending preaching services) as they seek God's salvation in Christ?

- How do the doctrines of *election* and *spiritual inability*, if true, practically translate into evangelistic method?

- Should ministers call sinners to *repent immediately*, or should they direct sinners to *wait to discern certain signs of genuine faith* in the heart before calling them to repentance and faith?

- Should ministers employ a method, such as an *anxious bench* or *altar call*, to call anxious souls to come forward publicly and receive spiritual counsel, or should they leave it up to individuals themselves to seek the counsel of spiritual advisers after a revival service?[11]

Second, there were questions related to the spiritual experiences individuals were expected to pass through in their journeys through the conversion process. These questions included the following:

- Is it necessary that individuals pass through a period of spiritual distress known as *conviction of sin* before they are ready for faith in Christ? If so, how much conviction is necessary?

- Is conversion *a lengthy process*, or does it normally occur in *a short period of time*?

---

[10]From the period of 1740–1840, *sinner* was a general term used to refer to all non-Christians or individuals who were not yet converted; it did not merely refer to a person who had committed a serious moral lapse.
[11]Many of the italicized terms in this list and the next were technical terms that ministers used widely. We will examine these terms more thoroughly in the chapters to come.

- What, specifically, are sinners to *do* to be saved? Do individuals *wait for God* to create in them a new heart, or are there *steps they can take* that render salvation more probable?

- What are the *essential marks of salvation*? How do individuals *truly know* that they love God and believe in Christ?

- Should converts experience an *assurance* of salvation *immediately* at the moment of belief, or is assurance the *fruit of Christian maturity*?

Revivalists in the First and Second Great Awakenings addressed these questions in their ministries. The different answers they gave drew them into debate with one another and generated several different schools of thought. These different traditions form the subject of this book. Thus, as we explore the theologies revivalists heralded in the First and Second Great Awakenings, our attention will be focused on the interplay of these three themes—their theologies of salvation, the ways they practically preached the gospel, and the conversion experiences they expected from those experiencing salvation. These three components constitute a given revival theology.

REVIVAL THEOLOGIES IN EARLY AMERICA: A THEMATIC OVERVIEW

This book is a historical theology of the significant traditions of revival theology that surfaced in North America from the First Great Awakening through the Second Great Awakening (roughly 1740–1840). This is a very complicated story, filled with numerous controversies and unexpected turns. To bring some coherence to what follows, our narrative will have three components: a starting point, a main trajectory of doctrinal development, and several side stories that add texture to the main narrative. In a nutshell the starting point consists in the "moderate evangelical" revival theology of the primary revivalists of the First Great Awakening, such as Gilbert Tennent, Jonathan Edwards, Jonathan Dickinson, and Samuel Davies, who preached a deeply pietistic form of Calvinism that they inherited from their Puritan predecessors. This will be the subject of chapter one.

The main trajectory of doctrinal development concerns the twists and turns associated with the Edwardsean theological tradition. Even though he was closely associated with the moderate evangelicals of the First Great Awakening, Jonathan Edwards contributed to the emergence of a new kind of Calvinism that in time gave rise to a revival theology that was distinct from the moderate evangelicals. The origins and transformation of the Edwardsean theological tradition will occupy numerous chapters in what follows, from its birth in Edwards's writings (chapter two) to its first mature expression in the writings of Edwards's disciples Joseph Bellamy and Samuel Hopkins (chapter three), its flourishing during the Second Great Awakening (chapter four), and its most extreme, and some would say unrecognizable, form in the revival theology of Charles Finney (chapter seven).

As we trace this narrative several side stories appear that, while not central to the development of the Edwardsean story line, are necessary to address in order to appreciate the diversity of American revival theologies during the Awakenings. These stories fall into two categories: stories of criticism and stories of revival theology in two of America's major popular denominations. First, several groups offered sustained criticism of the most popular revival theologies in the period of 1740–1840. In the First Great Awakening, radical revivalist Andrew Croswell mounted a vigorous critique of moderate evangelical revival theology based on the principles of "free grace" theology (chapter two), while in the Second Great Awakening we find the theologians at Princeton Theological Seminary and leaders of the Restoration Movement advancing two very different critiques of modern revivals (chapter eight).[12] Second, there are the histories of revival theology found among the Methodists and the Baptists (chapters five and six), two of the "popular" denominations that benefited immensely from the revivals of the Second Great Awakening. Together these side stories reveal that sustained and detailed discussion on the intricacies of revival theology was occurring throughout American evangelicalism in the First and Second Great Awakenings.

CHAPTER OVERVIEWS

Our exploration of early American revival theologies will follow a chronological path, beginning with the views advanced in the First Great Awakening and its

---

[12]As we will see in chapter two, revivalists were considered "radical" in the First Great Awakening if they advocated the following positions: that assurance is the essence of saving faith; that faith is particular (i.e., faith must be grounded in the particular apprehension that God has loved *me* in Christ); that employing the means of grace prior to salvation is not necessary to salvation and is potentially legalistic; and that conversions are normally powerful affairs that happen very quickly. Radical revivalists who advanced these views were often open to extraordinary manifestations of the Holy Spirit (being led by dreams, visions, or impulses). They also tended to ecclesiastical separatism. Many were labeled "antinomian" by the moderate evangelicals.

aftermath (chapters one through three). Chapter one introduces our starting point, namely, the moderate evangelical revival theology that emerged around the great revivals of the awakening (roughly late 1730s–1740s). Moderate evangelicals were predominantly "New Light" or *pro-revival* Congregationalists and Presbyterians who promoted revivals that were emotionally intense and theologically robust.[13] Most of the well-known leaders of the First Great Awakening, such as George Whitefield, Gilbert Tennent, and Samuel Davies, were moderate evangelicals. Their revival theology was strongly influenced by the Puritan tradition and was generally presented as a threefold process they summarized under the terms *conviction* (spiritual preparation for faith by the law and the means of grace), *conversion* (spiritual illumination, repentance, and faith), and *consolation* (the quest and attainment of assurance of salvation). Under such teaching, conversions were usually lengthy affairs.

Chapter two, "First Great Awakening Alternatives," will introduce our first "side story" as well as the beginning of the main trajectory of doctrinal development, the Edwardsean tradition. The chapter will analyze the revival theologies of an unlikely pair, Andrew Croswell and Jonathan Edwards, who each contributed specific themes to the discussion during the First Great Awakening, themes that differed from the moderate evangelicals. Their revival theologies were very different from each other. Croswell, the longtime minister of Boston's Eleventh Congregational Church, advanced a "free grace" revival theology that downplayed the "legal" preaching and lengthy preparatory convictions expected by moderate evangelicals. He maintained that conversions ought to happen quickly and that ministers should call sinners to repent immediately. His views, which were labeled "antinomian" by moderate evangelicals, never gained traction among the revivalists of the eighteenth century and thus never generated a longlasting tradition in American revival theology.

Edwards, by contrast, birthed an enduring tradition by introducing two extremely important elements to the history of revival theology. First, he amplified the theme of human agency in his soteriology, a feature I call the "voluntarist accent" of his theology. Second, he introduced a powerful spirituality of "disinterestedness" to

---

[13]Moderate evangelicals are distinguished from two other groups of the First Great Awakening: radical evangelicals, who advocated ecclesial separatism and "enthusiastic" revivals, and antirevivalists, who sharply criticized the awakening. For further description of these three groups, see Thomas S. Kidd, *The Great Awakening: The Roots of Evangelical Christianity in North America* (New Haven, CT: Yale University Press, 2007), xiv-xv.

the discussion, one grounded in an aesthetic vision of God that powered a selfless and activist desire to advance God's universal interests in the world. During Edwards's lifetime these features of his revival theology did not stand out significantly from the moderate evangelicals, but in time they took on a life of their own in the hands of his heirs, a group of pastors known as the New Divinity. After the First Great Awakening these New Divinity ministers transformed Edwards's insights into a full-blown theological system known as Edwardsean Calvinism. Chapter three will examine how Joseph Bellamy and Samuel Hopkins, the most notable of the New Divinity Edwardseans, transformed Edwards's insights into this new Calvinistic revival theology, which would influence American revivals well into the nineteenth century.

In the 1790s, a fresh new set of revivals began surfacing throughout America, forging what we now call the Second Great Awakening (1790–1840). The next three chapters explore the revival theologies that were well-known among the major evangelical denominations of the early decades of the awakening. First, in chapter four, we will continue the story of Edwardsean revival theology among New England Congregationalists and New School Presbyterians. Special attention will be given to how particular Edwardsean themes surfaced in their preaching as well as in converts' conversion narratives. Chapters five and six will examine the revival theologies found among two popular evangelical denominations of the Second Great Awakening that postured themselves as champions of the people rather than as defenders of Old World theological traditions. Chapter five examines the revival theology of early American Methodists, who reproduced John Wesley's doctrines and tailored them to the deeply emotional setting of America's rural revivals. Chapter six details the numerous revival theologies among early American Baptists. Baptists did not present a single, unified revival theology like the Methodists did. Rather, their leaders borrowed from the spectrum of revival theologies surveyed in the previous chapters.

The book winds down with an examination of the revival theology of the most popular revivalist of the Second Great Awakening, Charles Finney, and two very different criticisms of modern revivals. Chapter seven highlights Finney's work, which appeared in the later decades of the Second Great Awakening. Though not a formally trained theologian, Finney constructed a revival theology that attracted much attention. Essentially, he was a New School Presbyterian who borrowed extensively from a progressive form of the Edwardsean tradition and coupled it with his own persuasive revival methods, known as "new measures." His numerous writings on revival, which were severely criticized, represent the last original system of revival theology advanced in America.

Chapter eight treats two groups that offered different responses to modern revivals: the traditional Calvinist theologians of Princeton Seminary (Archibald Alexander and Charles Hodge) and the early leadership of the Restoration Movement (Alexander Campbell and Walter Scott). Both groups raised important theological criticisms of modern revivals, yet they offered very different visions of what to replace it with. Princeton's high Calvinists preferred a vision of Christian parenting and catechizing coupled with a cautious reappropriation of moderate evangelical revival theology of the First Great Awakening. The Restorationists, by contrast, advocated a "biblicist" approach to conversion that emphasized a plain, common-sense reading of Scripture devoid of the emotional fervor of many modern revivals. It also prominently featured the rite of baptism for the remission of sins as the crucial moment of Christian initiation.

For centuries revivals have both united and divided evangelical Christians. The element that unites each of the views treated here is perhaps the quest to identify the fundamentals of Christian initiation: Is it essentially experiential, volitional, ritualistic, sacramental, or perhaps some combination of each? As revivalists addressed these questions, they were essentially providing contrasting ideals of the nature of true Christian conversion and incorporation into the church. Over the course of time and across the spectrum of different evangelical traditions, we see these ideals slowly changing and developing. In this light, this book is fundamentally a theological history about what it has meant to "become a Christian" during the age of America's Great Awakenings.

CHAPTER ONE

MODERATE EVANGELICAL REVIVAL THEOLOGY IN THE FIRST GREAT AWAKENING

AMERICAN REVIVAL THEOLOGY BEGAN WITH A BANG, namely, with the spectacular revivals that composed the First Great Awakening of the early 1740s. This is not to say that revival theology did not exist beforehand. Indeed, its basic building blocks had been present among English-speaking churches for over a century by the time George Whitefield began his New England preaching tour in 1740. What was unique about the First Great Awakening, however, was that it helped widely disseminate a common revival theology throughout the American colonies through the solidification of an evangelical identity. Many historians date the birth of the modern evangelical movement to these decades (1730s–1740s).[1] With this common evangelical identity came a fairly uniform understanding of the nature of salvation, preaching the gospel, and conversion. In short, a uniform revival theology emerged in the wake of the First Great Awakening.

This chapter will examine the revival theology of the main leaders of the First Great Awakening, a group that I will call the moderate evangelical revivalists. As

---

[1]For background on evangelical origins and its early history, see Mark A. Noll, *The Rise of Evangelicalism: The Age of Edwards, Whitefield and the Wesleys* (Downers Grove, IL: IVP Academic, 2003); and David W. Bebbington, *Evangelicalism in Modern Britain: A History from the 1730s to the 1980s* (London: Unwin Hyman, 1989; repr., New York: Routledge, 2005).

we will see, their views provided the baseline for the future development of American revival theology. Before examining their views, however, we begin with a historical summary of the First Great Awakening in order to provide the needed historical context.

OVERVIEW OF THE FIRST GREAT AWAKENING

When George Whitefield, a twenty-five-year-old Anglican itinerant evangelist, arrived in Newport, Rhode Island, on September 14, 1740, he may not have realized that his visit would help ignite a period of intense spiritual renewal throughout the American colonies. But after his arrival, something extraordinary was unfolding before the eyes of the colonists as thousands were converting to Christ under his ministry. While the First Great Awakening (1740–1743) spanned the entirety of the American colonies, we will confine our attention to two geographic regions—New England and the Middle Colonies—because most of the ministers who wrote on revival theology hailed from these areas.[2]

In New England, Congregationalism had achieved denominational dominance by the early decades of the eighteenth century. Though they were descendants of the deeply pietistic English Puritan tradition, many Congregationalist ministers had come to the conclusion that its churches had lost their spiritual edge by 1700. Consequently, their preaching took on more of a prophetic accent as they began delivering sermons designed to expose societal decline and the rise of national faithlessness. The results of these efforts were encouraging, as congregations throughout the region began reporting periods of renewal. Samuel Danforth reported a youth revival in his town of Taunton, Massachusetts, in 1705. "[We] had *three hundred Names* given *to list under Christ*, against the Sins of the Times," he wrote in a letter. "The whole acted with such Gravity, and Tears and good Affection, as would affect [a] Heart of Stone. *Parents* weeping for Joy, seeing their *Children* give their *Names* to *Christ.* . . . Let God have the Glory."[3] Other revivals were reported in Windham, Connecticut, in 1721, and throughout the region after a great earthquake in 1727. Northampton ministers Solomon Stoddard and Jonathan Edwards saw no less than

---

[2]For an overview of the Great Awakening in Virginia and the Carolinas as well as its spread among Native Americans and slaves, see Thomas S. Kidd, *The Great Awakening: The Roots of Evangelical Christianity in North America* (New Haven, CT: Yale University Press, 2007), 189-266.

[3]Samuel Danforth, letter of March 5, 1705, in Thomas Prince, *The Christian History, Containing Accounts of the Revival and Propagation of Religion in Great-Britain and America* (Boston: S. Kneeland and T. Green, 1744), 1:111.

half a dozen periods of intense religious renewal spanning the years 1679–1735. Thus, when the awakening began in 1740 in the wake of Whitefield's preaching, everyone identified what was happening, because periods of religious renewal were a prominent feature of New England's historical memory.

We find a slightly different context in the Middle Colonies, those regions encompassing New York, Long Island, the Raritan Valley of central New Jersey, and southeastern Pennsylvania. There many Scots-Irish Presbyterian and Dutch Reformed immigrants settled, bringing with them patterns of piety that were shaped by Old World traditions. Theodore Frelinghuysen (1691–1747) is perhaps the best known of the Dutch Reformed immigrants. Born in Westphalia, Frelinghuysen was an established leader and revivalist among the Dutch Reformed in New Brunswick, where he mentored other ministers and led numerous revivals from the 1720s to 1740s.[4] Prominent among Presbyterian ministers of the time were those associated with a small seminary known informally as the "Log College" of Neshaminy, Pennsylvania.[5] Founded in the late 1720s by William Tennent (1673–1746), the college graduated a small but steady stream of ministers who would leave a significant mark on the revivals of the 1740s. Several of Tennent's sons—John, William Jr., and most notably Gilbert—studied there before taking charge of congregations in New Jersey. Prior to Gilbert's (1703–1764) rise to fame, he labored for more than a decade in New Brunswick, where he was mentored by Frelinghuysen, oversaw several revivals in his own congregation, and helped establish the pro-revival New Brunswick Presbytery in 1738.[6]

Other notable Log College graduates would establish their own academies. Samuel Finley (1715–1766) was a successful evangelist during the height of the awakening who settled in a church at Nottingham, Maryland, where he opened a small school for training ministers and leaders, one of whom was Benjamin Rush, the future physician, politician, and signer of the Declaration of Independence. Samuel Blair (1712–1751), another Log College graduate, ministered in New Londonderry, Pennsylvania, and oversaw an extraordinary revival in his congregation in 1740.[7] Blair also founded his own ministerial academy, which

---

[4]See Kidd, *Great Awakening*, 27-29; James Tanis, *Dutch Calvinistic Pietism in the Middle Colonies. A Study of the Life and Theology of Theodorus Jacobus Frelinghuysen* (The Hague: Martinus Nijhoff, 1967).

[5]Frank Lambert, *Inventing the "Great Awakening"* (Princeton, NJ: Princeton University Press, 1999), 55-62.

[6]Milton J. Coalter, *Gilbert Tennent, Son of Thunder: A Case Study of Continental Pietism's Impact on the First Great Awakening in the Middle Colonies*, Contributions to the Study of Religion 18 (New York: Greenwood Press, 1986), 27-54.

[7]Kidd, *Great Awakening*, 55.

graduated Samuel Davies (1723–1761), the great Presbyterian revivalist of Virginia. As the elder Tennent's health began to fail in the 1740s, arrangements were made to reorganize the college by his son Gilbert, along with Presbyterians Aaron Burr of Newark, Ebenezer Pemberton of New York, and the elder statesman of New Jersey Presbyterianism, Jonathan Dickinson (1688–1747) of Elizabethtown. The result was the founding of the College of New Jersey (later Princeton University).[8] This network of revival-friendly ministers who coupled education with a vision for revival virtually ensured the appearance of dozens of theological publications defending the awakening once revivals became a flash point of controversy in the 1740s.

Whitefield's preaching tour brought him through both New England and the Middle Colonies in the fall of 1740. Wherever he went, thousands apparently flocked to hear the young wonder. In Boston he preached in the pulpits of ministers who would later vigorously defend the awakening in print. On Saturday, September 20, he preached to "about eight thousand" on the common near the Old South Church (Third Congregational).[9] Old South's ministers, Joseph Sewall (1688–1769) and Thomas Prince (1687–1758), were vocal supporters of Whitefield's ministry and published numerous works designed to promote the awakening.[10] The next day Whitefield attended worship at Brattle Street Church (Fourth Congregational), where he heard Benjamin Colman (1673–1747) preach before dining with the church's assistant pastor, William Cooper (1694–1743).[11] Later that afternoon Whitefield preached in the Old Brick Church (First Congregational) before relocating again to the Boston Commons, where he preached to "about fifteen thousand." Old Brick's ministers, Thomas Foxcroft (1697–1769) and Charles Chauncy (1705–1787), demonstrate the complex makeup of Boston-area Congregationalism. Though they ministered amicably together for four decades,

---

[8]Bryan F. Lebeau, *Jonathan Dickinson and the Formative Years of American Presbyterianism* (Lexington: University Press of Kentucky, 1997), 172-86; Noll, *Rise of Evangelicalism*, 131.

[9]For details on Whitefield's Boston visits, see George Whitefield, *George Whitefield's Journals* (London: Banner of Truth Trust, 1965), 457-63, 471-74; Thomas S. Kidd, *George Whitefield: America's Spiritual Founding Father* (New Haven, CT: Yale University Press, 2014), 120-27. For details of Boston's Congregational Church and their ministers, see George W. Harper, *A People So Favored of God: Boston's Congregational Churches and Their Pastors, 1710–1760* (Lanham, MD: University Press of America, 2004).

[10]Most notable among these is Prince's *The Christian History*, a weekly periodical (1743–1745) that published accounts of current and past revivals in the colonies and Scotland.

[11]Founded by Colman in 1699, Brattle Street Church was a progressive Congregational alternative to a stricter high-church ecclesiology that characterized other Boston congregations. Under Colman and Cooper's leadership, Brattle Street remained committed to a broad evangelical Calvinism and to the revival.

the two held different opinions about the awakening, Foxcroft being its great supporter while Chauncy its most famous critic.

During these engagements, Whitefield preached powerful sermons that underscored the depths of human sin, the need to be born again, and a religion of the heart that stressed a personal, relational walk with God—all hallmarks of the nascent evangelical movement. While his sermons focused on these evangelical essentials, he did not hide the Calvinist scaffolding that framed much of his preaching.[12] Whitefield's theology had solidified around the Reformed "doctrines of grace" in the years 1739–1740, a result of his study of the Anglican divine John Edwards, the Scottish Presbyterian Thomas Boston, and the Dissenter Jonathan Warne.[13] While this would create much tension between him and John Wesley, the Arminian Methodist who had been somewhat of a mentor to Whitefield earlier, it did enable him to bring together a deep pietism, powerful preaching, and a Reformed vision of conversion and the Christian life. The fusion was a perfect recipe for his North American audience, many of whom were familiar with the broad outlines of orthodox Calvinism but who had never seen it bristle with life as it did in Whitefield's intensely searching orations.

Whitefield's revival theology, though not extensively delineated in his sermons, is fairly consistent with what we will explore below in greater depth.[14] His contribution to revival theology lies not so much in its content but in the way that his preaching helped create the conditions for a surge in writing on the topic. The awakening, sparked in great measure by his ministry, generated much controversy, which in turn led to the publishing of many writings that contained robust reflections on the nature of conversion, evangelism, and revival.

After ministering at Boston's Old Brick Church, Whitefield continued preaching the gospel for several weeks throughout the region. At one stop he noted that the crowd "was so exceedingly thronged, that I was obliged to get in at one of the windows." Leaving the Boston area, he traveled west through Concord,

---

[12]For a brief overview of Whitefield as a "Reformed Divine," see Lee Gatiss, "Introduction," in *The Sermons of George Whitefield*, ed. Lee Gatiss, The Reformed Evangelical Anglican Library 1.1 (Stoke-on-Trent, UK: Tentmaker Publications, 2010), 1:28-37.

[13]Kidd, *George Whitefield*, 86-88.

[14]See notes below where Whitefield's sermons are referenced in our treatment of moderate evangelical revival theology. For several representative sermons where he explicitly mentions some of the doctrines related to revival theology, see Whitefield, "The Lord Our Righteousness" (Gatiss, *Sermons*, 1:263-81), "Marks of a True Conversion" (Ibid., 1:384-401), "The Conversion of Zaccheus" (Ibid., 2:73-87), "Saul's Conversion" (Ibid., 2:168-84), and "On Regeneration" (Ibid., 2:276-89).

Worcester, and Brookfield before arriving at Northampton, where he delivered several sermons from Jonathan Edwards's pulpit. "Preached this [Lord's Day] morning, and good Mr. Edwards wept during the whole time of exercise. The people were equally affected; and, in the afternoon, the power increased yet more. Our Lord seemed to keep the good wine till the last. I have not seen four such gracious meetings together since my arrival."[15]

In October Whitefield moved south along the Connecticut River Valley, preaching at Westfield, Springfield, Hartford, Weathersfield, Middletown, and New Haven. From there he left New England and visited New York, New Brunswick, Philadelphia, New Londonderry, and Nottingham, Maryland. He was well acquainted with the Tennents, Samuel Blair, Samuel Finley, and other ministers who gladly welcomed the religious fervor that swelled in the wake of his visits. In November he persuaded Gilbert Tennent to follow up on his spectacular New England tour. While Tennent headed for Boston, Whitefield continued south, accompanied by James Davenport, a Congregationalist from Long Island.[16] Tennent's Boston tour in December 1740 would prove to be just as affecting, as thousands flocked to hear this "Son of Thunder" who excelled at deeply convicting "law-preaching." Others took the mantle of itinerancy, and within months New England and the Middle Colonies were traversed by numerous revivalists bringing good news to the spiritually poor, a phenomenon that would last for the next several years.

Though Whitefield would not return to the Northeast until 1745, he left a profound mark on the religious landscape of the region. His celebrity drew together many disparate trajectories in colonial American religious life. A new clerical identity featuring the passionate, extemporaneous preaching of the gospel by an itinerant minister captured the imagination of multitudes. The Puritan spirituality modeled in his *Journal* received a new lease on life. And the echo of the Great Awakening of the early 1740s was burned into the collective memory of many Christians who later came to yearn, pray, and labor for similar divine visitations in their own day. In short, modern evangelicalism in North America had been born.

It is difficult to imagine the excitement generated by Whitefield, Tennent, and the Great Awakening in general. We capture a glimpse of it in an often-quoted

---

[15]Whitefield, *Whitefield's Journals*, 472, 477. For details of Whitefield's visit to Edwards's Northampton, see George M. Marsden, *Jonathan Edwards: A Life* (New Haven, CT: Yale University Press, 2003), 201-13; Kidd, *George Whitefield*, 127-29.

[16]Whitefield, *Whitefield's Journals*, 489.

selection from the diary of Nathan Cole (1711–1783), a Connecticut farmer who, on receiving news that Whitefield would soon preach in Middletown, literally dropped his field tools and rushed twelve miles on horseback to make the engagement. Cole's vivid account bristles with energy and must be quoted at length:

> And when [my wife and I] came within about half a mile or a mile of the Road that comes down from Hartford weathersfield and Stepney to Middletown; on high land I saw before me a Cloud or fogg rising; I first thought it came from the great River, but as I came nearer the Road, I heard a noise something like a low rumbling thunder and presently found it was the noise of Horses feet coming down the Road and this Cloud was a Cloud of dust made by the Horses feet; it arose some Rods into the air over the tops of Hills and trees and when I came within about 20 *rods* of the Road, I could see men and horses Sliping along in the Cloud like shadows and as I drew nearer it seemed like a steady Stream of horses and their riders, scarcely a horse more than his length behind another, all of a Lather and foam with sweat, their breath rolling out of their nostrils every Jump; every horse seemed to go with all his might to carry his rider to hear news from heaven for the saving of Souls, it made me tremble to see the Sight, how the world was in a Struggle. . . .
>
> We went down in the Stream but heard no man speak a word all the way for 3 miles but every one pressing forward in great haste and when we got to [the] Middletown old meeting house there was a great Multitude *it was said to be 3 or 4000* of people Assembled together . . . I turned and looked towards the Great River and saw the ferry boats Running swift backward and forward bringing over loads of people and the Oars Rowed nimble and quick; every thing men, horses and boats seemed to be Struggling for life: *The land and banks over the river looked black with people and horses* all along the 12 miles. I saw no man at work in his field, but all seemed to be gone.
>
> When I saw Mr. Whitfield come upon the Scaffold he Lookt almost angelical; a young, Slim, slender, youth before some thousands of people with a bold undaunted Coutenance, and my hearing how God was with him every where as he came along it Solemnized my mind; and put me into a trembling fear before he began to preach; for he looked as if he was Cloathed with authority from the Great God; *and a sweet sollome solemnity sat upon his brow*[.] And my hearing him preach, gave me a heart wound; By Gods blessing: my old Foundation was broken up, and I saw that my righteousness would not save me.[17]

---

[17]Michael J. Crawford, ed., "The Spiritual Travels of Nathan Cole," *The William and Mary Quarterly* 33, no. 1 (1976): 93. See also Kidd, *Great Awakening*, 88-89, whose presentation of the details of Cole's conversion I follow here.

The event initiated a grand two-year struggle in Cole's life, one that brought him to the depths of spiritual despair and the brink of insanity. "Hell fire was most always in my mind; and I have hundreds of times put my fingers into my pipe when I have been smoking to feel how fire felt: And to see how my Body could bear to lye in Hell fire for ever and ever."[18] Later, however, his spiritual angst found resolution in a powerful conversion to Christ.

Cole's experience, though certainly an extreme example, does portray the profound degree to which many colonial Americans were affected by the awakening. Numerous journals, letters, and testimonies by laypersons and ministers witness that something profound was happening. Church registers witnessed a spike in either full communicant membership (Congregationalist, Presbyterian) or baptisms (Baptist), a sign that church leaders had discerned the new birth in a significant numbers of churchgoers.

Not everyone welcomed the awakening, however. Many had come to believe that an "enthusiastic" spirit had come to characterize the revivals, one that overly relied on direct leadings from the Holy Spirit, dreams, visions, and other hyperspiritual experiences as their ground for religious authority. Critics also noted how churches often split in the wake of revival because church members could not agree whether the awakening was from God or not. This group of critics came to be known as Old Lights, who defended an older church order they believed was being threatened by the revivals. Does God encourage disorder, division, and an excessive interest in spiritual impulses, they asked? Or does he encourage an ordered, established church grounded in the Word of God? Old Light leaders such as Samuel Mather, Mather Byles, and most notably Charles Chauncy pointedly raised these questions and collectively came to resist the revivals. By 1743 a public division between Old Lights and pro-revival New Lights had emerged among New England Congregationalists. Many of these churches split, with New Lights forming separate congregations.[19] Similar fault lines opened in the Presbyterian Church as the denomination split in 1741 between pro-revival New Side Presbyteries of New Brunswick and New York and Old Side Presbyterians of Philadelphia, a rift that would not heal until 1758. While it is clear that the awakening was a blessing to multitudes of colonial

---

[18]Crawford, "Spiritual Travels of Nathan Cole," 94.
[19]Kidd, *Great Awakening*, 174-88; C. C. Goen, *Revivalism and Separatism in New England, 1740–1800* (New Haven, CT: Yale University Press, 1962), 68-114.

Christians, it is also clear that it did not promote unity among churches where revivals were powerfully felt.

Perhaps the greatest example of this disunity and separatism is found in the ministry of James Davenport (1714–1758). A Long Island Congregationalist and onetime partner of Whitefield's, Davenport became the worst nightmare of both Old and New Lights because of his aberrant escapades. At the height of his radical phase (1740–1742), he had embraced every extreme of the radical revivalists: he claimed the ability to determine whether individuals were either saved or reprobated; he relied on dreams, visions, and impulses from the Holy Spirit in a way that appeared to bypass the need for scriptural authority; and he embraced a hyperspiritual antinomian theology of conversion. Davenport encouraged New Light churchgoers to separate from their parent churches. He even rejected large swaths of the Puritan tradition, which he infamously demonstrated in a book-burning ceremony in March 1743, where, in a fit of righteous indignation against the establishment, he burned his ministerial garb, including his trousers![20] Though Davenport later came to his senses and publically repented, the damage had been done. "It is at this Day enough to make the Heart of a sober and considerate Christian to bleed within him," Benjamin Colman lamented, "to hear of the sore *Rents and Divisions* made by Mr. *Davenport* and other a great Number of *Towns and Churches* thro' our *Provinces*: Almost *all* [the churches] on *Long-Island* are thus broken to pieces, and so are *many* in *Connecticut* and with us of the *Massachusetts* to a sorrowful Degree."[21]

The threat of unbridled radicalism and unrestrained emotionalism in Davenport's example challenged many New Light revivalists who sought to strike a balance between warm-hearted devotion and ecclesiastical unity in revival. In their efforts to avoid both the conclusions of the radicals on the one hand and the Old Lights on the other, New Light revivalists advocated a position that I will call their moderate evangelical revival theology.

MODERATE EVANGELICAL REVIVAL THEOLOGY

To a large degree, the revival theology the moderate evangelicals preached was basically Reformed theology (Calvinism) cast in a pietist accent. The moderate

---

[20]Lambert, *Inventing the "Great Awakening,"* 242-43.

[21]Benjamin Colman, *A Letter From the Reverend Dr. Colman of Boston, To the Reverend Mr. Williams of Lebanon, Upon Reading the Confession and Retractations of the Reverend Mr. James Davenport* (Boston: G. Rogers and D. Fowle, 1744), 6-7.

evangelical leaders of the First Great Awakening valued their Calvinist theological heritage, and they merged that with a strong emphasis on piety, devotion, and religious experience. In their minds Calvinism should not just be embraced intellectually; it should be experienced, felt, and known in the heart. Because of this, their revival preaching sought to enliven the heart and touch the religious experiences of those listening. Piety, or a robust sense of religious devotion, thus characterized their Calvinistic proclamation.

What are the components to this revival theology? Summaries of it abound in the primary literature and follow a general pattern that Peter Thacher, pastor of Middleborough, Massachusetts, succinctly summarized in three words: *conviction, conversion*, and *consolation*.[22] The process begins with conviction of sin, where individuals come to "a convincing and humbling sense of their sin, guilt, and impotency" and are "driven to despair of help from any refuges of their own."[23] Through prayer, seeking God, and utilizing the means of grace, sinners wait for God's work of regenerating grace. The second step, conversion, commences with a moment of spiritual illumination where the convicted sinner "sees that Christ is an All sufficient Saviour, able to save them to the utmost that come unto God by him."[24] This discovery emboldens the individual to venture forth in repentance and faith in Christ. The third part, consolation, comprises the young Christian's pursuit of spiritual maturity through the quest for assurance of salvation. Since these phases formed the framework of the moderates' revival theology, we will use them to structure our analysis of their views.

Conviction of sin: Preparing the heart for receiving Christ. Conviction of sin was the preparatory phase to salvation and the one that the moderate evangelical revivalists wrote about the most. Simply stated, conviction is when nonbelievers awaken to the guilt of sin in their lives. Those experiencing conviction are haunted by the sentence of divine condemnation as their consciences continually renew God's guilty verdict to their souls. This tumultuous spiritual unease demands action, and moderate revivalists laid out a detailed road map designed to

---

[22]Letter of Peter Thacher to Thomas Prince, December 21, 1741, printed in Prince, *Christian History*, 1:171. The ministers who wrote "the Attestation" to Jonathan Dickinson's *A Display of God's Special Grace* use the same three words; see Jonathan Dickinson, *A Display of God's Special Grace*, in *Sermons and Tracts, Separate Published at Boston, Philadelphia, etc.* (Edinburgh: M. Gray, 1793), 381. Also see Coalter, *Gilbert Tennent, Son of Thunder*, 18-19.

[23]Dickinson, *Display of God's Special Grace*, 425.

[24]Samuel Blair, *The Gospel Method of Salvation* (New York: William Bradford, 1737), 105.

guide convicted sinners safely to Christ. Our analysis of this topic will progress from the theoretical to the practical, noting first the moderates' theology of conviction and then the practical advice ministers prescribed to sinners who were in the midst of that conviction.[25]

To the moderate revivalists conviction of sin was generally considered a necessary prerequisite to experiencing salvation. They argued this on both rational and biblical grounds. Rationally, they maintained that God is a God of order who generally follows a wise and predictable course in his actions. Samuel Davies notes this with regard to the physical creation: while God is able to create the world instantly, he shows his preference for a protracted, orderly process that takes six days to complete. Similarly, he creates a human being in nine months rather than instantaneously. This same protracted process, Davies notes, characterizes God's supernatural work in the new birth. "In like manner, the Almighty proceeds in quickening us with spiritual life; we all pass through a course of preparation, though some through a longer [course], and some shorter."[26] The Bible provided the pattern of this "course of preparation." Moderates noted how Scripture consistently represents salvation as a work of liberation from a bondage that is palpably felt: the Son of Man came to seek *the lost*; the prodigal son's repentance came once *he realized his oppressive condition* apart from his family; *the sick* seek out the help of a physician, not the healthy; Christ bids those who are *weary and heavy laden* to come to him.[27] From these texts they concluded that sinners must come to experience the oppressiveness of sin in their lives and yearn for salvation in Christ before they are thoroughly prepared to repent and believe the gospel. Thus conviction was a vitally important prerequisite to salvation. "I cannot see," Jonathan Dickinson wrote, "how any person . . . can receive the Lord Jesus Christ upon gospel-terms, till he is at least brought to some sensible apprehension

---

[25]Works that address conviction of sin and the experience of conversion in general include Blair, *Gospel Method of Salvation*; Benjamin Colman, *The Wither'd Hand Stretched Forth at the Command of Christ, and Restored*, 2nd ed. (Boston: J. Draper, 1740); Jonathan Dickinson, *The True Scripture Doctrine Concerning Some Important Points of Christian Faith*, in *Sermons and Tracts*; Ebenezer Pemberton, *Practical Discourses on Various Texts* (Boston: T. Fleet, 1741); and Joseph Sewall, *The Holy Spirit Convincing the World of Sin, of Righteousness, and of Judgment* (Boston: J. Draper, 1741).

[26]Samuel Davies, "The Nature and Process of Spiritual Life," in *Sermons on Important Subjects* (New York: Robert Carter, 1845), 1:98.

[27]Sewall, *Holy Spirit Convincing the World*, 10-11. For a full exposition of the theology of conviction used by many New England ministers, see John Norton, *The Orthodox Evangelist* (London: John Macock, 1654), 129-40.

of the misery of his present state, and of his absolute necessity of a Saviour."[28]
Samuel Buell concurred. "[It] doubtless holds true that until Sinners see the Sinfulness of Sin, their lost State by Nature, the spirituality of the Law, their unwor-
thiness of divine Mercy, they will not come to Christ for Salvation; nor are they
like to have a Discovery of his Fullness and Glory."[29]

Three related doctrines broadened the moderate evangelical understanding of
conviction of sin. The first relates to the Reformed emphasis on the moral law.
Moderate evangelicals argued that the law served the purpose of revealing God's
holiness to sinners with the hopes that their consciences would be struck with the
devastating sentence of personal guilt and condemnation. Understood to be a
"transcript" of God's holiness, the law was preached to expose the great moral gulf
between God and the sinner. John Tennent explains that through the concurring
work of the law and the Holy Spirit there arises a "discovery of sin" in the heart
where "they see sin in its loathsome nature, [its] deplorable circumstances, and
dreadful consequences; they begin to see the holiness of God, the spiritual latitude of his law, and their own corrupt nature; then are they apt to cry out, Who
can stand before this great and dreadful God?"[30] The source of this "discovery of
sin" lay within the individual's own constitution, the conscience. As a "principle
natural to men," the conscience is designed "to give an apprehension of right and
wrong; and to suggest to the mind the relation that there is between right and
wrong, and a retribution."[31] Once attuned to the divine law, the conscience becomes "awakened to do its Office, and as it were says to the Sinner, *Thou art the
Man.*"[32] Like a spiritual Trojan horse in the sinner's heart, the wounded conscience
became a powerful ally of the moderates' ministry because, once awakened, it
threatened to overthrow the sinner's inner peace. "I remember in particular,"
David Brainerd reminisced about his period of conviction, when "I was walking
solitarily abroad, and the Lord opened to me such a sense of my sin and danger
that I feared the ground would cleave under my feet and become my grave; and

[28]Dickinson, *Display of God's Special Grace*, 395.

[29]Samuel Buell, *A Faithfull Narrative of the Remarkable Revival of Religion in the Congregation of East Hampton on Long-Island* (Aberdeen: 1773), 35-36. It should be noted that most moderates treated this conviction as a general rule of thumb, not a strictly applied law applicable in all situations.

[30]John Tennent, "Regeneration Opened," in *Sermons and Essays by the Tennents and Their Contemporaries*
(Philadelphia: Presbyterian Board of Publication, 1855), 273.

[31]Jonathan Edwards, "A Divine and Supernatural Light," in *Sermons and Discourses, 1730–1733*, ed. Mark
Valeri, WJE 17 (New Haven, CT: Yale University Press, 1999), 410-11.

[32]Sewall, *Holy Spirit Convincing the World*, 39.

send my soul quick into hell even before I could get home."[33] These experiences were not interpreted as signs of psychological disintegration but as positive indicators of the Spirit's work aiding the conscience to agree with God's law. Consequently, the worst thing they argued could happen in such circumstances was to lose these guilty impressions.

Original sin is the second doctrine that significantly informed the moderates' understanding of conviction. All the revivalists maintained that the sinner's natural posture toward God is one of rebellion. "The Heart of every Sinner is naturally shut and bar'd against the Lord Jesus Christ," John Webb noted. "Christ is not [a] welcome Guest to the Sinner himself."[34] This individual sinfulness, they pointed out, derives from the sin of Adam and Eve, our first parents. Because Adam sinned, the entire human race descending from him is guilty before God and worthy of eternal condemnation. "Upon *Adam's* Transgression," Samuel Blair wrote, "Guilt and Condemnation plainly and necessarily followed upon all the human Race."[35] Because all human beings stand under the guilt and condemnation of original sin, they are rendered spiritually impotent to do anything to change their circumstances. Sinners, in other words, are totally unable to seek God or remedy their situation because a settled bias against God governs the soul. In a sermon on Mark 3:5, where Christ heals a man with a withered hand, Benjamin Colman notes how sinners are *"by Nature as this Man [is] with a withered hand; labouring under a moral Weakness and Impotence, thro' the Loss of those spiritual Powers, which Man was certainly created with."*[36] Jonathan Dickinson agreed. In a sermon on the consequences of original sin, he questioned how it is possible

> to deserve the blessing of this renewed nature from God; when your whole conduct is one course of enmity against him, and indignity to him? . . . [If] God have mercy upon your soul, he will bring you to his footstool, with a most humble abasing sense of this your impotent and miserable, guilty and exposed state. He will bring you to be thus poor in spirit, if ever he gives you a title to the kingdom of heaven.[37]

---

[33]Jonathan Edwards, *An Account of the Life of the Reverend Mr. David Brainerd*, in *The Life of David Brainerd*, ed. Norman Pettit, WJE 7 (New Haven, CT: Yale University Press, 1984), 111.

[34]John Webb, *Christ's Suit to the Sinner, While He Stands and Knocks at the Door* (Boston: S. Kneeland and T. Green, 1741), 8.

[35]Blair, *Gospel Method of Salvation*, 16-17; Samuel Blair, *The Doctrine of Predestination Truly and Fairly Stated* (Philadelphia: B. Franklin, 1742), 10, 15; Dickinson, *True Scripture Doctrine*, 192-93.

[36]Colman, *Wither'd Hand*, 8.

[37]Dickinson, *True Scripture Doctrine*, 210.

In short, spiritual inability before God was the direct byproduct of the moderate evangelicals' understanding of original sin.

Election or predestination is the third doctrine that significantly informed their understanding of conviction of sin. As a prominent feature of Reformed theology, the revivalists utilized the doctrine of election to highlight the centrality of God's work in the salvation process. Every facet of human redemption— including the complete number of those to be saved and the personal strivings of faith itself—was explicitly decreed by God before the creation of the world and executed in time at his express direction.[38] Moderate revivalists defended the unconditionality of election, the view that God elects some for salvation merely on the basis of his own choosing, not on the basis of foreseen faith. They also maintained that the number of the elect is definite (it cannot be added to or detracted from) and that this doctrine mysteriously coheres with human freedom.[39]

Preaching election produced a number of practical results that worked to the revivalists' advantage. Though it is a doctrine of many "mysteries, and abstruse difficulties," it is not, Cooper noted, purely speculative: "No, it has a powerful influence upon vital religion."[40] Specifically, the doctrine practically exposes the true foundation of the heart, since it "cuts all the sinews of self-dependence, and leaves the sinner no other foundation to cast himself upon, but the sovereign mercy of God, through a redeeming Saviour."[41] Many ministers believed that protesting this doctrine was a sign that that person had not come to terms with God being in complete control of their redemption. It was only when sinners came to take this doctrine to heart that they were in a position to submit to God's decision and wait for his saving mercy.

Stepping back for a minute, we can take stock of the full extent of the revivalists' teaching. While they held that Scripture teaches a period of conviction prior to salvation, these three related doctrines added further depth to their views. God's law is designed to reveal the holiness of God and the heinousness of sin, all with the goal of smiting the conscience with the profound reality that "I am guilty." Original sin exposed the vast spiritual poverty of the sinner, resulting in the conclusion that "I am unable." And once the doctrine of election is internalized, the

---

[38]William Cooper, *The Doctrine of Predestination Unto Life, Explained and Vindicated* (Boston: J. Draper, 1740), 15, 99.

[39]Ibid., 15, 91-99; Dickinson, *True Scripture Doctrine*, 124.

[40]Cooper, *Doctrine of Predestination*, 8.

[41]Blair, *Doctrine of Predestination*, 38.

soul can only conclude that "I must submit to God's decision, even if it is does not end in my favor." Together these conclusions maneuvered the sinner's soul into the very uncomfortable position of guilt and a sense of helplessness. The revivalists did not consider this to be a morose, psychological detour leading sinners away from Christ; rather, they believed it to be a necessary prerequisite to saving faith.

Practically, how are ministers to counsel a person under a sense of conviction? At first glance, the theological mix described above might be construed as a recipe for spiritual lethargy and inactivity. Proclaiming human inability and divine sovereignty does not initially appear to motivate a person to action. Yet inactivity was the furthest thing from the minds of the moderate evangelical revivalists, because for them *inability was not equivalent to inactivity*. As a matter of fact their sermons overflowed with earnest calls to sinners to exert themselves on behalf of their salvation. While human effort was not understood to merit salvation in any way, the revivalists envisioned human striving to have a positive effect in bringing the soul into a position where salvation was more likely to take place. "God's decree does not at all take off the use of our endeavours," William Cooper directed, "for in the use of the means the very decree it self is to receive its accomplishment."[42] Jonathan Dickinson's exhortations that sinners exert themselves saturate his writings and play off the seemingly paradoxical tension implicit in striving and inability:

> Labor after a lively impression of your *incapacity* to produce this grace in yourselves. . . . Let a discovery of this your distressed case quicken you to greater diligence in *seeking* the influence of the blessed Spirit. . . . And labor to *exercise* faith in Christ. Though you cannot work this grace in yourselves; yet if ever you obtain it, you yourselves must use and exercise it. The principle is from God; but the act must be your own. If God bring you to exercise this grace, you must be *made willing in the day of his power*, and act with your free consent.[43]

Benjamin Colman agreed: "*It is no ways unjust or absurd for God to command us to do those things, which of our Selves we are unable to do, because he is able to make all Grace to abound to us, and to give us an Allsufficiency in all things.*"[44] Thus the moderates called sinners to vigorous endeavors for the gospel, actions they knew sinners had no power to exert, but ones that they knew God might bless with his gracious intervening. In sum, through the very act of reaching beyond themselves

---

[42]Cooper, *Doctrine of Predestination*, 98.
[43]Dickinson, *True Scripture Doctrine*, 269-70.
[44]Colman, *Wither'd Hand*, 19-20, 25-27.

to exert faith, the moderate revivalists noted that God often produced the miracle of belief in sinners who sought after the Lord.[45] Consequently, the revivalists called sinners to seek salvation in Christ by vigorously embracing a course of action that they believed rendered salvation more probable. What, specifically, are convicted sinners to do once they come under conviction of sin? The moderate revivalists were unanimous in their answer: apply the means of grace to your life!

The means of grace were a set of spiritual exercises that moderate evangelical revivalists prescribed to sinners seeking God's mercy. These exercises were basic spiritual disciplines—such as prayer, study of the Word, diligent attendance at worship services, and personal moral reformation—and were designed to draw the soul into a humble posture where God might produce the miracle of faith. The emphasis on the word *might* is key, because the revivalists argued that the means of grace were not automatic conduits of divine grace. "There is no certain or infallible connection," John Blair wrote, "between the most diligent and earnest attendance on the means of grace that unregenerate sinners are capable of, and their obtaining the saving grace of God. The issue of the matter is entirely from the sovereign mercy of God."[46] At the same time, they wanted to avoid the opposite extreme, which affirmed that God grants salvation ex nihilo to individuals who have no desire for salvation, no preparatory convictions, and no knowledge of gospel truths. Rather, their position was that God's normal course was to grant salvation to individuals in the context of employing the means of grace because the means specially fit the soul to receive Christ. God, in other words, does not work salvation *because* of the means of grace, yet he rarely ever works salvation in sinners *without* them. Through the means sinners come to an experiential acquaintance with their sin, their guilt, and their great need of salvation. They also gain a notional knowledge of scriptural truths and an acute awareness that they lack true faith. These become the intellectual and experiential materials that form a natural foundation on which a supernatural work of grace can be built should God's sovereign hand so move. This point explains the moderates' zealous advocacy of their use. "If we be partakers of Christ at all," Dickinson notes, "it must be by an active reception; by a faith accompanied with earnest, diligent seeking him in the ways of God's appointment."[47]

---

[45]Samuel Davies, "The Method of Salvation Through Jesus Christ," in *Sermons on Important Subjects*, 1:50-51.

[46]John Blair, "An Essay on the Means of Grace," in Tennent, *Sermons and Essays*, 219.

[47]Dickinson, *True Scripture Doctrine*, 261.

Lists of the various means of grace populate the exhortation sections of many sermons from the period. They reveal the great spiritual activism to which the moderate evangelicals called sinners. Gilbert Tennent briefly surveys the basic range of directives in a sermon on divine mercy: "Attend with diligence upon the preached word. . . . Bewail your sins against the mercies of God. . . . Try to reform your lives. . . . Pray earnestly and frequently to God for mercy, in the name of Christ, with fear and hope."[48] In an earnest plea that sinners "make it [their] present and active care, to obtain a saving conversion unto God," Jonathan Dickinson gives numerous directions to anxious souls seeking God. These include exhortations to meditate on the misery of their condemned state, to labor "after a humbling sense of your utter *inability* to relieve and save yourselves," to resolve to cast their soul on God's sovereign mercy, and to persevere in "a constant and diligent attendance upon all the *means of grace*, in order to have this change wrought in you."[49] Knowing that one's fate lies in the hands of God, the convicted sinner ultimately was exhorted to entreat the Lord for the gift of faith. "Who knows but the Lord may have mercy on, may abundantly pardon you?" Whitefield urged. "Beg of God to give you faith. And, if the Lord gives you that, you will by it receive Christ, with his righteousness and his all."[50]

As more individuals came under a powerful sense of conviction during the awakening, two issues arose that called for pastoral discernment. The first had to do with the degree of experiential conviction required before an individual was prepared to receive God's grace. This issue arose because it became clear to many pastors that not everybody experienced conviction in the same way or to the same degree. One individual passes through a period of great spiritual anguish, while others are "wrought on in a more gentle and silent Way."[51] Some come under conviction suddenly, "by a more *forcible impression*, filling the soul with greatest agony and distress," while others' convictions are "more *gradually* brought on; and with *lower degrees* of terror and amazement."[52]

When they addressed this problem, moderate evangelical revivalists generally focused their attention on the nature of the conviction process an individual

---

[48]Gilbert Tennent, "The Divine Mercy," in Tennent, *Sermons and Essays*, 46-47.
[49]Dickinson, *True Scripture Doctrine*, 209-11.
[50]Whitefield, "The Lord Our Righteousness," in Gatiss, *Sermons*, 1:279.
[51]Prince, *Christian History*, 1:159.
[52]Jonathan Dickinson, "The Witness of the Spirit, A Sermon Preached at Newark in New-Jersey, May 7, 1740," in *Sermons and Tracts*, 303.

experienced rather than on other factors, such as the intensity of conviction or a specific way one ought to experience it.[53] Joseph Sewall strongly cautioned against using one person's experience of conviction as a yardstick for determining the authenticity of someone else's experience, because numerous variables are at play in different people's lives, variables that will generate different conviction processes. Those converted in childhood might not remember their conviction, and the conviction of a scoundrel will most likely be more intense than that of an individual raised with a "pious education." In the final analysis, what mattered to Sewall was a recognition and wholehearted embrace of the fundamentals: the sinners' abhorrence of their own sin, a willingness to submit to Christ and trust in his righteousness, and a desire to see God as their greatest good. "I say, these Persons ought not to distress themselves, because they can't give such a distinct Account of the Time and Manner of this Work of Conviction, as some others can."[54]

A second issue that called for discernment had to do with the physical results that emerged from the intense convictions some individuals experienced during revivals. Sometimes the preaching was so convicting that "bodily effects" could be viewed among the crowd: persons crying out in the middle of a sermon under sharp pangs of conscience, or individuals so overcome with terror that they trembled and lost their ability to sit up or stand. Samuel Blair noted extraordinary responses from his preaching in the summer of 1740: "Several would be overcome and fainting; others deeply sobbing, hardly able to contain, others crying in a most dolorous manner, many others more silently weeping. . . . And sometimes the soul exercises of some, thought comparatively but very few, would so far affect their bodies, as to occasion some strange, unusual bodily motions."[55]

The moderate evangelicals addressed this problem with a mixture of wonder and caution. In a 1742 sermon, Joseph Sewall called his listeners to judge these surprising bodily manifestations by their effects and not write them off merely because of their extraordinary nature. Scripture, he noted, indicates that God produced similar effects, such as the Philippian jailer's trembling response to Paul and Silas (Acts 16) and the multitude that was deeply affected by Peter's sermon (Acts 2). He warns that we should not "presume to confine the *free* Spirit of God" by

---

[53]Samuel Davies, "The Nature and Process of Spiritual Life," 1:98-99; Buell, *Faithfull Narrative*, 21.
[54]Sewall, *Holy Spirit Convincing the World*, 23.
[55]Samuel Blair, *A Short and Faithful Narrative, of the Late Remarkable Revival of Religion in the Congregation of New-Londonderry, and Other Parts of Pennsylvania* (Philadelphia: William Bradford, 1744), 74.

disregarding bodily effects completely, nor are we to "excite these Screamings." Rather, gospel ministers are "to set the *Terrors* of the Law and *gracious Invitations* of the *Gospel* before Men *in the most powerful Manner* they are able; and then leave it to the only wise God to take his own Way, who can if he pleaseth order these Things to the awakening of others."[56] This required restraint and vigilance on behalf of the minister and an intimate awareness of his people's religious impressions through spiritual conferencing and counsel.

Overall, the moderates' elaborate doctrine of conviction represented an expansion of the experiential dimensions of Calvinism. Sinners must not just know but come to experience deeply the doctrines of law, sin, and predestination in their lives. Awakened sinners must actively employ the means of grace with a hopeful expectation that God might work true faith into their hearts. This process was often a lengthy affair, lasting days, weeks, or even months. What, we might ask, were they waiting for?

Conversion: The sinner's discovery of Christ. The reason the conviction process was so lengthy was that most would-be converts were waiting to discern the marks of the new birth in their hearts. For them, the experience of conversion did not commence with one's decision for Christ, as is common among today's evangelicals. Rather, it began when one discerned new principles of spiritual life within the heart: a new awareness of the beauty of Christ, new desires to love God, and a firm commitment to follow God's holy law. These principles, moderates taught, cannot be the product of human decision or natural principles; they can only be wrought in the soul by God's direct supernatural intervention. Because this spiritual transformation, technically known as regeneration, was discerned mainly through an examination of spiritual experiences, the revivalists went to great lengths to delineate the differences between legitimate and illegitimate conversion experiences. This section will examine the theology behind this delineation. First, we will explore their theoretical understanding of God's work of regeneration in the heart, where he brings new life to the individual. Second, we will examine how this plays out "on the ground" in the actual experience of conversion.

Moderate revivalists embraced a comprehensive understanding of regeneration, one that goes much deeper than an outward profession of faith or external conformity to Christian morality.[57] Rather, regeneration is the implantation of a

---

[56]Joseph Sewall, sermon fragment from February 26, 1742, printed in Prince, *Christian History*, 1:234-35.
[57]Tennent, "Regeneration Opened," 266-71.

new principle of life in the soul, wrought instantaneously by the Holy Spirit, where the subject subsequently possesses new capacities of spiritual perception and action. "Regeneration," summarized Jonathan Dickinson, "*is a new, spiritual, and supernatural principle; wrought by the Spirit of God in all the faculties of the soul, inclining and enabling unto the exercise of a life of faith in Christ; and new obedience to God.*"[58] John Blair agreed: "Regeneration is the communication of a principle of spiritual life to the soul of a sinner, naturally dead in trespasses and sins, by the agency of the Holy Spirit."[59] In their description of regeneration they emphasized two important and interrelated concepts: the notion that regeneration is instantaneous and the notion that it is a supernatural work of the Holy Spirit.

First, by noting that regeneration is an instantaneous work, the moderate revivalists underscored the radical division between converts and the rest of humanity. Just as there was no midpoint between death and life when Jesus called Lazarus from the tomb, so there is no halfway house between non-Christian and Christian status. Consequently, there can be no gradual phasing into a Christian state.[60] Regeneration occurs in an instant. Their affirmation of this point, however, did not eliminate all elements of gradualism in their revival theology, since most moderates acknowledged that it takes time to discern the reality of one's own regeneration. Samuel Davies noted that "the principle of life might be very weak at first, like the life of a new-born infant, or a fetus just animated in the womb."[61] Though aware of new spiritual insights and desires, such persons might remain confused as to whether they have been converted or not. Samuel Blair tells the account of a young woman who, after a lengthy period of conviction, had experienced "considerable sweetness" in contemplating the gospel. Yet because she had misconceptions about the nature of faith, she could not agree with Blair that she had been regenerated.[62] In sum, while moderate revivalists affirmed the instantaneous nature of regeneration, they also maintained that coming to an experiential conviction of it is sometimes a gradual affair.[63]

Second, by emphasizing that regeneration was the implanting of a "supernatural principle" in the soul, the moderates directed attention to the supernatural

---

[58]Jonathan Dickinson, "The Nature and Necessity of Regeneration, Considered in a Sermon from John iii.3," in *Sermons and Tracts*, 331.
[59]John Blair, "Observations on Regeneration," in Tennent, *Sermons and Essays*, 189.
[60]Dickinson, "Nature and Necessity of Regeneration," 343.
[61]Davies, "Nature and Process of Spiritual Life," 1:107.
[62]Blair, *Short and Faithful Narrative*, 81-82.
[63]Dickinson, "Nature and Necessity of Regeneration," 335.

origins of regeneration. Mere nature cannot produce supernatural results, they argued, and hence no human activity can effect regeneration. Whitefield noted that "in order to make Christ's redemption complete, [it is necessary] that we should have *a grant of God's Holy Spirit to change our natures* and so prepare us for the enjoyment of that happiness our Saviour has purchased by his precious blood."[64] Because regeneration is God's work alone, moderates followed the Reformed tradition in concluding that the soul is entirely passive in it.[65]

Paradoxically, while they indicated that the soul is passive in regeneration, this did not mean that the human subject is inactive in it. God's regenerating work is accompanied by human exertion: saving faith, evangelical repentance, and love for God are all spiritual activities expressed during the context of God's regenerating action. Thus from the human perspective there is spiritual activity occurring during the moment of regeneration. Dickinson explains this subtle distinction with reference to faith, illumination, and regeneration:

> Though regeneration be considered, as being in order of nature previous to faith; yet in order of time, they are always together. The same time that the eyes of the soul are opened, they look to Jesus, as the author of our eternal salvation. The same time that this new creature is formed, it lives; and acts faith in the Son of God. Whence we are said to be *created in Christ*, (Eph. ii. 10) i.e. to be immediately united to him by faith, at our new creation. Upon this account, the *new birth* and *faith* in Christ are spoken of in Scripture, as mutually implying each other.—The Divine light which shines into the soul in regeneration, not only gives a feeling apprehension of our own lost and perishing condition: But such a view of Christ's readiness to save; and his abundant fullness to supply all our wants, as constrains us to consent to the gospel offer; and encourages us to trust all our interests in his hands.[66]

Jonathan Edwards agreed. In a brief note on "efficacious grace," he observes that "we are not merely passive in it, nor yet does God do some and we do the rest, but God does all and we do all. God produces all and we act all. For that is what he produces, our own acts. God is the only proper author and fountain; we only are the proper actors. We are in different respects wholly passive and wholly active."[67] In short, while the soul is passive in the work of regeneration, it nonetheless is

---

[64]Whitefield, "On Regeneration," 2:283-84, emphasis added.
[65]Dickinson, "Nature and Necessity of Regeneration," 343.
[66]Ibid., 338-39.
[67]Jonathan Edwards, "Efficacious Grace, Book III," in *Writings on the Trinity, Grace, and Faith*, ed. Sang Hyun Lee, WJE 21 (New Haven, CT: Yale University Press, 2002), 251.

vitally active in the context of God's work because the exertions of repentance and faith are the direct results of the Spirit's exertions.

It is at this point where the discussion transitions from the divine perspective (regeneration) to the human (the experience of conversion). The doctrine of conversion, or turning to God in repentance and faith, was generally understood by the moderates to be the flip side to regeneration. "Now this, when considered as the effect of the Holy Spirit's agency, enabling or causing the soul to turn to God, is called regeneration; but when considered as an activity essential to spiritual life, and formally as the soul's act, is called conversion; but these are only different views and respects of the same thing."[68] While not every revivalist articulated the doctrine of conversion in the same manner, an overarching consensus can be observed in their writings as to its essential components. Conversion first begins when the mind is opened to a new and often aesthetic awareness of the gospel. This spiritual illumination is followed by a transformation of the will, where there arises a resolution to part with sin (repentance) and a willingness to trust Jesus Christ (faith). While they distinguished these diverse components in the conversion process, the moderates noted that these phases were a packaged deal, the result of God's one work of regeneration.[69]

For the moderate revivalists, true conversion begins when the mind is "savingly enlightened" to see gospel truths as they really are. Jonathan Dickinson employed multiple terms to describe this phenomenon: the mind comes to a "lively view," a "realizing sight," or a "sensible discovery" of "divine things."[70] Based on Scripture verses that speak of "seeing" and "knowing" God in a special way, they maintained that knowledge via spiritual illumination was qualitatively different from mere intellectual assent to the truths of the gospel, though they often confessed difficulty in articulating the precise nature of this difference.[71] The illumined soul, Edwards explained, has "a true sense of the divine excellency of the things revealed in the Word of God, and a conviction of the truth and reality of them." This knowledge possesses a beauty that is "divine and godlike," rendering it virtually impossible to deny. "This evidence, that they, that are spiritually enlightened, have

---

[68]Blair, "Observations on Regeneration," 193.

[69]For instance, see Sewall, *Holy Spirit Convincing the World*, 91.

[70]Dickinson, *True Scripture Doctrine*, 215, 220-23.

[71]In a sermon on spiritual illumination, Jonathan Edwards points to Ps 119:18; Mt 11:25-27; Jn 14:19; 17:3; Gal 1:15-16; 2 Cor 4:6; 1 Jn 3:6; 3 Jn 11, among others, as biblical texts supporting a doctrine of spiritual illumination. See Edwards, "Divine and Supernatural Light," 417-19.

of the truth of the things of religion, is a kind of intuitive and immediate evidence. They believe the doctrines of God's Word to be divine, because they see divinity in them."[72] No new knowledge or spiritual faculties are given to the illumined soul.[73] Rather, the revivalists spoke of this knowledge in aesthetic terms, where converts love what they perceive in the gospel. Whereas before their regeneration the gospel message was merely an intellectual set of propositions, now that same knowledge is loved for its inherent beauty and worth. "Formerly," John Tennent indicates, "the face of Christ was veiled from the soul, as the face of Moses from the Israelites; but now he sees something of his peerless beauty, and transcendent excellency.... Christ is to him as the apple tree among the trees of the woods, as the rose of Sharon, and the lily of the valley.... All other enjoyments are as dross in comparison to him."[74]

Edwards likened this difference to that of two kinds of people beholding a country landscape. The natural person beholds the trees and fields as in the night, when objects are very faint "and therefore he has but little notion of the beauty of the face of the earth." The spiritual person, by contrast, sees the landscape under the brilliance of the daytime sun, "where the ideas appear with strength and distinctness; and he has that sense of the beauty of the trees and fields given him in a moment." No matter how hard the natural person tries to study the nighttime landscape, his resulting knowledge would still be colorless and abstract, not the rich, affecting visage beheld by the daytime observer.[75]

With the mind illuminated, the will consequently shifts into gear by expressing a twofold response: turning away from sin (repentance) and depending on Christ for salvation (faith). Moderate evangelicals first described faith as possessing both intellectual and volitional aspects, implying an affectionate assent of the mind to the contents of the gospel, the free consent of the will to embrace Christ, and a complete dependence on him for deliverance.[76] "*Faith in Christ*," Jonathan Dickinson summarized, "*is such an assent to the Christian revelation, as brings us heartily and fully to receive him as he is therein exhibited to us, and to depend on him only for salvation upon gospel terms.*"[77] Because faith and illumination are two sides of the

---

[72]Edwards, "Divine and Supernatural Light," 413, 415.

[73]Dickinson, *True Scripture Doctrine*, 215.

[74]Tennent, "Regeneration Opened," 275-76.

[75]Jonathan Edwards, "Miscellanies," no. 408, in *The "Miscellanies," (Entry Nos. a-z, aa-zz, 1-500)*, ed. Thomas A. Schafer, WJE 13 (New Haven, CT: Yale University Press, 1994), 470.

[76]Blair, *Gospel Method of Salvation*, 98; Davies, "Method of Salvation Through Jesus Christ," 44-46.

[77]Dickinson, *True Scripture Doctrine*, 256.

same coin, and because they are the first acts of a regenerate soul, faith becomes the foundation of genuine, evangelical repentance.[78]

Like faith, the moderates described true repentance in all-encompassing terms primarily because the nature of regeneration is all-encompassing. Having truly seen the glory of God in the gospel of Christ, the enlightened soul, drawn to Christ in faith, simultaneously senses the intrinsic evil of sin and the utter incompatibility of sin with God's holy ways. A sense of profound shame, grief over personal sin, and godly sorrow arises in the heart, leading to a hatred of sin and a thorough resolve to rid the heart of its presence.[79] This first act of evangelical repentance, accompanied by spiritual illumination and faith in Christ, lays in the soul a new foundation for a life of penitent faith. "In short, every true penitent is a critic upon his own heart; and there he finds constant cause for repentance while in this imperfect state."[80]

These descriptions of true faith and repentance suggest the existence of criteria that helped moderate revivalists distinguish between true conversions and false. The fundamental difference noted between the two lay in that true conversions arise from spiritual illumination, whereas false conversions do not. True repentance and faith "see" the glory of God, the amiableness of Christ, the pleasantness of faith, and are drawn after these spiritual objects in love. False repentance, by contrast, is not motivated by love but by fear, which leads a person merely to seek relief from guilt and punishment. Such persons do not hate sin itself but merely its punishment. "It is not sin they hate, but hell," observed Samuel Davies. "Were it possible for them to enjoy their sins, and yet be happy, they would never think of repenting."[81] Whitefield, similarly, noted how worldly sorrow can generate great religious emotions of apparent remorse, as in the cases of Esau and Judas. Yet in the end, "their sorrow was only extorted by a fear of hell, and a despairing sense of impending ruin."[82] Ultimately, false faith does not seek continual subjection to Christ but rather finds contentment only in a loose and general hope of mercy. Once again Jonathan Dickinson nicely summarizes this fine distinction:

---

[78]Jonathan Dickinson, *Familiar Letters to a Gentlemen, upon a Variety of Seasonable and Important Subjects in Religion*, 3rd ed. (Edinburgh: R. Fleming, 1757), 124; Samuel Davies, "The Nature and Necessity of True Repentance," in *Sermons on Important Subjects*, 2:302.

[79]Samuel Blair, *A Persuasive to Repentance: A Sermon Preached at Philadelphia, Anno 1739* (Philadelphia: W. Bradford, 1743), 16-18.

[80]Davies, "Nature and Necessity of True Repentance," 295.

[81]Ibid., 296.

[82]George Whitefield, "The True Way of Beholding the Lamb of God," in Gatiss, *Sermons*, 2:416.

Here then you see an apparent *Difference* between a true and a false Faith; the one realizes the great Truths of the Gospel by a lively and feeling Discovery of them, giving the *Light of the Knowledge of the Glory of God in the Face of Jesus Christ.* The other gives by a lifeless and unactive Assent to these important Truths.—The one influences the Heart and Affections, and by *beholding with open Face, as in a Glass, the Glory of the Lord, changes the Soul into the same Image, from Glory to Glory*; the other only swims in the Head, and leaves the Heart in a State either of Security or Despondency.—The one is an abiding Principle of divine Life, from which there flow Rivers of living Water: The other is transient and unsteady, and leaves the Soul short of any spiritual Principle of Life and Activity.[83]

It took time to discern these criteria in people's hearts, a point that accounted for lengthy conversion experiences. The common sentiment was that one dare not claim that God had accomplished his work in the heart until these kinds of motions were identified in the soul. This created a few wrinkles for pastoral discernment, since some individuals presumed to be gracious when they really were not, while others refused to acknowledge their salvation even when the minister thought they should be rejoicing. In his narrative of the 1737 revival at New Londonderry, Samuel Blair related examples illustrating both of these problems, noting how one man of fifty years of age, "a sober professor" of Christianity, had for many years believed himself to be converted when Blair thought otherwise. By contrast, another woman enjoyed spiritual sweetness in pondering the gospel and the person of Christ for two years before she was finally convinced that God had regenerated her heart. In handling these different cases, Blair would be frank with those he deemed unconverted. Conversely, with individuals who he believed were truly converted, he remained "very cautious of expressing to people my judgment of the goodness of their states," presumably because converts' search for assurance forged in their souls a process vital to their spiritual maturity.[84]

The difficulties in distinguishing true spiritual experiences from counterfeit occupied much of Jonathan Edwards's writing. In a brief pamphlet titled "Directions for Judging of Persons' Experiences," he lists key indicators of a true work of

---

[83]Dickinson, *Familiar Letters to a Gentleman*, 103.

[84]Blair, *Short and Faithful Narrative*, 77, 80-85. He notes that one exception to this rule of reticence was in the case of individuals whose convicting distress was so deep that it blinded them from discerning God's saving work in the soul. In such cases Blair would "use greater freedom" in confirming to them their state of salvation.

the Spirit in the soul for use in spiritual conferencing. Evangelical conviction, he noted, does not merely tantalize the imagination or the speculative understanding, but is soundly wrought in the frame of an individual's will and heart, leading to a hatred of sin. The truly convicted sinner is convinced of sins of heart and life and agrees with God's justice in their condemnation. Evangelical illumination must be grounded in a sense of the beauty and excellency of divine things—the sufficiency and excellency of Christ—which engenders joy in God, a longing for holiness, and a willingness to bear all things for the sake of Christ.[85] Edwards's list, which was sort of a sketch of his volume on the *Religious Affections*, was indicative of the kind of discernment ministers employed during the awakening when determining the validity of the Spirit's work in an individual.

Discernment was also on the minds of those undergoing conversion. Hannah Heaton (1721–1793), a young Connecticut farm woman, came under deep conviction of sin after hearing Whitefield and Tennent preach. Her period of conviction included wrestling with suicidal thoughts, believing that she had committed the unpardonable sin, and lamenting over her humanity: "Oh how i did invy toads or any creature that had no souls to perish eternally." After some time she attended a local worship service, where "the power of god [came] down. Many were crying out [on] the other side of the room what shall I do to be saved? . . . A great melting of soul [came] upon me" as she came to see the justice of God in her damnation in a new light. "It seemd to me i was a sinking down into hell. I thot the flor i stood on gave way and i was just going but then i began to resign." In her resignation she came to accept her eternal fate—"lord it is just if i sink in to hell"—and for a few moments she noted a quiet calm: "I was nothing i could do nothing nor i desired nothing." Hearing someone quote Matthew 11:28 ("Come unto me, all ye that labour and are heavy laden"), she sensed a new thirst after Christ and began to plead for divine mercy. Just then a new view of Christ was opened to the eyes of her soul. "Me thot i see jesus with the eyes of my soul stand[ing] up in heaven. A lovely god man with his arms open ready to receive me his face full of smiles he lookd white and ruddy and was just such a saviour as my soul wanted." Subsequently, Heaton's heart melted in mourning over the fact that she had been refusing the Savior for so long. A love for Christ inflamed her soul—"Jesus appeared altogether lovely to me now. My heart went out with love

---

[85]Jonathan Edwards, "Directions for Judging Persons' Experiences," in WJE 21:522-24.

and thankfulness and admiration"—and she began going about the room inviting others to Christ.[86] Heaton's firsthand account of the spiritual illumination that subsequently drew her lovingly to Christ mirrors the conversion pattern that moderate revivalists preached.

David Brainerd's conversion narrative demonstrates a similar pattern. In 1739, Brainerd, the future missionary to Native Americans, grew concerned over his soul's eternal destiny and began to seek God. After several months of employing the means of grace, he came under a deep sense of conviction yet grew increasingly vexed over his spiritual inability. "I could not find out how to believe or come to Christ, nor what faith was." After consulting Solomon Stoddard's *Guide to Christ*, Brainerd was greatly helped by the author's directions on conviction, but when it came to trusting in Christ, "he failed, he did not tell me anything that I could do that would bring me to Christ, but seemed at last to leave me as it were with a great gulf between me and Christ, which I seemed to have no direction to get through."[87] This lack of direction, of course, was by design, for it was intended to draw the soul's posture face-to-face with its spiritual impotence. In his helpless distress Brainerd gradually came to recognize "that I deserved nothing but damnation," and he began to lose hope in the efficacy of prayer and spiritual duties.[88] It was at this time in July 1739 that Brainerd found himself attempting to pray one evening when something new happened.

> [Then], as I was walking in a dark thick grove, "unspeakable glory" seemed to open to the view and apprehension of my soul. By the glory I saw I don't mean any external brightness, for I saw no such thing, nor do I intend any imagination of a body of light or splendor somewhere away in the third heaven, or anything of that nature. But it was a new inward apprehension or view that I had of God; such as I never had before, nor anything that I had the least remembrance of it.[89]

From this point he came to "wonder" and "admire" at God's glory and the way of salvation, and he heartily repented and trusted in Christ. While his spiritual struggles would continue throughout his missionary service, a ridge had been crossed in the summer of 1739. He no longer saw himself as a sinner seeking

---

[86]Hannah Heaton, *The World of Hannah Heaton: The Diary of an Eighteenth-Century New England Farm Woman*, ed. Barbara E. Lacey (DeKalb: Northern Illinois University Press, 2003), 6-7, 9.

[87]David Brainerd, *Life and Diary of Brainerd*, in WJE 7:123.

[88]Ibid., 130.

[89]Ibid., 138.

salvation but as a convert working out the implications of his salvation in the midst of a tumultuous life and ministry. And like in Heaton's conversion narrative, the crucial divide was identified as the moment when a new affective view of God was opened to the gaze of his soul, leading to repentance and faith.

Consolation: The quest for assurance. For the moderate evangelicals, conversion was not the final goal of their ministerial labors among their flocks; Christian maturity was. A common barrier to spiritual maturity for many new converts was their struggle over the assurance of their salvation. Since this problem dealt directly with identifying a work of the Spirit in the heart, the topic frequently surfaced in their writings. Assurance thus became a prominent feature of their revival theology.

In crafting their position on assurance, the moderates sought to distinguish their views from those of the radical evangelical revivalists. As we shall see in the next chapter, radicals believed that regeneration is such a powerful experience that it is virtually impossible to doubt one's salvation. Saving faith and assurance of salvation are one and the same experienced reality. Consequently, radicals argued that those who doubt probably do not have true faith. Relatedly, radicals argued that sanctification, though important to the Christian life, provides no evidence that an individual has been justified. Only the experience of faith does. Moderate evangelicals found numerous problems with these positions and responded to them with a doctrine of assurance that acknowledged the coexistence of doubt and faith, one that affirmed the view that assurance is a product of Christian maturity and sanctification. Their broad consensus on assurance involved several features.

First, moderate revivalists maintained that faith and doubt can simultaneously reside in a converted heart. They offered several reasons for why a genuine Christian might doubt his or her salvation. At the top of the list was spiritual sloth. "We teach," Solomon Williams wrote, "that 'tis the Duty of all to [make one's calling and election sure]: And that although there are comparatively *few*, who attain *Assurance*, yet it is thro' their own Sloth and Negligence that they do not."[90] Sinfulness can also cloud a Christian's confidence, so much so that it is "hard to distinguish between the remains of sin in the children of God, and the reign of sin in refined hypocrites."[91] Certain personality traits, such as meekness

---

[90]Solomon Williams, *A Vindication of the Gospel-Doctrine of Justifying Faith* (Boston: Rogers and Fowle, 1746), 57.
[91]Dickinson, "Witness of the Spirit," 316.

or a proclivity to "melancholy" (or depression), might also lead believers to be overly cautious in concluding that they have been saved because of an excessive fear of being self-deceived.[92] Together, these points provided solid reasons for concluding that the experience of saving faith should be distinguished from the experience of assurance.

Second, when they explored the relationship between faith and assurance, moderate evangelicals generally noted that assurance is a fruit of faith and is thus something that is experienced after expressing saving faith. Referencing Romans 5:1 and 1 Peter 1:8, Jonathan Dickinson noted that the biblical pattern shows faith giving rise to other fruits of the Spirit, such as peace with God, unspeakable joy, and, by extension, assurance of salvation: "[It] is evident from the *Nature* of Things . . . that the *Act* must necessarily precede the *Evidence* of it; and consequently our first receiving the Lord Jesus Christ must necessarily precede our Knowledge or grounded *Persuasion* of it."[93] Solomon Williams agreed. He maintained that faith essentially has an objective orientation because it "goes out to the promise" of the gospel and rests on Christ's completed work. Assurance, by contrast, looks inward to the heart and is essentially a distinct spiritual operation that consists in discerning the works of grace in the heart—namely, the exercises of faith and the analysis of one's growth in sanctification. In several ways, the moderate revivalists maintained that assurance is derivative of or consequential to faith. Consequently, one should not be surprised to find some Christians experiencing assurance long after they truly believe.

Last, the moderates addressed the process of seeking assurance. This path basically comprised two important elements: self-examination and sanctification. Examining one's own spiritual progress was one way a confused or doubting saint could seek assurance of salvation. Much of Jonathan Edwards's *Religious Affections* was devoted to this purpose. At the risk of oversimplifying his argument, Edwards held that gracious affections possess a benevolent disposition, engendered by the Holy Spirit, which inspires a host of other "religious affections" (or spiritual desires) in the soul. These include a selfless love of God's moral excellency, a certitude in the divinity of the gospel, and other virtues (humility, tenderness of spirit) that create in the saint a spiritual appetite for more grace. This list of affections can be used by confused saints to test one's own religious experiences. If

---

[92]Ibid., 316-17.
[93]Dickinson, *Familiar Letters to a Gentleman*, 183-84.

echoes of these graces are present in the soul, then one should rejoice. Similarly, Dickinson called confused Christians to self-examination in their pursuit of assurance. "Make it a daily business to *examine yourselves, whether you be in the faith*," he urged.

> Search and try whether you have these gracious influences of the Spirit in your soul, or not. Set apart time on purpose. You will do well to take the help and assistance of some good book, that most plainly and clearly sets the genuine marks of the new creature before you; and to your self-examination join fervent prayer, that God would graciously shew you your state as it is. In this way a truly sanctified person will be like[ly] to discover that he is such.[94]

Directions like these illustrate how the moderates called Christians to take stock of their spiritual health in light of the Scripture's portrayal of true faith. Yet this was only half of the story in seeking assurance.

The other half of seeking assurance was through the pursuit of sanctification. Both Dickinson and Edwards noted that Scripture gives no assurance to a Christian who is not pursuing a Christlike life. Consequently, all other avenues to assurance are useless without a lively pursuit of sanctification. "Assurance is not to be obtained so much by self-examination," Jonathan Edwards wrote, "as by action." Actively seeking to grow more in virtue, grace, and holiness through a conscious campaign against sin can only strengthen one's awareness of grace in the heart.

> And therefore many persons in such a case [of doubt] spend time in a fruitless labor, in poring on past experiences, and examining themselves by signs they hear laid down from the pulpit, or that they read in books; where there is other work for them to do. . . . The accursed thing is to be destroyed from their camp, and Achan to be slain; and till this be done they will be in trouble. 'Tis not God's design that men should obtain assurance in any other way, than by mortifying corruption, and increasing in grace, and obtaining the lively exercises of it.[95]

This position explains why the last sign in Edwards's *Religious Affections*, "Christian practice," was the sign to which he devoted the greatest amount of space. Jonathan Dickinson likewise encouraged doubting Christians to know

---

[94]Dickinson, "Witness of the Spirit," 320-21.
[95]Jonathan Edwards, *Religious Affections*, in *Religious Affections*, ed. John E. Smith, WJE 2 (New Haven, CT: Yale University Press, 1959), 195.

that assurance is attainable, and he urged them to pursue it diligently through sanctification. "If you are slothful and remiss, you must expect to be dark and doubtful about your state. . . . Be in earnest, attending upon all the means of grace and life; and wrestle with God, with insatiable desire and importunity, that he would *lift up the light of his countenance* upon your souls; and give you the *Spirit of adoption*."[96]

In short, the pursuit of assurance comprised the same spiritual activities that occupied the sinner's search for salvation, namely, using the means of grace. Because of this, assurance of salvation was often understood to be a lengthy process, one that was months or possibly years in the making and that required a Christian's conscious and earnest effort. As fruit requires time to ripen, so too does assurance.

SUMMARY

In this opening chapter we have spent a considerable amount of time analyzing the revival theology of the First Great Awakening's moderate evangelicals. This is for good reason. Their work drew together prominent themes from the Puritan theology of conversion, which they zealously promoted in the context of a vast intercolonial awakening. Because the awakening gave birth to the evangelical movement in North America, their revival theology became the central understanding of conversion that many American evangelicals embraced. Put another way, when North American evangelicals considered the subject of conversion in the mid-eighteenth century, they generally thought in the terms outlined in this chapter.

The central features of their revival theology can be summarized as follows. Moderate evangelical revival theology was Reformed theology with a strong pietist accent, designed to bring Reformed soteriology into contact with individuals' religious experience. Specifically, the doctrines of the moral law, original sin, and election were preached to inculcate the necessary spiritual preliminaries to receiving the gospel:

- The law was meant to portray God's holiness so that sinners might experience their true guilt before a holy God.

- Original sin and election were doctrines intended to make sinners aware of their spiritual inability before God and the need to place their all into his hands.

---

[96]Dickinson, "Witness of the Spirit," 320.

Guilty sinners, deeply aware of their need for grace, were said to be under "conviction of sin" and were urged by ministers to employ the means of grace (prayer, Scripture reading, moral reformation), entreat God for the gift of faith in Christ, and wait for him to bestow a new heart.

Conversion followed conviction. If God was pleased to grant salvation to the individual, he sent his Holy Spirit to regenerate the heart, an act that was instantaneous, supernatural, and a completely divine work, even though the sinner was actively employing the means of grace in the midst of the process. On the ground, the individual experienced conversion in the following way:

- Spiritual illumination, or a new sense of Christ and the gospel, opened up the mind and heart to see divine things in a different way.

- Repentance of sin followed out of a hatred for sin and love of God's holiness, not out of a fear of punishment.

- Faith in Christ, a gift bestowed by God, established a covenantal relation between God and the convert, where the new believer enjoys the blessings of redemption.

The new believer then embarks on a process of growth in grace, leading to the full consolation of one's assurance of salvation. While the moment of regeneration is instantaneous, and while sometimes converts underwent a quick work, most moderate evangelicals considered the conversion process to be a lengthy affair, taking days or several weeks to complete under the spiritual guidance of a trained pastor.

In the chapters to come we will see how this basic revival theology was transformed as new issues and controversies arose among evangelicals. Before moving away from the First Great Awakening, however, we shall examine two variants that appeared during the period: the radical revival theology of little-known pastor and revivalist Andrew Croswell and the extensive theological reflections on the nature of revival provided by Jonathan Edwards. I will argue that the variations they introduced to the discussion provided material that generated new trajectories. Their revival theologies were, in essence, harbingers of things to come.

CHAPTER TWO

FIRST GREAT AWAKENING
ALTERNATIVES

The **REVIVAL THEOLOGIES** *of* **ANDREW CROSWELL**
and **JONATHAN EDWARDS**

IN THE COURSE OF THE FIRST GREAT AWAKENING, several alternatives to moderate evangelical views emerged as ministers published their
sermons and treatises on the great revivals. In this chapter we will examine two
ministers who advocated alternative positions that, in time, would alter the
history of revival theology in America. The first of these, Andrew Croswell
(1709–1785), is an obvious candidate for examination. Croswell, who sharply
criticized moderate evangelicals, was a vigorous champion of the revival theology held among the radical fringe of the New Lights. His views gave voice to
themes that would become increasingly popular among evangelicals of a later era,
including an emphasis on free grace, "particular" faith, and a shorter pathway to
conversion and assurance.

Second, we will examine Jonathan Edwards and his revival theology. This
might come as a surprise: Why examine Edwards's views in a chapter treating
"alternatives" to moderate evangelical revival theology when we categorized him
as a moderate evangelical in the last chapter? The reason for this is not hard to
discern. Edwards was a profound thinker whose original reflections on the
nature of religious experience left a deep impression on evangelicals for generations to come. In his revival theology, he introduced two topics that would
prove to be extremely important in the history of revival theology: his emphasis

on voluntarism, or what I call the voluntarist accent of his theology, and his powerful spirituality of disinterestedness. These two features did not set Edwards apart from the moderate evangelicals during his lifetime. But later, in the hands of his successors, these positions helped forge a uniquely American school of Calvinism known as the New Divinity movement or the Edwardsean theological tradition. In order to understand that story line, which we will discuss in later chapters, we first need to come to grips with Croswell's and Edwards's views.

THE FREE GRACE REVIVAL THEOLOGY
OF ANDREW CROSWELL

For much of his adult life, Andrew Croswell ministered on the margins. As pastor of Boston's Eleventh Congregational Church for almost four decades, Croswell cultivated a reputation as a radical New Light who vigorously promoted an understanding of the gospel that emphasized spiritual passivity and the reception of God's grace displayed in Christ. Sinners who yearn for regeneration are not to prepare themselves for salvation by using the means of grace, he argued, because God gives his grace to the world freely, with no strings attached. Similarly, doubting Christians are not to labor for assurance because faith alone grants Christians assurance, not the cultivation of a holy life. Moderate evangelicals strongly opposed Croswell's teachings because they believed he downplayed the centrality of the moral law in both the salvation process and in the Christian life. Because of this, they labeled Croswell's theology "antinomian," a term he denied, but one that stuck to his reputation throughout his life.[1]

Croswell had not always been on the fringes of New England Congregationalism. Born in Charlestown, Massachusetts (1709), Croswell was a Harvard graduate (1728) who was ordained at the Second Congregational Church of

---

[1]Antinomianism is the position that argues that Christians are not obligated to follow or preach the Old Testament moral law because they stand under the gospel of Christ. Thus they are against (*anti-*) the law (*-nomos*, Greek for "law"). In the context of the First Great Awakening, antinomianism was associated with quick conversion experiences, a lack of concern for using the means of grace in the conversion process, and a heightened spirituality that asserted that assurance is the essence of saving faith. For the historical and theological backgrounds to antinomianism, see Mark Jones, *Antinomianism: Reformed Theology's Unwelcome Guest?* (Phillipsburg, NJ: P&R, 2013); and Theodore Dwight Bozeman, *The Precisianist Strain: Disciplinary Religion and Antinomian Backlash in Puritanism to 1638* (Chapel Hill: University of North Carolina Press, 2004).

Groton, Connecticut, in 1736.[2] During his decade there he supported Whitefield, promoted the awakening, and published his first work, which defended Whitefield against the criticism of the Anglican antirevivalist Alexander Garden.[3] In 1741, however, he invited James Davenport to preach in his pulpit. This event precipitated Croswell's conversion to New Light radicalism.[4] Like Davenport, Croswell came to advocate revival techniques that were considered shocking for the time: long, protracted meetings that sometimes lasted twenty-four hours; the cultivation of deeply emotional services that sometimes degenerated into religious frenzies; and advocacy of nonordained persons to "exhort" (or preach to) the congregation. He quickly denounced any criticism of his methods as satanic, and he concluded that many ministers, even moderate evangelicals, were unregenerate.[5]

For forty years Croswell funneled his ideas into several dozen short treatises and published sermons that promoted what I will call his free grace revival theology. The blessings of salvation are freely granted to humankind, he argued, and must be freely received. Individuals need not spend weeks in spiritual labors preparing for salvation only to spend years seeking assurance. These blessings are given freely and instantaneously. He forged these views in several treatises written during the 1740s, the most important being *What Is Christ to Me, If He Is Not Mine?* (1745).[6] In 1746 he moved to Boston, where he became minister of Eleventh Congregational, a church composed of separatist-leaning Bostonians. Up to his death in 1785 he remained a true defender of free grace revival theology.

Croswell's opposition to moderate evangelical revival theology. In order to get a clear understanding of Croswell's views, it is necessary that we begin with his critique of moderate evangelical revival theology. Throughout his ministry, Croswell voiced serious concerns with the standard way moderate New Lights preached the gospel. In his mind their practice was fraught with contradictions and errors that wound up leading sinners away from faith by cultivating a legalistic spirit of works-righteousness.

---

[2]For biographies on Croswell, see Clifford Kenyon Shipton, *Sibley's Harvard Graduates: Biographical Sketches of Those Who Attended Harvard College* (Cambridge: Massachusetts Historical Society, 1951), 8:386-407; Leigh Eric Schmidt, "'A Second and Glorious Reformation': The New Light Extremism of Andrew Croswell," *The William and Mary Quarterly* 43, no. 2 (1986): 214-44.

[3]Andrew Croswell, *An Answer to the Rev. Mr. Garden's Three First Letters to the Rev. Mr. Whitefield* (Boston: S. Kneeland and T. Green, 1741).

[4]Schmidt, "'Second and Glorious Reformation,'" 218.

[5]Shipton, *Sibley's Harvard Graduates*, 8:389-94.

[6]Andrew Croswell, *What Is Christ to Me, If He Is Not Mine?* (Boston: Rogers and Fowle, 1745).

The core of Croswell's critique of moderate evangelical revival theology can be summarized as follows. First, Croswell found their method to be inherently confusing because it called sinners to spiritual "works" (the means of grace) while at the same time calling them to a faith that receives Christ without works. Such a message is confusing at best and deadly at worst. Repeatedly, Croswell noted how moderate revivalists called people to trust Christ and then "[drove] them to their duties" with multiple directions of using the means of grace and scrupulous self-examinations, only to tell them not to trust in these duties. What can a normal churchgoer make of such a complex message? "It is as if a Woman should be rocking a Child to Sleep and should whisper once in a while, *Child you must not go to Sleep*, and then go on rocking again as fast as ever." He found the practice to be inherently fraught with tension: "The plain English of what they say is no better than this, viz. *We do invite Sinners to come to Christ immediately, but yet we do not invite them to come immediately.*"[7]

Second, Croswell argued that the counsel moderate evangelicals gave to sinners diverted their attention away from Christ and toward the shifting sands of their own religious experiences. The process of discerning the signs of a heart thoroughly prepared for the gospel was a fundamental feature of moderate evangelical revival theology, as we noted in the last chapter. Croswell, however, maintained that this process essentially takes one's eyes off of Christ as the remedy to our sinful plight. "Instead of *looking out of himself* for Salvation; his Business will be to keep *looking within* for the *horrible Preparation*; 'till at length, not being able to get the *unattainable Attainment*, he will be brought to the very Borders of Despair."[8] Evangelism should primarily focus sinners' attention on Christ, he contended, not on one's own religious experiences.

Third, Croswell believed that standard conversion experiences were too lengthy under the moderates' spiritual direction. Moderate evangelicals directed convicted sinners to employ the means of grace and wait to discern signs of spiritual renewal in their hearts. The process took time, involving periods of prayer, searching, introspection, and conferencing with a wise minister. Croswell was convinced that this whole process was unbiblical. "How long a time were those

---

[7] Andrew Croswell, *Mr. Croswell's Reply to a Book Lately Publish'd, Entitled, A Display of God's Special Grace* (Boston: Rogers and Fowle, 1742), 10-11.

[8] Andrew Croswell, *A Letter to the Reverend Alexander Cumming* (Boston: D. and J. Kneeland, 1762), 22; see also Andrew Croswell, *Free Justification Through Christ's Redemption* (Boston: T. & J. Fleet and Green & Russell, 1765), 12.

thousands under convictions, who were wrought upon by Peter's preaching? How long the woman of *Samaria*, the jailor, or *Zaccheus*? . . . [Likewise a] man may go into a christian assembly stupid and unconcerned about the one thing needful, and yet go home to his house justify'd, and an heir of heaven."[9]

Overall, the spiritual activism, introspection, and waiting inherent within moderate evangelical revival theology led Croswell to the conclusion that the system made grace too costly for the convert. The New Testament, by contrast, portrays grace as freely offered to sinners. Consequently, Croswell embarked on an alternative path in his evangelistic method.

During the awakening Croswell was notorious for calling sinners to bypass the lengthy requirements of legal preparations and respond immediately to the call of the gospel. "Sinners are in Danger of being devoured by the Wrath of God before [the] Sermon is done," he warned. "Why then should they not be call'd immediately to get into the *City of Refuge* before the *Avenger of Blood* overtakes them? . . . Why then should not Ministers call upon all the *Prisoners of Hope* who are in equal Danger, to *get into the strong Hold immediately*?"[10] While he affirmed that conviction of sin is a necessary prerequisite to receiving God's grace, he noted that the period of conviction does not need to be a lengthy one. Rather, conviction can be wrought in the soul in a moment by calling sinners to submit to Christ immediately. "And what is more likely to give them this necessary Conviction than their being commanded in the Name of the great God to come to Christ *immediately*?"[11] When asked what a person is to do to find salvation in Christ, Croswell bypassed the lengthy list of disciplines the moderates counseled and pressed sinners immediately to believe the gospel. "But see to it that you don't take up with meer legal Holiness, a keeping the Commandments of God, without the Faith of Jesus: But first believe on the Lord Jesus Christ with all your Hearts, and then Obedience to God's Commands will as naturally flow from your Faith, as Light flows from the Sun."[12]

Immediate conviction, the call to believe now, the bypassing of lengthy preparatory convictions—these all became the hallmarks of Croswell's evangelistic method. What was the theological basis for his practice? Croswell did not just

---

[9]Croswell, *Free Justification*, 22-23.

[10]Croswell, *Croswell's Reply*, 9.

[11]Ibid., 7.

[12]Andrew Croswell, *Heaven Shut Against All Arminians and Antinomians* (Boston: Rogers and Fowle, 1747), 20.

criticize the moderates and then simply turn to the Bible to find examples of quick conversions and calls to immediate repentance. He presented a thoughtful system that served as a theological alternative to moderate evangelical revival theology. Two positions undergirded his views: his teaching that God universally "grants" the blessings of the gospel to humankind and his doctrine of particular faith. The first position, which I will call his universal grant theology, relates to how Croswell was able to exhort sinners to trust Christ immediately. The second position, his doctrine of particular faith, concerns his understanding of the nature of saving faith and illustrates the kind of spirituality he expected true converts to experience.

Croswell's universal grant theology. When Croswell preached the gospel, he encouraged sinners to believe that Christ and the blessings of his forgiveness are already theirs for the taking. No preparatory requirements are necessary in order to possess the gospel's blessings; sinners only need to believe Christ. Moderates balked at this practice because it appeared to affirm that salvation is a gift that everyone everywhere possesses regardless of faith, sanctification, or holy living. Yet Croswell did not affirm that sinners *possess* the benefits of Christ and forgiveness. The reason for this had to do with a subtle but very important distinction he introduced to the discussion. "What *we* hold is that all Men should be *pressed to believe* that Christ and Forgiveness are *theirs*, not *in Possession*, but in *Right* or *Grant* only: These two Propositions are *essentially* different."[13] On the one hand, encouraging sinners to believe that Christ and forgiveness are theirs before they have believed is indeed an absurd proposition, for "'tis impossible a Man should believe that that which *was not his*, is *now his*, and in *his Possession*, without believing that he *hath received* it."[14] What Croswell did want to affirm, however, is that in the gospel offer every human being, no matter how wretched, has just as much of a right to the blessings of the gospel as another. Individuals do need not to wait to discern signs of saving faith before taking the encouragement that they have been saved. Rather, sinners in any state of unbelief need to be pressed now to believe because Christ and his salvific benefits are "theirs by right or grant" in the gospel offer. To put it another way, sinners do not *possess* the benefits of salvation in the gospel offer prior to faith, but in a real sense it is *theirs for the taking in the offer*. This position is what we will call Croswell's universal grant theology.

---

[13]Croswell, *What Is Christ to Me?*, 35.
[14]Andrew Croswell, *A Second Defence of the Old Protestant Doctrine of Justifying Faith* (Boston: Rogers and Fowle, 1747), 30.

Croswell illustrated this right that sinners have to the benefits of the gospel in several places. In *What Is Christ to Me, If He Is Not Mine?*, he asks his readers to consider a king who graciously declares that a group of condemned traitors might procure a royal pardon if they would come to him and "receive such Kindness at his Hands." Under these circumstances, is it not sensible to conclude that "all those Traitors [have] a *Right*, and one just as good a *Right* as another to the King's Pardon and Favour?"[15] Even though only some of the traitors might respond favorably to the declaration, it is an objective fact that the rest still possess the right to the royal favor, since it is truly theirs by royal grant.

Similarly, in another illustration, Croswell asks the reader to consider a rich man offering a beggar a piece of gold. "Take this Money, *it is yours*," the rich man declares. "The Beggar believes him, sees the Money to be *his*, and immediately takes Possession: He doth not *take Possession*, to *make it his own*, but sees it to be his own already by *free Gift*, and therefore *takes Possession*." It is in taking possession of the offer where the beggar experiences the blessings of the gift, even though the gift is his by grant before taking it. "This Similitude," Croswell continues, "answers exactly to the Sinners believing Christ for Forgiveness to be *his*, and his receiving them *as his*."[16]

In order to understand Croswell's strategy here we need to step back to gain a broader perspective of what he is trying to do. Croswell saw himself as a staunch defender of Calvinism, the divine decrees, and the Protestant emphasis on justification and the freeness of grace. Like many Calvinists of his day, he strongly believed that Arminianism in all its forms was a "soul-destroying" system that encouraged works-righteousness and denied the doctrine of justification by faith.[17] Yet throughout his writings he cautioned against applying the doctrine of election directly to the practice of evangelism because Scripture appears to present Christ to the world positively and in universal terms: he is the "Saviour of the world" (1 Jn 4:14), one given as "a covenant of the people, for a light of the Gentiles" (Is 42:6). "Whosoever will, let him take the waters of life freely" (Rev 22:17). Croswell notes how Christ says, "Look unto me, and be ye saved, all the ends of the earth" (Is 45:22), and that Paul preached to all that "through this man is preached unto you the

---

[15]Croswell, *What Is Christ to Me?*, 36; see also 21 for a similar illustration.
[16]Croswell, *Second Defence*, 30.
[17]Though he did affirm that there are Arminian believers. See Croswell, *Heaven Shut*, 11.

forgiveness of sins" (Acts 13:38).[18] If the particularizing doctrine of election is true, and Croswell believed it was, then how does one account for Scripture's universal presentation of Christ to the world? Croswell nowhere grounded the universal presentation of Christ in a theology of universal atonement. Rather, he adopts this theology of the universal grant of the gospel for this purpose: God has freely given the benefits of Christ's salvific work *objectively* to humankind. It *is* theirs objectively, whether they believe or not, yet without their belief they will not experience any of its blessings. This doctrine—not election—must be the primary animator of one's evangelistic preaching. "We must not blend the grant and the decree together," he maintained. "Tho' the apostles held the divine decree, they preached justification as freely as if there had been no decree at all."[19]

This objective gifting or granting of the gospel to all humanity, Croswell maintained, captures the positive stance God has toward the sinful world in the sending of his Son. Eternal life is neither withheld from sinners (as if they have no right to it), nor is it their possession (as if they have it already in their impenitent state); rather, it has been corporately granted to them virtually in the offer. Consequently, every human being in particular has warrant to lay claim to the offer of salvation in Christ. "For this only is *properly* and *strictly* [the] Gospel, viz. That God *gives Eternal Life* to Sinners *in Christ Jesus*, not *if* they will believe, but *whether they believe or no*: tho' without their believing, or *taking* the *unspeakable Gift* will *profit them nothing*, but only be a Means of their receiving the *greater Damnation*."[20]

Croswell did not invent his universal grant theology but borrowed it from a group of Scottish ministers known as the Marrow Brethren. Several decades earlier the Marrow Controversy (1718–1722) rocked the Church of Scotland over issues that pertained to evangelistic preaching, issues such as the relationship between assurance and saving faith, preparation for grace, the sinner's warrant for trusting Christ, and the extent of Christ's atoning work. After Thomas Boston republished Edward Fisher's *The Marrow of Modern Divinity* in 1718, denominational leaders in the Church of Scotland rejected numerous "antinomian" themes they found in the text. At issue was the appropriateness of the evangelistic method in Fisher's work, which encouraged sinners to "be verily persuaded in your heart

---

[18]Croswell, *What Is Christ to Me?*, 36. In keeping with the biblical text that all of the revivalists used in the period between 1740 and 1840, I cite the King James Version of Scripture when making direct references to Scripture in the text.

[19]Croswell, *Free Justification*, 7; see also Croswell, *What Is Christ to Me?*, 36.

[20]Croswell, *What Is Christ to Me?*, 19; Croswell, *Second Defence*, 15.

that Jesus Christ is yours, and that you shall have life and salvation by him; that whatsoever Christ did for the redemption of mankind, he did it for you."[21] Boston defended this evangelistic method in lengthy footnotes he attached to Fisher's text. He noted that in properly presenting the gospel it is vital to affirm, following Fisher's words, "that Jesus Christ is yours," because this "is the foundation of faith, and the ground and warrant of the ministerial offer." Boston comments,

> By this offer, or deed of gift and grant, Christ is ours before we believe; not that we have a saving interest in him, or are in a state of grace, but that we have a common interest in him, and the common salvation, which fallen angels have not, Jude 3; so that it is lawful and warrantable for us, not for them, to take possession of Christ and his salvation.[22]

Boston and a group of celebrated evangelistic ministers, including James Hog, James Webster, and Ebenezer Erskine, all defended the practice found in Fisher's *Marrow* but were strongly opposed by others who charged them with antinomianism. The controversy led to the reprimanding of the Marrow Brethren, a move that in time contributed to the formation of the separate Associate Presbytery in 1732. Croswell was familiar with the writings of this group and saw himself as a champion of their views, a point that explains his advocacy of their doctrine of the universal grant.[23]

In sum, the doctrine of the universal grant of the gospel significantly affected Croswell's evangelistic ministry. In his preaching, it allowed him to get to the good news of the gospel message faster because of the way it positively presents God's stance toward the sinful world. Though sin is infinitely heinous, yet God is for you in Christ and in the gospel. Evangelistic preaching need not linger at length on sin, the law, and divine wrath. In spiritual direction, it allowed him to bypass the long train of duties that moderate evangelicals exhorted sinners to follow to prepare themselves for receiving Christ. Sinners no longer need to wait to be thoroughly prepared to receive Christ because God has already given him to them by a royal

---

[21]Edward Fisher, *The Marrow of Modern Divinity: In Two Parts*, ed. Thomas Boston (London: Thomas Tegg and Son, 1837), 98.

[22]Ibid., 99.

[23]On several occasions Croswell lists the writers he thinks are safe guides on the subject of conversion and evangelistic preaching. He specifically names Thomas Boston and "the Erskines" (Ebenezer and Ralph), who were part of the Marrow Brethren, as well as Walter Marshall and James Hervey. See Andrew Croswell, *The Heavenly Doctrine of Man's Justification Only by the Obedience of Jesus Christ* (Boston: Green and Russell, 1758), vii-viii, xiii-xiv; and Croswell, *Letter to the Reverend Alexander Cumming*, 29.

grant. And with regard to the central call of the evangelist, the doctrine of God's universal grant allowed Croswell to press sinners to take hold of Christ immediately: do not wait for God to give you a new heart; repent and believe the good news now!

The doctrine of the universal grant of the gospel was a central feature of his revival theology, yet it formed only a part of his total views; his understanding of the nature of saving faith also factored prominently in his revival theology. While the doctrine of the universal grant affected his evangelistic method, his doctrine of particular faith transformed his understanding of the spirituality associated with conversion.

Croswell's doctrine of particular faith. Croswell's doctrine of particular faith became the foundation of a potent evangelical spirituality that prominently featured a sensible awareness of Christ's forgiveness and the exclusion of spiritual doubt. Particular faith affirms that *assurance is the essence of saving faith.* This seemingly simple point entails numerous beliefs that contrasted sharply with moderate evangelical revival theology.

According to Croswell, saving faith is "particular" in the sense that the believer apprehends the mercy of God in the gospel as being personally directed to the self. Thus, when an individual trusts Christ for salvation, that person does not merely look to Christ as the world's Savior but as *my Savior.* Though Christ died for sinners in general, particular faith perceives more: that Christ died for *my sins.* It is this personal appropriation of the gospel's promises that makes saving faith saving. "The *Faith of God's Elect* must be a *particular* Faith, whereby a man not only believe Jesus Christ to be the Saviour of *Sinners in general,* but the Saviour of *himself,* a most vile and miserable Sinner."[24]

Croswell believed that moderate evangelicals failed to preach the complete gospel because they merely presented an objective message of redemption— "believe in Christ who saves sinners"—rather than the full message of particular faith—"believe in Christ who is *your Savior.*" Croswell found the moderate evangelical understanding, which he called "general faith," to be woefully inadequate. He not only likened it to the nominal faith of many Christian ritualists, but he also believed that general faith inculcates legalism and works-righteousness because it encourages spiritual duties that are practiced apart from true faith.[25] The only way to avoid these "soul-killing" pitfalls, he noted, is to articulate a robust

---

[24]Croswell, *What Is Christ to Me?*, 18.
[25]Ibid., 6.

understanding of particular faith. "[Justifying faith is] not only a general Belief of the Articles of Faith, that Christ was dead and rose again for them that believe; but it is an *assured* stedfast *Confidence*, where by every Man *particularly* doth apply *to himself* the general Promises of God."[26]

Croswell linked two important doctrines to his understanding of particular faith. First, he argued that, in the process of spiritual illumination just prior to saving faith, an individual must apprehend God as personally loving them before true faith can be exerted. In other words, an awareness that "God loves me" must be the foundation for my trust in Christ. Basing his argument off 1 John 4:19 ("We love him, because he first loved us"), Croswell maintained that this perception of divine love is the only proper ground of saving faith. "When we exercise Love towards God, we *do*, and *must*, in Proportion to our *loving him*, look upon him to be *a God loving us*. Not that we love him only *for* loving *us* (*such Lovers* are *Haters of God*) but yet the Idea of his *loving us*, is not *excluded*."[27] A perceived awareness of divine love *for me* grounds the sinner's personal faith response.

To twenty-first-century evangelicals, this might seem like a very basic point: we come to love God because we sense that he loves us personally in the gospel call. But in the eighteenth century this was not a settled point; in fact, there were those who found Croswell's ideas to be deeply unsettling. Joseph Bellamy and Alexander Cumming, two ministers from the New Divinity tradition, contested Croswell's point because they believed it promoted self-interest and selfishness. They pointed out that all individuals would "love" God if God fixes his infinite love and blessing on them. Such "love" is self-interested and expects something in return, a far cry from the selfless portrait of love we find in Scripture. True love for God, Bellamy noted, must have a disinterested, objective foundation, grounded in the inherent worthiness of God rather than in the personal benefit we receive from him. Thus Bellamy argued that in the process of conviction and illumination sinners must come to a point where they perceive God's objective holiness so clearly that they conclude that they are personally damned.[28] In other words, before one can see God as one's Savior, one must first come to see him as a personally damning God.[29]

---

[26]Ibid., 12.

[27]Ibid., 24; see also Croswell, *Second Defence*, 20-21.

[28]This theme is covered in Bellamy's first dialogue in Joseph Bellamy, *Theron, Paulinus, and Aspasio; Or, Letters and Dialogues upon the Nature of Love to God, Faith in Christ, Assurance of a Title to Eternal Life*, in *The Works of Joseph Bellamy, D.D.* (Boston: Doctrinal Tract and Book Society, 1853), 2:165-85.

[29]We will explore these topics when we examine the New Divinity tradition in chapter three.

Croswell found Bellamy's doctrine to be ridiculous and practically impossible. How can a damning God be the object of love? "We can't love any one with a Love of *Complacence*, without apprehending him to be one who *loves us*, or at least, *would love us* upon sufficient Acquaintance with us."[30] He noted that such "dreadful Divinity" also runs counter to Scripture:

> God's Word don't represent him as the Object of Love, consider'd as a God that will damn us: But as a pardoning God thro' Jesus Christ, who bore our Sins in *his own Body on the Tree, and hath made Peace for us by the Blood of his Cross*. . . . [God did this] to draw our Hearts in love to him, [and] he tells how ready he is to pardon and pass by our Transgressions, and that he is full of Love and Kindness thro' Jesus Christ the Son of his Love. He styles himself Love.—*God is Love*. God in Christ is Love, an Ocean of Love, without any Bottom, and without any Shore. And accordingly we are said to love him, *because he loved us first*.[31]

For Croswell, it is clear that particular faith entailed a view of God that underscored divine love as the leading attribute in the proclamation of the gospel.

A second doctrine Croswell linked to his understanding of particular faith is the doctrine of assurance. If saving faith is defined as "trusting in Christ as *my Savior* who personally *loves me*," then there is no space for doubting, because the very concept of assurance is embedded in the definition of faith. To take out the particular aspect of the definition ("Christ is *my* Savior") destroys the concept of faith altogether. Consequently, as soon as individuals exert true faith in Christ, they experience assurance of their salvation. The "manifestation or persuasion of our justified estate," Croswell writes, "is essential to the exercise of saving faith. . . . It seems to me, the greatest absurdity in the world to suppose that the soul should trust Jesus Christ for salvation, and love him, and not be sensible of it. May I could as easily believe that the Saints now in Heaven don't know they are there."[32]

Croswell's stance calls into question the very existence of doubting Christians. Theoretically, doubt can have no place in the heart of an individual whose particular faith assures that "Christ has forgiven *my* sins." Consequently, those who doubt must not have true faith. Yet Croswell did admit that true Christians might sometimes doubt, and thus he offered advice to such "deserted believers." Specifically, doubting Christians are not to take encouragement in their sanctification

---

[30]Croswell, *What Is Christ to Me?*, 24.
[31]Croswell, *Letter to the Reverend Alexander Cumming*, 7-8.
[32]Croswell, *Croswell's Reply*, 11, 12.

and spiritual attainments. Sanctification, in other words, does not verify one's state of justification. Rather, doubting Christians are to seek the "immediate light" of God's countenance, which will assure them that they are indeed God's own children.[33] "If any tell him how *holily and unblameably he hath walk'd*, he will say, *miserable Comforters are ye all. A Christ* is what he wants; a *Christ* is what he must have: A *Christ* is what he *will* have: None but *Christ*: None but *Christ*; is the Language of his Soul."[34] In short, assurance is not attained through the action of sanctification, as the moderate evangelicals urged. Rather, it is experienced through a vibrant sense of faith in Christ and of his reciprocal love.

Moderate evangelicals found Croswell's views hard to swallow because of the self-centeredness they discerned in his formulations. Solomon Williams spoke for the majority. It is a mistake, he noted, to place assurance at the center of justifying faith, because by doing so individuals essentially make their own spiritual experiences an object of faith. True justifying faith should have only *objective* spiritual realities as their objects, namely, the gospel promises and the person and work of Jesus Christ. It should not add *subjective* components ("Christ is *my* Savior; God *loves me*"), because in doing so we logically make our subjectivity an aspect of justifying faith: "I believe in Christ *and* that I am one of his children." This understanding of faith, moderates noted, is found nowhere in Scripture. "There can be no foundation for a sinner's trust in God," Williams noted, "but the promise of God."

> And as there is no promise of salvation made in the bible to any particular sinner by name, therefore a particular persuasion that Christ is mine etc. cannot have any direct object; there being no such promise for that person's faith to stand upon. So that this can be no trusting in Christ. My believing though ever so firmly that Christ is my friend, or that God loves me, has nothing in it of the nature of trusting; it is only a persuasion of my mind. . . . To trust Christ, merely because I believe him to be my friend, or savior, is not to trust him on his promise, but on my own persuasion; which is no trusting at all, in the sense of Scripture.[35]

Joseph Bellamy agreed: "In true faith, nothing is believed but what is plainly revealed in the Holy Scriptures. But in [an antinomian understanding of] faith, the

---

[33]Croswell, *Heaven Shut*, 19-20.

[34]Croswell, *Croswell's Reply*, 19.

[35]Solomon Williams, *A Vindication of the Gospel-Doctrine of Justifying Faith* (Boston: Rogers and Fowle, 1746), 39.

main things believed are nowhere contained in the Bible. 'Pardon is mine, grace is mine.'"[36] For Bellamy and Williams, the end result of asserting that assurance is the essence of saving faith is a faith in one's religious experience ("grace is mine; God loves me"), not true faith grounded in the objectively displayed promises of Scripture.

Stepping back for a second, the differences between the spiritualities of Croswell and his opponents are clear. They arose because members from each side emphasized different themes found within the Reformed tradition. On the one hand moderate evangelicals presented a *spirituality of moral and religious activism* performed in the light of justification by faith, which resulted in lengthy directions prescribed to those seeking salvation or assurance in Christ. Calling any of these directions into question immediately raised the suspicion of antinomianism and cheap grace. Croswell, by contrast, emphasized more of a *spirituality of reception* that accentuated the blessings of what God has already worked on behalf of sinners in Christ—that in Christ God has granted salvation and eternal blessings to the world and that through faith alone sinners receive these blessings, not by any human exertion. Croswell's approach led him to a deep suspicion of any human activity that might interfere with the flow of God's free blessings. Both of these themes drew from theological positions present within the Reformed theological tradition. Their differences lie in emphasis.

Croswell was one of the few colonial American writers of his generation who published from a free grace perspective. In spite of this he was not a lone wolf. Similar views were found among other radical evangelical New Lights who found in free grace spirituality an attractive alternative to the protracted rigors of moderate evangelical revival theology.[37] This tradition, however, cultivated an anti-intellectual ethos that reveled more in the ministry of the Spirit than in the production of books. Consequently, we do not find an extensive legacy to Croswell's theology from 1740–1840. With his death in 1785, the tradition of free grace revival theology effectively came to an end.

---

[36]Bellamy, *Theron, Paulinus, and Aspasio*, 222.
[37]See Goen's exploration of the doctrines of the Separate Congregationalists in C. C. Goen, *Revivalism and Separatism in New England, 1740–1800* (New Haven, CT: Yale University Press, 1962), 115-58, though see especially 150-54.

JONATHAN EDWARDS: AMERICA'S REVIVAL THEOLOGIAN

The outlines of Jonathan Edwards's life and ministry are well-known.[38] Born October 5, 1703, in East Windsor, Connecticut, young Jonathan grew up in a family of eleven children, the only son of the Reverend Timothy and Esther (Stoddard) Edwards. Destined for a ministerial vocation, he attended Yale College and briefly led two congregations before settling in Northampton, Massachusetts, as the ministerial assistant to his aged grandfather Solomon Stoddard in 1727. That same year he married seventeen-year-old Sarah Pierrpont, and together they not only brought eleven children into the world but witnessed two spectacular seasons of revival over the next thirty years. His time at Northampton (1727–1750) coincided with the Connecticut Valley Awakening of 1735 and the First Great Awakening of the early 1740s, events he meticulously analyzed in *A Faithful Narrative of the Surprising Work of God in the Conversions of Hundreds of Souls in Northampton* (1737) and in his classic revival treatise *Religious Affections* (1746). His second pastorate at Stockbridge, Massachusetts (1751–1758), engaged him in missionary efforts to the region's Native Americans as well as authoring treatises that would have a profound effect on the history of theology in America, including *Freedom of the Will* (1754) and *The Great Christian Doctrine of Original Sin Defended* (1758). Called in 1758 to be president of the struggling College of New Jersey (later Princeton University), his life was sadly cut short after a smallpox inoculation, designed to protect him from a local outbreak, actually gave him the disease. He died on March 22, 1758.

Edwards was essentially a bridge figure in the history of American revival theology. On the one hand, he was a moderate evangelical who advanced the fundamental features of that system, including its emphasis on the means of grace, prayerful waiting on the Lord, and lengthy conversions—points we noted in the last chapter. At the same time, however, his theological profundity led him to experiment with new answers to old questions, answers that ultimately laid the foundation for a new trajectory in American revival theology known as the New Divinity tradition. In this section we will examine two features that formed the basis of this new trajectory. First, we will explore the prominence that Edwards gave to the will in salvation, what I shall call the *voluntarist accent* in his theology. Second, we will investigate an important aspect of his analysis of true

---

[38]For an excellent biography on Edwards see George M. Marsden, *Jonathan Edwards: A Life* (New Haven, CT: Yale University Press, 2003).

religious experience, what I shall call Edwards's *disinterested spirituality*. These
two features did not drastically alter his own revival practices, but in the hands
of his theological successors they were developed in such a way that forged the
New Divinity tradition.

***The voluntarist accent: Edwards on the imputation of Adam's sin and the
freedom of the will.*** Edwards prominently featured the human will in his theology.
Though he was a staunch Calvinist, he so closely aligned divine and human agency
in his work that it is often hard to distinguish between the two. We saw this earlier,
where we noted Edwards's take on efficacious grace: "We are not merely passive
in it, nor yet does God do some and we do the rest, but God does all and we do
all. God produces all and we act all. For that is what he produces, our own acts.
God is the only proper author and fountain; we only are the proper actors."[39] Similarly, he notes that justifying faith is not merely the passive recognition of what
God has done for us in Christ, but it is our active uniting with Christ, "our part"
in the covenant of grace, which establishes the person's union with Christ.[40] This
prominence of the active human will throughout his thought constitutes the voluntarist accent in Edwards's theology.[41]

This section will examine how the voluntarist accent helped shape two areas
of his revival theology: his understanding of the imputation of Adam's sin and his
theology of the freedom of the will. Here Edwards sought to recast the standard
Reformed positions on these topics. His aim was to show that we are not merely
passive inheritors of original sin and an unable will. Rather, *we* are directly responsible for our participation in Adam's sin and for our own spiritual inability.

One of Edwards's main goals in *Original Sin* (1758) was to defend the traditional position of the imputation of Adam's sin to his posterity. This doctrine is
vital to revival theology because it serves as a theological prequel to the doctrine
of redemption: salvation from sin and its punishment presupposes that all are in
sin and exposed to eternal wrath. Weakness here can signal weakness in one's

---

[39]Jonathan Edwards, "Efficacious Grace, Book III," in *Writings on the Trinity, Grace, and Faith*, ed. Sang Hyun
Lee, WJE 21 (New Haven, CT: Yale University Press, 2002), 251.

[40]For multiple definitions of faith, see Jonathan Edwards, "Faith," in WJE 21:417-25; for his language referencing "our part" in the covenant of grace, see Jonathan Edwards, "Justification by Faith Alone," in *Sermons
and Discourses, 1734–1738*, ed. M. X. Lesser, WJE 19 (New Haven, CT: Yale University Press, 2001), 158,
201.

[41]While it is clearly related, I am not referencing the technical distinction between voluntarism and intel-
lectualism prevalent in New England moral philosophy in the seventeenth and eighteenth centuries. By
voluntarist accent I merely refer to the prominence Edwards gives to the active will in the redemptive
process.

theology of salvation. The challenge facing Christian theologians through the centuries has been to articulate a robust understanding of sin that captures the way Scripture unites all humanity with Adam's fallenness (Rom 5; 1 Cor 15). The specific question to be answered has been this: What, exactly, unites Adam and his posterity (or his descendants)? The answer to this question reveals the medium for imputing (or crediting) Adam's sin to his offspring.

At the risk of oversimplifying, we can identify three different answers offered through the centuries. The first, the Pelagian view, maintains that what unites Adam and his posterity is that they share the medium of *a sinful context*. As new generations are propagated, they enter into an already sinful environment and thereby pick up wicked habits by imitation. Consequently, as persons individually transgress God's commands, they inherit a guilt similar to Adam's and fall under condemnation.[42] Guilt is consequential to each person's individual "fall." This simple answer was deemed heretical by the Council of Ephesus in 431 due to its undermining of the necessity of supernatural grace. Why does anyone need God's grace if, theoretically, all that is required for salvation is a sin-free environment? By contrast, orthodox Christianity deemed sin to be much more of a radical problem, not merely environmental.

With the rejection of the Pelagian position, Christian theologians moved on to offer better answers to the question of what unites Adam and the human race. As George Park Fisher indicates, two answers predominated throughout the medieval and early modern periods: the Augustinian theory and federal theory of imputation.[43] Taking cues from classical philosophy, the Augustinian theory maintained that Adam and his posterity share the medium of a *corrupt human nature*. When Adam transgressed, his sin brought corruption to human nature, and consequently every new instantiation of that nature (namely, every new human being) participates in this corruption and, by implication, Adam's guilt.

The federal theory, by contrast, located the unity of Adam and his offspring in the concept of a shared *covenantal bond*. In this position, Adam is understood

---

[42]Though technically they do not share in Adam's guilt, merely their own.

[43]George Park Fisher, "The Augustinian and the Federal Theories of Original Sin Compared," in *Discussions in History and Theology* (New York: Scribner, 1880), 355-409. Though written in the 1860s, Fisher's work is still a reliable study. For more recent studies on the history of original sin, see H. Shelton Smith, *Changing Conceptions of Original Sin: A Study in American Theology Since 1750* (New York: Scribner, 1955); Tatha Wiley, *Original Sin: Origins, Developments, Contemporary Meanings* (New York: Paulist Press, 2002); and part two of Hans Madueme and Michael Reeves, eds., *Adam, the Fall, and Original Sin* (Grand Rapids: Baker Academic, 2014).

as the "federal" or covenantal head of humanity, the one who legally represents the entire human race before God. This relationship is similar to the legal relationship between a head of state and its citizens: when the head of state declares war against an enemy, technically the entire citizenry is at war. Similarly, God holds the entire human race responsible for the actions of its covenantal head, Adam. Subsequent to Adam's failure, God imputes his sin to the entire race because it is in covenantal union with Adam. Subsequently, a corrupt human nature arises from this imputation, leading members of the human race to commit their own actual sins and incur their own individual guilt. Sinners thus partake of a double guilt: Adam's (via covenantal imputation) and their own (arising from their own sinful choices).[44]

While there are differences between these two views, both consider imputation to be logically antecedent to the individual's choice. Human beings, in other words, enter the world guilty and liable to condemnation for a transgression that they did not actively commit. Progressive theologians balked at the shocking inequity they discerned in these traditional Reformed positions. English Presbyterian minister John Taylor noted that "a Representative, the Guilt of whose Conduct shall be imputed to us, and whose Sins shall corrupt and debauch our Nature, is one of the greatest Absurdities in all the System of *corrupt Religion*. . . . [Anyone] who *dares* use his Understanding, must clearly see this is unreasonable, and altogether inconsistent with the Truth, and Goodness of God."[45]

Edwards apparently felt the weight of this criticism. Consequently, he sought to advance another solution to the link between Adam's original apostasy and ours, one that connected Adam's transgression with our actual willing. He proposed that Adam and his posterity share what we might call a *divinely established moral union*, whereby God constitutes a union between Adam's transgression and the first exercise of will in each of his posterity.[46] God, in other words, unites Adam's original apostasy and the initial moral exertions of every member of the human race into one complex moral act.[47] In attempting to explain this concept,

---

[44]Fisher, "Augustinian and Federal Theories," 356-60; Smith, *Changing Conceptions of Original Sin*, 1-9.

[45]John Taylor, *The Scripture Doctrine of Original Sin*, 3rd ed. (London: J. Waugh, 1750), 108-9.

[46]The details of Edwards's position are difficult to untangle but can be found in a short section of Jonathan Edwards, *The Great Christian Doctrine of Original Sin Defended*, in *Original Sin*, ed. Clyde A. Holbrook, WJE 3 (New Haven, CT: Yale University Press, 1970), 389-94.

[47]We should not think of this as a random connection Edwards concocts just to save the doctrine of imputation. He is attempting to construct a theoretical basis for the moral unity of the human race because Scripture appears to present humankind in this manner (Rom 5; 1 Cor 15).

Edwards resorts to a fascinating thought experiment in which he asks us to envision every member of the human race as existing simultaneously with Adam. "Let us suppose," he writes in a lengthy footnote,

> that Adam and all his posterity had *coexisted* . . . [and are constituted by God to be] *one* complex person, or *one* moral whole: so that by the law of union there should have been a *communion* and *coexistence* in acts and affections; all jointly participating, and all concurring, as *one whole*, in the disposition and action of the head.[48]

Not only do all human beings exist at one time in this thought experiment, but also God has effected a harmony of will among everyone, similar to a restless flock of birds in late fall that swarms about as if following an invisible law of nature. Consequently, when Adam (the head) sinned, the rest of humanity (as the body) concurred. Because all are complicit in the act, all equally share in the guilt: the sin and guilt of the head belongs to, or is imputed to, the aggregate, because all were active accomplices to the crime.

When we transition from this imaginative thought experiment (the coexistence of all humanity with Adam) to the actual way that human beings descend from Adam (propagation through generations), Edwards maintains that we essentially have the same situation.[49] Rather than uniting their wills *spatially* across a coexistent humanity (in the thought experiment above), God unites them *temporally* across the generations such that their initial moral exertions *are* their concurring with Adam's original apostasy. Thus, as soon as human beings come into existence, their initial moral acts, united to Adam's, immediately concur with Adam's transgression, and on that basis they become guilty of Adam's sin.[50] Because their initial moral acts are divinely linked to Adam's original transgression, the guilt they possess is a *shared* guilt: it is both Adam's guilt, because as the head of the race he committed the original transgression, and their guilt, because by union of will they consented to Adam's transgression and are active participants in it. In short, our first sins are the extended act of Adam's original transgression.

When Edwards tried to explain how it is possible that our first sins can be united to Adam's transgression, he resorted to another theory, this time with

---

[48]Edwards, *Original Sin*, 391.

[49]"Now, difference of the *time* of existence don't at all hinder things succeeding in the same order, any more than difference of *place* in a coexistence of time." Ibid., 392.

[50]From that point on, individuals proceed to produce their own acts of virtue or vice, for which they alone are individually responsible.

regard to the origin of evil in the human race.[51] Initially, Adam was created in perfect harmony with his maker: he possessed both *natural* principles (such as self-love) and *supernatural* principles (divine love, the consequence of the Holy Spirit's indwelling), which together would guide his life in perfect fidelity to God. Through an act of negative efficiency, in which God withdrew the presence of these supernatural principles, Adam's natural principles turned inward—the principle of self-love became selfishness—leading to sin, rebellion, and the fall. Because God was not positively active in Adam's moral implosion, Edwards argued that he cannot be blamed with sin. From this point on in the history of the human race, Adam's descendants receive the same nature he had after his fall, one devoid of the Spirit's supernatural principles. Consequently, at the moment they are created, the natural principles of their humanity turn inward in a moral exertion of nascent selfishness and sin. It is this moral act, Edwards notes, that is divinely linked with Adam's original transgression and literally *is* their consent to it.

Two observations are important to note at this juncture. First, in Edwards's theory we find no imputation of a completely alien guilt.[52] "Imputation" results from the shared transgression originating in the harmony of will that God established between Adam and his posterity. Second, for both Adam and his posterity the imputation of guilt is logically *consequential* to the transgression. "The apostasy is not theirs, merely because God *imputes* it to them; but it is *truly* and *properly* theirs, and on that ground, God imputes it to them."[53] This point distinguished Edwards's position from the federal view of imputation, which asserted that the imputation of Adam's sin is antecedent to any moral transgressing on the part of his posterity.

The upshot of Edwards's creative approach to original sin is that it simultaneously landed him in both traditional and progressive theological camps. On the one hand, several characteristics of his theory echoed traditional features. That Adam's posterity inherits a nature devoid of the Holy Spirit, subject only to the natural principles of self-love, strongly resonates with the traditional Augustinian view that we inherit a corrupt nature. Also, Edwards's intentional affirmation of imputation aligned him with Reformed orthodoxy in a day when many theological progressives

---

[51]See his entire discussion in Edwards, *Original Sin*, 380-83.

[52]*Alien* here is used in the sense that it is the imputation of the guilt of another individual, namely Adam's. Conversely, when evangelicals speak of the doctrine of justification, they often speak of the imputation of an alien righteousness to the believer, namely Christ's.

[53]Edwards, *Original Sin*, 308. See also 390-91, where Edwards makes this point several times.

were discarding the doctrine of imputation altogether. Furthermore, he believed his formulation had found a way around the central progressive critique against the Reformed position, namely that Calvinism entails the offensive notion that human beings come into the world condemned for an alien sin in which they played no active role. Edwards not only demonstrated (to his satisfaction) that the human race is indeed complicit in Adam's sin, but he did so within the structure of a decidedly predestinarian theology. Together, these moves were designed to strengthen the Reformed position on original sin. He thus can continue preaching for conversion as a moderate evangelical because he has reaffirmed central aspects of the doctrine of original sin, albeit in a creative way.

At the same time a progressive element appears in his theory. In constituting Adam's transgression and his posterity's into one moral whole, Edwards minimized the distinction between inherited, original sin and actual, individual sin.[54] Edwards's clever way of uniting these two distinct elements might have demonstrated how it is possible that the human race is truly responsible for Adam's sin, but there was a significant price to pay for such a move. The more original sin is identified with actual sin, the more it can be deemed a theologically meaningless concept, as it becomes virtually indistinguishable from the actual sins of Adam's offspring, a view that could approximate the Pelagian position if pushed to an extreme degree. Edwards, of course, did not succumb to this danger. His commitment to both imputation and the Reformed tradition prevented him from moving in this direction. Yet a door was opened by his views, one that was propelled by the voluntarist accent in his thought, and that was to be opened wider by his theological heirs.

In Edwards's doctrine of the freedom of the will we find the same voluntarist accent at work. In *Freedom of the Will* (1754), a work designed to counter Arminian notions of free will, Edwards sought to demonstrate how the concepts of freedom and human responsibility are perfectly consistent with the Calvinistic doctrine of inability. Many modern theologians, inspired by Enlightenment notions of liberty and freedom, had grown hostile to the concept of human inability because it aroused fears of fatalism and Thomas Hobbes's materialism. A nondeterministic, "Arminian" view of the will that emphasized human ability was increasingly becoming attractive as a viable alternative to Calvinism. Edwards

---

[54]This became the strategy of many of Edwards's New Divinity followers; see E. Brooks Holifield, *Theology in America: Christian Thought from the Age of the Puritans to the Civil War* (New Haven, CT: Yale University Press, 2003), 144; and Gerald R. McDermott and Michael J. McClymond, *The Theology of Jonathan Edwards* (New York: Oxford University Press, 2012), 605.

believed that this approach to understanding human volition was unbiblical and deeply flawed. Consequently, he sought to oppose it by critiquing the views of three representatives of the "modern prevailing notions" of free will: pseudo-deist Thomas Chubb, Anglican anti-Calvinist Daniel Whitby, and Calvinist dissenter and hymn writer Isaac Watts.[55] Edwards wove into his critique a fresh restatement of what he took to be the Calvinist view: nonbelievers, he maintained, are truly complicit in their inability, and because of this they are at fault in their unbelief.

Much of his argument in *Freedom of the Will* turns on the way Edwards defined the topic's central concepts.[56] The will, he noted, is not a separate subset of the inner person but rather is merely the choosing mechanism of the mind. *The will, in essence, is the mind choosing.*[57] This holistic definition of the will and its relation to the broader human mind enabled him to maintain that persons have freedom, not wills. How does the will make a choice? For Edwards, *the will is as the greatest apparent good is.*[58] As soon as the human mind perceives which course of action would bring the greatest apparent benefit to the self (which is discerning the "greatest apparent good"), the will is activated and a choice is made.[59] The will does not have a separate "mind of its own," as if it has a power to counter what the mind discerns to be the greatest good, for by definition the will *is* as the greatest apparent good is.[60]

If the will is not a separate entity of the inner person but rather the volitional extension of the mind's perception of the greatest apparent good, then in what sense is the will free? Edwards responded that the will is indeed free, but in a specific way. *Freedom is basically the power to do as one pleases* or the ability to carry out one's desires uninhibited.[61] When I am presented with a decision between two choices for dessert—chocolate cheesecake or Brussels sprouts—my tastes

---

[55]For details exploring the backgrounds to Edwards's work on the will, see Paul Ramsey, "Editor's Introduction," in *Freedom of the Will*, ed. Paul Ramsey, WJE 1 (New Haven, CT: Yale University Press, 1957), 1-128; Allen Guelzo, *Edwards on the Will: A Century of American Theological Debate* (Middleton, CT: Wesleyan University Press, 1989), 54-86.

[56]For an excellent overview of Edwards on the will, see Allen Guelzo, "Freedom of the Will," in *The Princeton Companion to Jonathan Edwards*, ed. Sang Hyun Lee (Princeton, NJ: Princeton University Press, 2005), 115-29. I rely on Guelzo's treatment at points in my analysis below.

[57]Jonathan Edwards, *Freedom of the Will*, in WJE 1:137-40.

[58]Ibid., 142-44.

[59]Emphasis is made on the "apparent" good because many choices appear, at the moment of decision, to bring a "good" that in reality is not the greatest objective good. The man struggling to quit cigarettes might know that his objective good is to avoid smoking, yet he lights up anyway because at that moment he has perceived that smoking would bring him greater satisfaction than refraining.

[60]Edwards, *Freedom of the Will*, 159.

[61]Ibid., 163.

incline me to one over the other (cheesecake "pleases me" over the other option), and if there is no natural impediment barring the course of action, then the resulting choice is executed in freedom. No sense of compulsion is experienced in choosing the cheesecake. It is important to note what Edwards did not include in the definition. Freedom is not the power to counter "what I please," because by definition freedom *is* doing what I please. What pleases me is a function of the fundamental orientation of my soul, the sum total of my tastes, biases, and values. We might call this orientation our "character"; Edwards called it our "disposition." It is the soul's disposition that conditions what we perceive to be our greatest apparent good. Our freedom is thus limited by our soul's disposition.[62] Subjectively, I experience freedom in choosing the cheesecake for dessert; no one coerced me. Objectively, my freedom is bound by the disposition of my soul—I am a cheesecake-loving, Brussels-sprouts-hating individual. I cannot counter or change the prevailing disposition of my soul simply because *I do not want to*. Why would I ever want to have Brussels sprouts for dessert over cheesecake? In sum, I am free and do as I please, but "what pleases me" is a function of my soul's disposition, something that I cannot alter (nor would I want to).

Edwards applied these concepts to the Reformed position of spiritual inability. Because sinful human beings by nature have no disposition to submit to God, they will never see Christ as their greatest good and consequently will never choose to follow him. This statement coheres with the standard Calvinist view of inability. Edwards wanted to go deeper, however, and demonstrate that sinners really are morally complicit in their inability. To achieve this, Edwards introduced to the theology of inability a distinction that became the hallmark of an Edwardsean theology of revival, the distinction between the sinner's *natural ability* to follow Christ and one's *moral inability* to do so.[63] From one angle, Edwards noted that the choice to follow Christ is theoretically possible for all sinners. The basic reason for this is that sin does not eradicate the existence of the will in a human being. All human beings, whether sinners or saints, possess wills by nature. The New Testament often associates redemption with volitional terms—sinners *follow, trust,* or *believe in* Christ unto salvation, acts that involve the will. Therefore

---

[62]Edwards's use of the concept of disposition, which appears throughout his notebooks and other works, is not that prevalent in the text of *Freedom of the Will*. It is inferred from his discussions of the virtuous or evil nature of certain individuals, as well as the excellent and holy disposition of God and Jesus Christ. See Edwards, *Freedom of the Will*, 160, 277-94, 337-42.

[63]Edwards's description of these concepts can be found in ibid., 156-62.

the choice to follow Christ is a theoretical option available to anyone who has a will. The sinner could choose Christ just like I theoretically could choose Brussels sprouts for dessert. Edwards called this theoretical ability the sinner's *natural ability* to follow Christ.

This, of course, is not the entire story. From another angle, Edwards realized that sinners' natural ability would never result in true faith because their sinful dispositions so incline them away from God that they would never see "following Christ" as their greatest good. Lacking the perception that "Christ is my greatest good," the gospel will never be seen as pleasing to the soul, and consequently the individual will never freely follow Christ. Edwards called this the sinner's *moral inability* to follow Christ because it pertains to the moral disposition of the soul animating the individual's character. Consequently, while nonbelievers possess all the natural resources needed to follow Christ (natural ability), they will never do so because their sinful dispositions always incline them away from God (moral inability). In short, though they *can* follow Christ, they *will not* do so because of their sinful dispositions.

Edwards gave a helpful illustration to demonstrate how this distinction works.[64] Imagine two seditious prisoners who are both personally offered a royal pardon on the condition that they approach their king standing outside their cells and humbly beg him for mercy. The first prisoner heartily repents and zealously accepts the offer, yet is prevented from bowing before the king because no one unlocked the doors to his cell. His is a natural inability because he *cannot* come even though he is willing. Nobody would blame him for missing the pardon offered by the king because his inability was natural, not moral. This, Edwards maintained, does not represent the kind of inability nonbelievers possess. That describes the other prisoner, who, in spite of the fact that his chains are removed and the door opened, refuses to prostrate himself before the king out of a seething hatred for his majesty. His inability has nothing to do with any natural impediments; the only thing he lacks is the moral desire to humble himself, confess, and gladly receive the king's pardon. In short, while this prisoner *can* be freed, he resolutely *will not* do so out of spite. His inability is a moral inability, arising from the vicious hatred wrought in his character. Consequently, though his inability is just as strong as the first prisoner's, everyone would agree that he is completely blameworthy for refusing the king's gracious offer.

---

[64]Ibid., 362-63.

By organizing his theology of the will around these categories, Edwards believed he had drawn together the diverse and oftentimes conflicting components of human volition into one coherent system. Freedom is preserved: at no point is it threatened. Persons do as they please; they get what they want if no natural impediments keep them from their desires. Because they are free agents, they consequently are held responsible for their actions. At the same time, inability is affirmed. Nonbelievers are held in bondage to sin, not against their wills but with the full complicity of their wills. Their sinful dispositions, working behind their wills, always incline them away from the gospel, because in their minds they do not see Christ's forgiveness as their greatest apparent good. Furthermore, they are blameworthy in the midst of their inability.[65] It is not that they cannot choose Christ (they can; they have a genuine natural ability); it is rather that they will not choose him because of sin (they have a moral inability and a hatred of Christ). Last, divine sovereignty in salvation is preserved, because only God can transform the sinner's nature by granting the soul a new disposition that sees God as their greatest good. Edwards believed he had found a way to unite freedom, responsibility, inability, and sovereignty into one consistent system.

Similar to his theology of imputation, Edwards's theory of the will reveals the voluntarist accent in his thought. *We* are complicit and volitionally involved in our spiritual inability, just like *we* are morally complicit with Adam in his original transgression. In both original sin and the freedom of the will, Edwards's goal was to demonstrate how human liberty can be understood to be consistent with Calvinist concepts (the imputation of Adam's sin, human inability) that were generally not associated with freedom, responsibility, and culpability. In demonstrating this consistency, however, Edwards was obliged to introduce new categories to the discussion, categories that earned mixed reviews by Calvinists of later generations. For original sin, Edwards's theory of the moral union between Adam's transgression and his posterity's enabled him to assert that all of humankind is justly responsible for Adam's sin, but the construct had the potential to dissolve the vital distinction between original sin and actual sin. For the freedom of will, the natural ability/moral inability distinction might have shown how it is that everyone is complicit and blameworthy in their inability, but it granted a theoretical ability to the sinner that made some Calvinists squirm due to its potential to denigrate divine sovereignty. These seeds took

---

[65]Ibid., 295-301.

root in Edwards's theological heirs, from which flourished a fascinating species of Calvinism that, as we shall see in the next chapter, developed in interesting and perhaps unanticipated directions.

On seeing God: The nature of Edwards's "disinterested" spirituality. Edwards's revival theology was not only influenced by the prominence of the will throughout his thought; it was also informed by his own vision of the nature of authentic Christian experience. Edwards advanced a version of spirituality that laid particular emphasis on the objective beauty of "divine things," by which he meant God, the person and work of Jesus Christ, the gospel, and the great themes of the Christian religion. According to Edwards, Christian saints are so enthralled with the beauty of God and his ways that they take little or no notice of themselves; their interests lie completely with God—his ends, his desires, his ways. In short, true saints are "disinterested" in themselves because they are completely preoccupied with enjoying God. I call this God-centered, self-denying portrayal of Christian experience Edwards's *disinterested spirituality*. While this theme is certainly found in the broader Puritan tradition as well as in other Christian traditions, it finds unique expression in Edwards's writings. Disinterestedness factored prominently in his doctrine of assurance and his theology of religious affections as well as his critique of antinomianism. It also heavily informed the spiritual vision and revival theology of the Edwardsean theologians who followed him.

The origins of Edwards's concept of disinterestedness are found in his theology of knowing God. When a sinner is regenerated and converts to Christ, Edwards argued that the Holy Spirit initiates a radical transformation of the person's perception of divine things such that they "see" God.[66] This is not a seeing with human eyes. Rather, "seeing God" is the result of Christians being enabled intellectually to discern a sublime and heavenly beauty in truths revealed in Scripture. In other words, when the saints meditate on the scriptural truths of Christianity— such as the character of God, the divine wisdom displayed in the gospel, the fitness of faith unto salvation, the advance of the gospel in the world, or any number of other points related to biblical divinity—they discern in these diverse objects a remarkable symmetry that is inherently beautiful. This inherent beauty

---

[66]For places where Edwards writes about spiritual sight, see his sermon "The Pure in Heart Blessed" in *Sermons and Discourses, 1730–1733*, ed. Mark Valeri, WJE 17 (New Haven, CT: Yale University Press, 1999), and two important "Miscellanies" entries, nos. 777 (on the "Happiness of Heaven") and 782 (on the "Sense of the Heart"), in Jonathan Edwards, *The "Miscellanies" (Entry Nos. 501-832)*, ed. Ava Chamberlain, WJE 18 (New Haven, CT: Yale University Press, 2000), 427-34, 452-66.

Edwards termed the *excellency* of divine things.[67] "To see God is this: it is to have an immediate and certain understanding of God's glorious excellency and love."[68] When the Holy Spirit opens the spiritual eyes of converts to behold divine excellency, there is elicited from their hearts a sense of love, desire, and communion with God. Edwards called this subjective sense of love the heart's *religious affections*.[69] In short, the central idea animating his doctrine of knowing God can be summarized as *the heart's affective sense of the excellency of divine things*.

Divine excellency and the affections they engender in the hearts of true saints are concepts found throughout Edwards's writings. In "A Divine and Supernatural Light," he defines spiritual illumination as "a true sense of the divine and superlative excellency of the things of religion."[70] In the *Religious Affections* Edwards devotes several distinguishing signs of authentic religious experience to this concept. "Those affections that are truly holy," he notes in sign three, "are primarily founded on the loveliness of the moral excellency of divine things. Or (to express it otherwise), a love to divine things for the beauty and sweetness of their moral excellency, is the first beginning and spring of all holy affections."[71] His conversion narrative represents a first-person example of the heart's affections for divine excellency. After experiencing periods of religious anxiety as a young man, Edwards came to a point, after meditating on 1 Timothy 1:17 ("Now unto the King eternal, immortal, invisible, the only wise God, be honour and glory for ever and ever. Amen"), where he came to see things in a much different light. "As I read the words," he noted,

> there came into my soul, and was as it were diffused through it, a sense of the glory of the divine being; a new sense, quite different from anything I ever experienced before. Never any words of Scripture seemed to me as these words did. I thought with myself, how excellent a Being that was; and how happy I should be, if I might enjoy that God, and be wrapt up to God in heaven, and be as it were swallowed up in him. I kept saying, and as it were singing over these words of Scripture to myself; and went to prayer, to pray to God that I might enjoy him; and prayed in a manner

---

[67]Jonathan Edwards, "The Mind," in *Scientific and Philosophical Writings*, ed. Wallace E. Anderson, WJE 6 (New Haven, CT: Yale University Press, 1980), 332-38.

[68]Edwards, "Pure in Heart Blessed," 64.

[69]Jonathan Edwards, *Religious Affections*, in *Religious Affections*, ed. John E. Smith, WJE 2 (New Haven, CT: Yale University Press, 1959), 96-99.

[70]Jonathan Edwards, "A Divine and Supernatural Light," in WJE 17:413.

[71]Edwards, *Religious Affections*, 253-54, yet see the entire section (240-91).

quite different from what I used to do; with a new sort of affection. But it never came into my thought, that there was anything spiritual, or of a saving nature in this.[72]

These examples demonstrate the objective nature of Edwards's spirituality. Similar to an art connoisseur at the Louvre for the first time, Edwards maintained that the Christian's spiritual attentions are drawn completely away from the self and its concerns by becoming totally preoccupied with the display of God's inherent beauty and excellency. This other-centeredness resulted in a spirituality that is almost spectator-like in nature, replete with a vocabulary that privileges visually oriented terms. Saints *behold* the *display* of divine *glory discovered* to their souls. They *apprehend* God's excellency in *views* of divine *light* and are desirous for the *magnification* of God's renown. These visual terms formed the fundamental grammar of an Edwardsean understanding of knowing God.

The corollary to this God-centeredness is a disinterestedness in the self and its concerns. What this means is that converts are not primarily preoccupied with their own interests, desires, and good (i.e., "What benefit do *I* receive from knowing God?"). They rather are focused solely on God's excellency and purposes in the world because God's universal interests have displaced their own private ones. This idea forms the core of what I am calling Edwards's disinterested spirituality, and it was fundamental to his discernment of a saving work of the Spirit in individuals as well as his doctrine of assurance. In *Religious Affections* it formed the central concept to his second sign of authentic spirituality. "The divine excellency and glory of God, and Jesus Christ, the Word of God, the works of God, and the ways of God, etc. is the primary reason, why a true saint loves these things; *and not any supposed interest that he has in them.*"[73] If one's spiritual joys arise solely from a sense of the "interest" or good one receives from God—such as a sense that "God loves *me*" or an awareness that "*I* am saved"—then such joy is a self-interested love, one that revolves around the private sphere of the individual's concerns. Such affections ultimately form no part of true religion. True affections arise completely from a delight solely in the display of God's excellencies. This does not mean that the saint derives no joy from an awareness of the great blessings redemption in Christ brings. Rather, it means that for Edwards these self-concerns are of secondary importance in the saint's spiritual consciousness.

[72]Jonathan Edwards, "Personal Narrative," in *Letters and Personal Writings*, ed. George S. Claghorn, WJE 16 (New Haven, CT: Yale University Press, 1998), 792-93.
[73]Edwards, *Religious Affections*, 240, emphasis added.

The soul that truly loves God is primarily preoccupied with God's inherent worth and excellency.

Edwards applied disinterestedness to his discernment of true grace in the heart. In his conversion narrative quoted above, we see him incorporating the concept in the last sentence. In the midst of experiencing the "new sense" of the beauty of divine things, he notes almost in an aside that "it never came into my thought, that there was anything spiritual, or of a saving nature in [these experiences]." His own wonder in God's glory drew the gaze of his soul completely away from concerns over his own salvation. Similarly, he noted the same theme in counseling sessions he had with newly converted saints who had not yet come to an awareness that they had experienced salvation.

> It has more frequently been so amongst us, that when persons have first had the Gospel ground of relief for lost sinners discovered to them, and have been entertaining their minds with the sweet prospect, *they have thought nothing at that time of their being converted.* . . . There is wrought in them a holy repose of soul in God through Christ, and a secret disposition to fear and love him, and to hope for blessing from him in this way. *And yet they have no imagination that they are now converted, it don't so much as come in their minds.*[74]

In the midst of "entertaining" the "Gospel ground of relief for lost sinners," Edwards discerned in these folks a "secret disposition to fear and love [God through Christ]." Their souls are not primarily concerned with the personal benefits of the gospel; "they have no imagination that they are now converted, it don't so much as come in their minds" primarily because they are "entertained" with the wisdom of God displayed in the gospel message. When Edwards sensed this kind of disinterestedness in the heart of an individual, he believed he had reliable evidence that the person had experienced a true work of grace.

Edwards's disinterested spirituality affected the broader contours of his theology. We can only sketch these implications here. First, it affected his doctrine of assurance. In contrast to Croswell, Edwards maintained that assurance ought not to be the immediate concern of the new convert. Assurance is a reflexive act of the soul, a conclusion that is a byproduct of beholding the inherent beauty of divine things. It grows as saints grow in sanctification and in the clarity of their

---

[74]Jonathan Edwards, *A Faithful Narrative of the Surprising Work of God in the Conversion of Many Hundred Souls in Northampton*, in *The Great Awakening*, ed. C. C. Goen, WJE 4 (New Haven, CT: Yale University Press, 1972), 173, emphasis added.

"views" of God. This point aligned him with the moderate evangelical approach to assurance. Consequently, Edwards stood resolutely against any "antinomian" version of justification that sought to embed assurance in the very definition of justifying faith. Second, Edwards's disinterested spirituality laid the foundation for an activist ethic of self-denial. If authentic Christian experience is fundamentally disinterested in the self's concerns and completely interested in God's, then the Christian life that arises from this should follow the same pattern: God's ends in the world (the spread of the gospel) and the ultimate concerns of others (their salvation) take center stage in the Christian's aspirations and desires. As we shall see in the next chapter, Edwards's followers developed these insights into a full-blown ethical system known as disinterested benevolence.

SUMMARY

As eager supporters of the First Great Awakening, both Croswell and Edwards contributed to the growing body of literature that analyzed revivals theologically. Their revival theologies represent two variations of the moderate evangelical revival theology described in chapter one.

Croswell's free grace revival theology was wary of the spiritual activism inherent in moderate evangelical revival theology, with its zealous advocacy of the means of grace and its lengthy conversions. Croswell believed these practices directly countered the Protestant teaching of justification by faith. In contrast, he advanced the following set of positions:

- Ministers are to encourage sinners to *believe the gospel immediately* because God has *universally granted Christ's salvation blessings indiscriminately* to the entire world. These blessings are theirs by grant or right; they only need to receive them.

- Faith is understood as *particular*, meaning that when one believes in the gospel, that person believes that Christ is not merely the Savior of the world but rather that he is "my" Savior.

- Assurance of salvation is necessarily entailed in both the definition and experience of saving faith. It is ridiculous to posit that individuals can believe in Christ and not know that they are Christians.

- Authentic conversions are short affairs that highlight the powerful transformation the Spirit works in the heart. Converts know the exact moment the Holy Spirit brought them from spiritual death to life.

Edwards's revival theology, by contrast, painted a much different picture from Croswell's. His work supported moderate evangelical revival theology, but he introduced two broad themes that would have a significant impact on the revival theologies of future generations:

- The *voluntarist accent* of his thought amplified the theme of human agency in his revival theology. This accent appears in two areas:

  » first, in original sin, where Edwards shows how human beings are actively complicit with Adam in the fall; and

  » second, in his portrait of the will, where he demonstrates how sinners possess both a moral inability to choose Christ and a natural ability to repent and believe. Thus even in a highly predestinarian theology sinners are the ones to blame for their sinfulness, not God or his decrees.

- A *spirituality of disinterestedness* also pervades Edwards's revival theology, a feature that surfaces in several discussions on the nature of true Christian affections:

  » The true Christian possesses an *objective spirituality* that takes the eyes of the soul off one's self and its interests and fixes them onto "views" of God's moral beauty seen in the gospel.

  » Sometimes new Christians are so overwhelmed with the moral beauty of God in salvation that they are not even aware they have been converted.

  » Assurance of salvation is a *reflexive act* of the soul, a byproduct of beholding God's inherent beauty and great worth.

Croswell's theology lived on in the radical, separatist wings of the New Light movement throughout the middle third of the eighteenth century. This tradition published very little, mostly due to an anti-intellectual ethos pervading much of the movement. It is therefore very difficult to trace the history of this tradition with any degree of accuracy. Edwards's theology, on the other hand, birthed an entire theological tradition in America known as the New Divinity movement or simply Edwardseanism. These Edwardsean ministers took Edwards's views and made further modifications to them, which brought new developments in the history of revival theology. We will begin to examine this story in the next chapter with our analysis of the New Divinity.

CHAPTER THREE

REVIVAL THEOLOGY IN THE NEW DIVINITY MOVEMENT

WHILE THE FIRST GREAT AWAKENING BROUGHT GREAT BLESSING
to the churches in colonial America, it also brought division. By the middle of the
eighteenth century many churches throughout New England were polarized over
the awakening. Some orthodox Calvinists, seeing the havoc that the awakening
brought to the region's Congregational churches, grew cold to revivals. They remained committed to Calvinism and to a warm-hearted piety, but they closed
their hearts to fantastic revivals. In time these churches and their ministers
became known as Old Calvinists. At the other end of the spectrum were many
New Lights who were drawn toward radical evangelical revival theology and separatism. In the middle were those like Edwards who sought to remain within the
Congregational establishment as pro-revival New Lights. In the 1750s these cen-
trists were dwindling in number as ministers were drawn to the poles. With Edwards's death in 1758, a gaping hole opened in New Light leadership among Congregationalists who sought to remain within New England's ecclesial order.[1]

Into this void stepped Joseph Bellamy and Samuel Hopkins, two ministerial
protégés of Edwards who carried his theological vision into the next generation.

---

[1]For studies that cover the New England theological landscape after the Great Awakening, see William
Breitenbach, "Unregenerate Doings: Selflessness and Selfishness in New Divinity Theology," *American
Quarterly* 34, no. 5 (1982): 479-502; E. Brooks Holifield, *Theology in America: Christian Thought from the
Age of the Puritans to the Civil War* (New Haven, CT: Yale University Press, 2003), 127-56.

During their long ministries they founded a movement among rural Congregationalists that grew from a handful of ministers in 1760 to roughly a quarter of all
New England Congregationalist clergy by the turn of the nineteenth century.
They saw themselves as consciously building on Edwards's legacy. Like him, they
were both zealously pro-revival and rigorously theological. They strongly opposed
the free grace theology of New Light Separates, the nonrevival views of the Old
Calvinists, and all forms of Arminianism. And in the midst of controversies with
these groups, they crafted positions that forged a different kind of Calvinism, a
"new divinity," as it was originally derided by its opponents.[2] That name, however,
stuck as the movement grew, and for the next century the New Divinity, or the
Edwardsean theological tradition, flourished in New England and beyond.[3] As
Sydney Ahlstrom has noted, it was "the single most brilliant and most continuous
indigenous theological tradition that America has produced."[4]

This chapter will cover the central features of New Divinity revival theology in
the latter half of the eighteenth century. I will show how the unique features of
New Divinity revival theology arose from the two points we explored in Edwards's
Calvinism in the last chapter. First, the New Divinity embraced Edwards's spirituality of disinterestedness and transformed it into a full-blown theological ethic.
Second, they embraced the voluntarism in Edwards's doctrines of original sin and
human ability, a move that ironically led to both the demise of the means of grace
and the elevation of immediate repentance. This subject will occupy the first
section of this chapter.

From there I will demonstrate how the New Divinity commitment to these
two Edwardsean ideas led to a reconfiguration of several Reformed doctrines.
Among these, three stand out. New Divinity ministers first expanded on the doctrine of original sin along lines laid down by Edwards himself. Sin is "in the

---

[2]Joseph A. Conforti, *Samuel Hopkins and the New Divinity Movement: Calvinism, the Congregational Ministry,
and Reform in New England Between the Great Awakenings* (Grand Rapids: Christian University Press,
1981), 71.

[3]The numerous labels given to the theological descendants of Edwards can be confusing. To simplify things,
I will use the terms *Edwardsean theology* and *Edwardseanism* to refer comprehensively to the entire tradition from 1750 to 1840. *New Divinity* will refer specifically to those Edwardseans in the latter half of the
eighteenth century (Bellamy, Hopkins, and their contemporaries) and their heirs in the early nineteenth
century. In the 1820s, an innovative branch of the New Divinity appeared that came to be associated with
Yale Divinity School and the writings of Nathaniel William Taylor. This group came to be known as the
New Haven Theology. Though there were differences between these groups, they were all "Edwardsean"
to varying degrees.

[4]Sydney E. Ahlstrom, *A Religious History of the American People*, 2nd ed. (New Haven, CT: Yale University
Press, 2004), 405.

sinning," not in the inheritance of an alien guilt that is antecedent to our actual existence. Second, many New Divinity revivalists embraced a view of the atonement that few evangelicals outside the New Divinity had advocated: the moral government theory of the atonement. And third, New Divinity revivalists articulated a very activist version of the doctrine of justification that demonstrated the necessity of holiness to one's justification.[5] By 1800, when the Second Great Awakening was taking off, New Divinity revival theology had come of age and was significantly different from the moderate evangelical revival theology of the First Great Awakening.

BELLAMY, HOPKINS, AND NEW DIVINITY REVIVAL THEOLOGY

One cannot read Joseph Bellamy (1719–1790) and Samuel Hopkins (1721–1803) without being struck by the fact that Jonathan Edwards's spirit hovers over their writings. This, no doubt, is due to their not only being mentored by Edwards as Yale postgraduates, but also maintaining close ties with him after settling into their long pastorates.[6] In their many writings they extended their mentor's theological vision. Among these, two works stand out: Bellamy's groundbreaking *True Religion Delineated* (1750), which is considered the first New Divinity treatise, and Hopkins's massive *System of Doctrines* (1793), which was the first systematic theology published in the United States.[7]

Disinterested benevolence: The New Divinity on God-centered virtue. Much of Joseph Bellamy's and Samuel Hopkins's theology is structured by a universal theory of virtue that Hopkins called *disinterested benevolence*. Simply stated, true

---

[5]For studies that examine the theology of the New Divinity, see Bruce Kuklick, *Churchmen and Philosophers: From Jonathan Edwards to John Dewey* (New Haven, CT: Yale University Press, 1985), 43-65; Holifield, *Theology in America*, 127-56; Douglas A. Sweeney and Allen C. Guelzo, eds., *The New England Theology: From Jonathan Edwards to Edwards Amasa Park* (Grand Rapids: Baker Academic, 2006); Oliver D. Crisp and Douglas A. Sweeney, eds., *After Jonathan Edwards: The Courses of the New England Theology* (New York: Oxford University Press, 2012).

[6]Bellamy ministered in Bethlehem, Connecticut, for more than half a century (1738–1790), and Hopkins led two churches over the course of sixty years in Great Barrington, Massachusetts (1743–1769), and Newport, Rhode Island (1770–1803). For biographical details, see Mark Valeri, *Law and Providence in Joseph Bellamy's New England: The Origins of the New Divinity in Revolutionary America* (New York: Oxford University Press, 1994); Conforti, *Samuel Hopkins and the New Divinity*.

[7]Joseph Bellamy, *True Religion Delineated; Or, Experimental Religion, as Distinguished from Formality on the One Hand, and Enthusiasm on the Other, Set in a Scriptural and Rational Light*, in *The Works of Joseph Bellamy, D.D.*, vol. 1 (Boston: Doctrinal Tract and Book Society, 1853); Samuel Hopkins, *System of Doctrines*, in *The Works of Samuel Hopkins, D.D.*, vols. 1 and 2 (Boston: Doctrinal Tract and Book Society, 1852).

virtue is "universal benevolence, or friendly affection to all intelligent being."[8] They argued that this concept captured Scripture's teaching on the essence of divine love. As such, it occupied a prominent place in their revival theology.

Love finds its origin in God, who loves with a disinterested, or other-centered, affection. "God is love:" Bellamy noted, "he has an infinite propensity to do good, and that in cases where there is no motive from without to excite him."[9] God's love leads him to bestow goodness on all creatures, even those who care nothing for divine benefits. He "loves to make his sun rise and his rain to fall upon the evil and unthankful. He loves to fill the hearts of all with food and gladness, and to strew innumerable blessings round a guilty God-hating world; yea, out of his great goodness, he has given his only Son to die for sinners."[10] God's benevolence, however, does not mean that sinners never experience the negative side of God, namely his justice, wrath, and eternal condemnation. This is because divine benevolence is exercised toward the entirety of creation at large and not toward individuals in particular. When God exercises disinterested affection toward creatures, he does so with an eye to the harmony and good of the entire system of being. By giving human beings life and blessing them with innumerable goods, he demonstrates a disinterested affection to them personally. Yet in the end, their rejection of his holiness ultimately results in their personal condemnation, because justice, exercised in eternal condemnation, is a "good" in the entire system of created being.[11] This portrait of divine love reveals two aspects that are central to the doctrine of disinterested benevolence: First, true love is *other-centered*, that is, it genuinely seeks the good of others, not its own. Second, true love is *universal in scope*, that is, it is a love that reaches out to the widest possible circle, encompassing the universality of existence.[12] The New Divinity took this pattern of divine love and made it the ideal of redemptive human virtue. The redeemed heart, in other words, loves God and others with an affection that takes its cues from this divine pattern of disinterestedness. Let us unpack this concept piece by piece.

First, true love for God originates in divine illumination, when a person comes to behold God's inherent beauty. Bellamy noted that "when we see [God's] infinite

---

[8]Samuel Hopkins, *An Inquiry into the Nature of True Holiness*, in *The Works of Samuel Hopkins, D.D.* (Boston: Doctrinal Tract and Book Society, 1852), 3:16.

[9]Bellamy, *True Religion Delineated*, 124; Hopkins, *True Holiness*, 40-41.

[10]Bellamy, *True Religion Delineated*, 124-25.

[11]Damnation, then, is a facet of God's disinterested benevolence toward creation.

[12]Both Bellamy and Hopkins used the terms *virtue* and *benevolence* as synonymous terms with *love*.

dignity, greatness, glory, and excellency, and begin rightly to esteem him, then his conduct, in all this, will begin to appear infinitely beautiful and ravishing, and worthy to be rejoiced and exulted in."[13] The pattern of divine beauty is encoded in the moral law, which Christ summarized in the greatest commandment (i.e., loving the Lord with all our hearts, souls, and minds, and loving our neighbors as ourselves; Mt 22:37-40). Consequently, when God opens the mind to see divine beauty in the moral law, that person is enabled to love God for who he truly is. Divine illumination thus becomes the necessary foundation of all true love to God. Without it, loving God is impossible: "In all cases, so far as we see beauty, so far we love, and no further."[14]

Second, true love is other-centered. What this means is that true virtue is *disinterested* in the self's needs and goods and wholly preoccupied with the good of others. A disinterested love to God loves him for who he is, not because he has loved us. "This obligation which we are under to love God with all our hearts resulting from the infinite excellency of the divine nature is binding *antecedently to any consideration of advantage or disadvantage, of rewards or punishments, or even of the positive will and law of God himself.*"[15] To love God simply because he loves us reflects a heart that loves God for his benefits, not from a true insight into his inherent excellency. This, Bellamy argued, is a recipe for false religion and a sign that the heart has not been freed from the bondage of sin. True love to God must be disinterested in the self and its benefits and solely interested in God and his worthiness.

Last, Bellamy and Hopkins's understanding of true love to God implied universal goodwill or benevolence to all intelligent beings. Once the saint loves God for his inherent worth, that love will lead the soul to love all that God loves. Since God's primary posture toward the moral world is one of benevolence to all, the saints' love will likewise follow suit. Private affection, or a love that extends to a limited sphere of interests (i.e., merely to one's family and/or friends), is really none other than self-love in disguise, rendering an individual no better than an unbeliever. By contrast, "disinterested benevolence is pleased with the public interest,—the greatest good and happiness of the whole."[16]

---

[13]Bellamy, *True Religion Delineated*, 19; see also Hopkins, *System of Doctrines*, 1:376.
[14]Bellamy, *True Religion Delineated*, 16.
[15]Ibid., 50.
[16]Hopkins, *System of Doctrines*, 1:379.

It was this type of robust love—one that arises from beholding the beauties of God's moral excellencies and one that seeks the good of the entire moral world at the expense of one's own personal interests—that occupied the New Divinity's understanding of what the regenerate heart looks like. When they preached the gospel and counseled individuals who were under a sense of conviction, they were on the lookout for signs of benevolent hearts that loved God disinterestedly. Bellamy and Hopkins used this doctrine to inform their revival theology in at least two ways.

First, Bellamy employed the doctrine of disinterested benevolence to oppose the erroneous spirituality he discerned in antinomian writers. In the late 1750s, an antinomian controversy flared up over the publication of a book by James Hervey titled *Theron and Aspasio, or, A Series of Dialogues and Letters, upon the Most Important and Interesting Subjects* (1755).[17] For several years, English writers from across the evangelical spectrum—including John Wesley, John Brine, Robert Sandeman, as well as Bellamy and Croswell—contributed lengthy treatises to the controversy, which drew Bellamy and Croswell into direct opposition with each other.[18] The point of contention between Bellamy and Croswell centered on the nature of the convert's love to God. Does a Christian's love for God arise from an objective insight into God's inherent moral beauty, as Bellamy maintained, or does it arise from a subjective sense of God's particular love to the self, as Croswell argued? In short, do Christians love God for who he is or for what he does for us? To Bellamy this seemingly subtle distinction was in essence two completely different foundations for the Christian faith. They are "two kinds of faith. . . . However in appearance they may be alike, yet in reality [they] are essentially different throughout."[19] He explored these differences in a dialogue titled *Theron, Paulinus, and Aspasio* (1759), a work that pits Paulinus, who represents Bellamy's views, against two antinomian proponents, Theron and Aspasio.[20]

---

[17]James Hervey, *Theron and Aspasio, or, A Series of Dialogues and Letters, upon the Most Important and Interesting Subjects* (London: John and James Rivington, 1755).

[18]Croswell's and Bellamy's contributions are as follows: Andrew Croswell, *The Heavenly Doctrine of Man's Justification Only by the Obedience of Jesus Christ* (Boston: Green and Russell, 1758); Andrew Croswell, *A Letter to the Reverend Alexander Cumming* (Boston: D. and J. Kneeland, 1762); Joseph Bellamy, *Theron, Paulinus, and Aspasio; or, Letters and Dialogues upon the Nature of Love to God, Faith in Christ, Assurance of a Title to Eternal Life*, in *The Works of Joseph Bellamy, D.D.*, vol. 2 (Boston: Doctrinal Tract and Book Society, 1853); Joseph Bellamy, *A Blow at the Root of the Refined Antinomianism of the Present Age*, in *The Works of Joseph Bellamy, D.D.*, vol. 1 (Boston: Doctrinal Tract and Book Society, 1853); Joseph Bellamy, *Remarks on the Revd. Mr. Croswell's Letter to the Reverend Mr. Cumming* (Boston: S. Kneeland, 1763).

[19]Bellamy, *Theron, Paulinus, and Aspasio*, 224.

[20]As noted in the title, Bellamy's dialogue was a direct response to Hervey's work.

In the dialogue, Bellamy explores the foundation of antinomian spirituality. "Is it not impossible," Theron, the antinomian, asks Paulinus, "[that] we should love God before we see that he is our reconciled Father and Friend in Jesus Christ? We must [first] know that our sins are forgiven, and be well persuaded that God is reconciled to us, before we can love him." With this question Bellamy confronts the reader with the central issue. Antinomian advocates had maintained that one's love for God must first arise from a subjective sense that God has first loved us in the gospel.[21] Once aware of God's love "for me," the person believes in the offer of reconciliation in Christ and reciprocates love to God out of gratitude. Theron describes this pattern by relaying his testimony of conversion: "[I first] had the love of God, as a reconciled God, manifest to my soul. [Second,] Hereupon I believed that God was my reconciled God and Father. [Third,] And so I loved God because he first loved me."[22]

Paulinus, who voiced Bellamy's views, found this order to be completely backwards. "God never manifests himself, as a reconciled God and Father, to any of the children of men, until they are first reconciled to him."[23] According to Bellamy, God does not, in the process of conversion, first reveal his love to fallen humanity. Rather, in their path to conversion, God first reveals his holiness and justice to sinners in the moral law. This is the sinner's first true encounter with God. Subsequently, by coming to see God's holiness through illumination, sinners not only come to agree with God's just sentence on the self ("I justly deserve hell"); they also come to detest sin and desire to part with it. It is only at this point that individuals are completely in a state of disinterestedness, that is, they are disinterested in their own good and become completely "interested" in God and his holy ways. This insight becomes a holy foundation for repentance and faith in Christ. Experiencing God's love takes place only after the process of true repentance and faith has been completed.

When he compared Theron's and Paulinus's conversions, Bellamy came to the conclusion that they were two very different spiritualities. "There is an essential difference between being charmed with the beauty of the divine goodness, and being ravished merely to think that God loves me. The one will infallibly change

---

[21]This essentially is Croswell's view, as we saw in the last chapter. Bellamy judged Croswell's free grace revival theology to be antinomian.

[22]Bellamy, *Theron, Paulinus, and Aspasio*, 179. As we saw in the last chapter, Croswell cited 1 Jn 4:19 as the biblical foundation for this approach: "We love him, because he first loved us."

[23]Ibid., 167.

us into the divine image, agreeable to Matt. v. 44, 45, 48; the other will never raise us higher than to the publican's standard, (ver. 46, 47)."[24] In sum, Bellamy argued that the experience of salvation must begin with a sense of God's holiness, justice, and wrath *prior to* an awareness of his love for the soul.[25] The antinomian route to God, by contrast, merely encourages the principle of self-love and fundamentally does not lead the soul to God.

Like Bellamy, Samuel Hopkins also employed the doctrine of disinterested benevolence extensively in his writings. He contended that God loves with a costly, disinterested love "in giving his Son to die for sinners, that they might live through him."[26] Christ's love for humankind reflected the same pattern: "His love to men was, in the highest degree, disinterested benevolence, as it was love to enemies, and such a regard for their good as to lead him to be willing to take their misery on himself, and bear it all, that they might escape and live forever."[27] Christians likewise are commended to patterns of love that reflect the selflessness inherent in disinterestedness. True love "seeketh not her own" (1 Cor 13:5) but hates one's own life in this world (Jn 12:25). Disciples are charged to take up their crosses daily and follow Christ (Lk 9:23). They are not merely to tolerate their enemies; they are to love them (Mt 5:43-47). Such a love unites individuals to "the grand community of the universe."[28]

The unique feature in Hopkins's articulation of disinterestedness lies in the radical degree to which he believed it could be experienced during the conversion process. Hopkins argued that sinners under conviction of sin can come to a point where they are so disinterested in themselves that they actually desire their own damnation for the sake of the greater good.[29] This question of one's "willingness to be damned for God's greater glory" is not as farfetched as one might initially think. He noted that many individuals came to entertain such a notion in the midst of an agonizing conviction process. Furthermore, he observed a similar

---

[24]Ibid., 181.

[25]Ibid., 179-80. Consequently, Bellamy had to offer an alternative interpretation of 1 Jn 4:19 ("We love him, because he first loved us"). The love with which God first loved us is not to be understood as our subjective sense of his love to us prior to conversion. Rather, it is the objective action of his electing love ("sovereign grace . . . which he exercised in awakening, convincing, and converting elect sinners"), which forms the basis for the saints' responsive love to God. See Bellamy, *Theron, Paulinus, and Aspasio*, 179-80.

[26]Hopkins, *True Holiness*, 41.

[27]Ibid., 44-45.

[28]Ibid., 31; for similar comments, see Hopkins, *System of Doctrines*, 1:379-85.

[29]See Hopkins, *True Holiness*, 59-61. Joseph Bellamy, by contrast, denied that this is the sinner's duty; see Bellamy, *Theron, Paulinus, and Aspasio*, 263.

sentiment in the apostle Paul with regard to the Jewish race: "For I could wish that myself were accursed from Christ for my brethren" (Rom 9:3). Consequently, he believed that it is possible to come to a place in the conviction process where we might desire to "give up ourselves wholly to [God], to be for his use, that his ends may be answered by us, and he be, in the highest degree, blessed and glorified, . . . let what will become of us."[30] If God so chooses to execute his wrath on us (which is just), then the disinterested heart says, "Amen!" "Therefore, however great and important is our whole interest, temporal and eternal, we ought to be willing to give it all up, if it is inconsistent with the highest interest, the greatest glory of Him who is at the head of the universe, and the sum of all being and perfection, and true benevolence will do this."[31]

God-centered virtue, codified in the theory of disinterested benevolence, was a fundamental feature of New Divinity views. It served as the foundation of their analysis of true Christian experience, and as we shall see below, it shaped the conversion narratives of individuals who converted in the midst of their revivals. It was, however, only part of the Edwardsean inheritance that informed the revival theology of the New Divinity. In the next section we will examine other New Divinity doctrines that drew inspiration from the voluntarist accent in Edwards's writings and led to a transformation of their revival theology.

Edwardsean anthropology and immediate repentance. While Edwards's theology of disinterestedness shaped the New Divinity's understanding of the spirituality of conversion, it was his theological anthropology, or the doctrines related to the theology of humanity (such as sin, original sin, and human ability), that transformed his disciples' practice of preaching. Samuel Hopkins extensively drew out the implications of Edwards's anthropology in his polemical writings against Old Calvinists. In order to see the significance of these themes to Hopkins's thought, it is important first to explore the historical backgrounds of his encounter with Old Calvinists.

After the great revivals of the 1740s had simmered, New England Congregationalism went through an informal restructuring process. Many of the larger established churches had grown weary of the awakening's divisiveness.

---

[30]Hopkins, *True Holiness*, 60.

[31]Ibid., 61. True benevolence is a desire peculiar only to the regenerate. Thus, while someone may evince a legitimate desire to be damned for the sake of God's universal good, that individual will never experience damnation. Consequently, Hopkins held that the willingness to be damned was a sign of true grace in the soul.

Consequently, many ministers defaulted to a pious, confessional Calvinism they believed characterized their seventeenth-century forebears. These Old Calvinists championed Reformed theology and advocated the use of the means of grace in conversion but eschewed the emotionalism of revivals. Hopkins, however, believed that Old Calvinists advocated a model of conversion that was detrimental to evangelism. At the top of his list of grievances was their *positive* portrayal of the "unregenerate doings" of sinners: those activities, such as the means of grace, that nonbelievers employ in seeking salvation prior to their conversion. Does God look favorably on these unregenerate doings? Are the blessings of the gospel, in other words, positively connected in any way with these activities? Old Calvinists suggested a positive connection between the means of grace and salvation.[32] Hopkins disagreed, believing that such a view directly leads to a "glaring absurdity and contradiction." He argued that "[if] the promises of the gospel are made to the doings of unregenerate sinners then they have a title to God's favor and eternal salvation, antecedent to faith. . . . They are therefore, at the same time, interested in the all the divine promises, under God's favor and smiles . . . and yet under all the curses written in God's book."[33] His encounters with Old Calvinist arguments led him back to Edwards, where he found resources that ultimately led Hopkins to the doctrine of immediate repentance.

Hopkins held two aspects of Edwards's theological anthropology, each informing his understanding of unregenerate sinners. First, he reaffirmed Edwards's privative view of the nature of the fall. Fallen human beings lack the supernatural principle of divine love in their hearts. Devoid of the Spirit's presence, the sinner operates only with natural motives and principles guided by self-love, a formula that necessarily gives rise to selfishness, sin, and condemnation.[34] Second, in an effort to counter Arminian criticisms of Calvinistic inability, Hopkins reaffirmed Edwards's distinction between the natural ability and the moral inability of the unregenerate. While it is true that sinners will not choose the gospel because they lack the supernatural principle of love, it is also true that their refusal of Christ is freely willed, the result of their desire to seek their own selfish ends via self-love. No one compels them in their rejection; they are solely at fault. Theoretically, they

---

[32]Samuel Hopkins, *The True State and Character of the Unregenerate*, in *The Works of Samuel Hopkins, D.D.*, 3:300-302.

[33]Samuel Hopkins, *An Inquiry Concerning the Promises of the Gospel*, in *The Works of Samuel Hopkins, D.D.*, 3:238.

[34]Hopkins, *System of Doctrines*, 1:209-10.

could comply if they wanted to do so. If you were able to look inside and examine their souls, you would find all the necessary components of a human nature capable of loving and serving God. Because they have natural ability, there is "no difficulty" in complying with the terms of the gospel. The only thing lacking is "an inclination and true desire to accept the salvation offered. . . . If sinners perish under the gospel, it is through their own obstinate, continued, voluntary refusal to accept of, or truly desire and ask for, [the] offered salvation."[35]

The combination of these positions led Hopkins to embrace a negative and even harsh understanding of sinners. Simply put, if there is no love of God's holiness in the unregenerate heart, then every action, no matter how pious or virtuous, is to be regarded as wholly wicked and evil. "The unregenerate sinner is an enemy to God," he argued. "The whole bent and all the exercises of his heart are in opposition to God's true character, and no influences on his mind, whether by the Spirit of God or anything else, antecedent to regeneration, or any change whatsoever, do in the least degree remove this opposition and enmity."[36] Since there is no halfway house between the unregenerate and the regenerate, no one should think God regards the unregenerate positively, no matter how desirous or sincere the seeker may be of obtaining salvation.[37] Thus, when Hopkins encountered Old Calvinists portraying the means of grace in a positive light, he naturally recoiled at the idea. By contrast, he affirmed that unregenerate sinners and all their actions are wholly regarded by God as sinful, wicked, and worthy of eternal condemnation. Consequently, Hopkins drew out several implications from these reflections.

First, he argued that the promises of the gospel found in Scripture—and specifically the promise that those who repent and believe shall be saved—are promises made *only to the regenerate*. He asserted that Scripture makes no promise of eternal life to the unregenerate who diligently use the means of grace or who sincerely desire salvation.[38] The simple reason for this is that the unregenerate are carnally minded and at enmity with God (Rom 8:7-8). The only legitimate condition of the gospel is repentance and faith, and the only individuals capable of exerting such exercises are those who have been regenerated by the Spirit of God.

---

[35]Hopkins, *Promises of the Gospel*, 248-49; Hopkins, *True State of the Unregenerate*, 296.
[36]Hopkins, *True State of the Unregenerate*, 292.
[37]Hopkins, *Promises of the Gospel*, 207.
[38]Ibid., 237.

"We may, therefore, be sure the apostles did not believe there were any promises made to [unregenerate] doings short of repentance and faith in Christ."[39]

Second, Hopkins adopted a negative stance toward the means of grace. If all the "doings" of the unregenerate are sinful and done with selfish motives, then the means of grace fall under this category. Hopkins took this logic a step farther in a way that shocked Old Calvinists: he argued that sinners' use of the means of grace compounds their guilt rather than allays it. "On the whole, [a sinner] becomes not less, but more vicious and guilty in God's sight, the more instruction and knowledge he gets in attendance on the means of grace."[40] The reason for this is that the means of grace are, in a sense, holy things, and a sinner's use of them is essentially sinning in "more direct and immediate" proximity to God. "Every sin is more or less aggravated and criminal according as it is committed more directly and immediately against God or not."[41] To support his point Hopkins pointed to biblical texts such as Hebrews 2:2-3; John 15:22; and Matthew 11:20-24, which imply that greater knowledge and exposure to the truths of the gospel render sinners even more sinful. Thus Christ regards Chorazin, Bethsaida, and Capernaum as more evil than Tyre, Sidon, and Sodom because they rejected the gospel implicit in Christ's mighty works.[42] Consequently, one should not take comfort in adopting a lengthy course of the means of grace with the hopes that God will someday regenerate. The awakened should approach the means with trepidation and fear, knowing that they are increasingly compounding their sinfulness and guilt before God.

Finally, Hopkins adopted this negative stance toward the means of grace because he believed they distracted attention away from the biblical conditions of eternal life, namely repentance and faith. While the means are necessary in that through them sinners learn of the claims of the gospel on their lives,[43] Hopkins saw that they could easily be abused by ministers urging their use.

> Instead of calling upon all to repent and believe the gospel . . . the most they do, with relation to unregenerate sinners, is to exhort and urge them to these doings, which are short of repentance. They teach them to use means in such a manner as rather tends to defeat the proper ends of means, and so as that they become a means of

---

[39]Ibid., 240.
[40]Ibid., 263.
[41]Hopkins, *True State of the Unregenerate*, 305.
[42]Ibid., 308-9, 321.
[43]Hopkins, *Promises of the Gospel*, 260-62.

blinding their eyes, rather than of instruction; it tends to lead them to rest in means, and make a Savior of them.[44]

Because of this, Hopkins made it clear that once sinners have become aware of the gospel claims through the means of grace, they are to be called immediately to repentance and faith, not to some continued course of moral reformation and spiritual duties. Scripture nowhere calls sinners to these duties; rather "God commands all men, every where, to repent and believe the gospel."[45] When we add to this scriptural warrant the fact that sinners have a natural ability to repent and believe, then the conclusion is clear: the minister's main task with regard to unbelievers is to call them to repent immediately and believe the gospel.

Immediate repentance, then, became the practical result of Hopkins's reflections on Edwardsean anthropology. It must be noted that he arrived at this conclusion by a much different route from Andrew Croswell and the free grace revivalists. While Croswell stressed the universal grant of the gospel offer, Hopkins, by contrast, derived immediate repentance from trajectories present in Edwards's theology. Lacking a principle of divine love, the sum total of a sinner's actions and intentions only amounts to a sinfulness that is vicious in God's sight. Convicted sinners must employ the means only so far as to get a knowledge of the gospel's claims on their lives. Once there, they are to be exhorted immediately to repent of their selfishness and believe. Protests of inability to comply with the gospel are to be answered with the famous Edwardsean emphasis: "You indeed can comply only if you will. The only thing preventing you from receiving eternal life is your stubborn obstinate heart. Repent and believe in Christ!" While Hopkins's version of immediate repentance theoretically implied a faster conversion experience, in actuality the sinner still had to wait for God's work of regeneration. Only then could the sinner truly repent and believe with disinterested, benevolent motives fueled by a principle of divine love.

Toward the end of the eighteenth century, Hopkins's arguments were winning the hearts of many New England ministers, so much so that "Hopkinsianism" became synonymous with New Divinity theology. His views on the unregenerate, natural ability, and immediate repentance, coupled with the Edwardsean ideal of disinterested benevolence, drove New Divinity revival theology. The cluster of

---

[44]Ibid., 272.
[45]Hopkins, *System of Doctrines*, 1:501.

these theological ideas, forged in the context of the New Divinity's rural revivals, affected other areas of their theology. In the next section we will examine how these views transformed the broader vistas of New Divinity Calvinism.

ROUNDING OUT NEW DIVINITY REVIVAL THEOLOGY

As the Edwardsean theological tradition matured, New Divinity leaders realized that Edwards's core insights could be applied to other doctrines in ways that could "update" Calvinist theology. The New Divinity saw themselves as committed New Light Calvinists: they prized the sovereignty of God in salvation, the spiritual theology of the Puritans, and the great revivals of the First Great Awakening. Yet as children of their own age they believed that particular points of traditional Calvinism were out of step with their day. Consequently, they sought to reconfigure Calvinism in such a way to render it more amenable to reason, more consistent with humanity's sense of justice, and ultimately more in alignment with their reading of Scripture. Insights gleaned from Edwards's theology paved the way to this reconfiguration.

This section will examine three doctrines in which we see this reconfiguration evident: original sin, the atonement, and justification. While New Divinity leaders freely borrowed much from their mentor, the voluntarist accent in Edwards's thought had the most profound impact on the New Divinity. As we will see, the New Divinity took this Edwardsean insight and developed it into a powerful principle that saturated their thought. We can term this *the principle of personal merit*, which states that ethical merits (and, by contrast, demerits) are personal, individual things that cannot be shared between persons. If this concept is true, then it calls the traditional understanding of imputation into question: sinners cannot be held responsible for the sins of another person (like Adam's) antecedent to their own actual participation. Likewise, saints cannot claim an alien righteousness from Christ apart from their own personal participation in holy affections and acts. This section will explore their valiant attempt to do what had not been done before: to articulate a pious and vigorously revivalistic version of Calvinism that *lacked* a traditional understanding of imputation.

Our examination will feature the writings of Bellamy and Hopkins as well as other New Divinity ministers, such as Jonathan Edwards Jr. (1745–1801), minister at New Haven, Connecticut, and later president of Union College; Nathanael Emmons (1745–1840), pastor in Franklin, Massachusetts, who personally mentored close to ninety ministerial candidates; and Timothy Dwight (1752–1817), pastor of Green-field, Connecticut, who later presided over seasons of revival as president of Yale College. These New Divinity leaders formed the core of a growing cadre of evangel-icals committed to Edwards, revival, and the spread of the gospel. Together they carried the torch of Edwardsean theology through the Revolutionary period and into the nineteenth century.

Original sin. The New Divinity held the doctrine of original sin in high regard. "This doctrine lies at the foundation of all revealed religion," preached Nathanael Emmons, "and to deny it, is virtually to deny the whole of divine revelation."[46] This regard, however, did not extend to embracing all the facets of the Calvinist, federal theory of imputation.[47] Because they were countering an established view, we find the New Divinity prefacing their discussions on original sin with a neg-ative description of what their views are not before offering a positive description of what they actually affirmed.

Negatively, imputation is not to be understood as the transfer of Adam's spe-cific sin and guilt to his posterity. "Neither our reason nor experience, therefore, will allow us to believe that Adam made men sinners by causing them to eat of the forbidden fruit, which they never saw, in a place where they never were, and at a time before they existed."[48] The principle of personal merit and demerit formed the basis for their rejection of the federal theory of imputation. "It seems to be a clear dictate of common sense, and also a plain doctrine of scripture," John Smalley writes, "that blameworthiness is ever personal; and that a transfer of pun-ishment from the guilty to the innocent—from the transgressor to one who has never transgressed, at least without the free consent of the latter, is a palpable vio-lation of justice."[49] Scripture, they argued, concurred with the insights of reason: "There is no passage in the whole Bible which declares that we are guilty of the sin of Adam, or that this is so imputed to us as to render us guilty, antecedent to any

---

[46]Nathanael Emmons, "Original Sin," in *The Works of Nathanael Emmons, D.D.*, ed. Jacob Ide (Boston: Crocker & Brewster, 1842), 4:495.

[47]Bellamy was one of the few New Divinity theologians who appears to have held to the traditional federal rendering of original sin. See Bellamy, *True Religion Delineated*, 155-56. Hopkins retained a version of Edwards's view that the entire human race is constituted as a moral whole, but he wanted to emphasize our active complicity in Adam's sin; see Hopkins, *System of Doctrines*, 1:218; also see Peter Jauhiainen, "Samuel Hopkins and Hopkinsianism," in Crisp and Sweeney, *After Jonathan Edwards*, 116.

[48]Emmons, "Original Sin," 488. Jonathan Edwards Jr., "Remarks on the Improvements Made in Theology by His Father, President Edwards," in *The Works of Jonathan Edwards, D.D.*, ed. Tryon Edwards (Andover, MA: Allen, Morrill & Wardwell, 1842), 1:486-87.

[49]John Smalley, *Sermons, on a Number of Connected Subjects* (Hartford, CT: Lincoln and Gleason, 1803), 179.

sin of our own."[50] Thus, according to the New Divinity, Scripture, common sense, and divine justice all align to dethrone the federal theory of the imputation of Adam's sin. Some other theory must be advanced that unites the depravity of humankind with that of Adam's.

Positively, when turning to what they affirmed, we find the New Divinity advocating a more modest connection between Adam's sin and that of the human race, one that bypasses the need to postulate the imputation of an alien sin. Essentially, they maintained that *human beings necessarily sin at their first existence as a direct consequence of Adam's transgression.* They argued that there exists a necessary connection between Adam's sin and that of the race, a connection grounded in God's decree. God set up the moral order such that if Adam sinned, so too would the human race. "By divine constitution," Hopkins wrote, "there is a certain connection between the first sin of Adam and the sinfulness of his posterity; so that as he sinned and fell under condemnation, they, in consequence of this, became sinful and condemned."[51] This connection is "certain" because God constituted the human race in this way. Consequential to Adam's transgression, sin will necessarily arise voluntarily in every human heart from the moment they come to exist. Biblically, they based this connection on a plain reading of Romans 5. "The meaning of these passages," Timothy Dwight wrote in reference to Romans 5:12, 18-19, "is, I think, plainly the following: that by means of the offence, or transgression of *Adam*, the judgment, or sentence of God, came upon all men unto condemnation; because, and solely because, all men, in that state of things, which was constituted in consequence of the transgression of *Adam*, became sinners."[52] While Adam's transgression made all to become sinners, all became sinners voluntarily. Consequently, all are liable to eternal condemnation due to their own sin. The New Divinity came to believe they had established a necessary connection between Adam's sin and that of the race without having to posit the imputation of an alien sin (Adam's) to all of humankind.

When they explained the mechanics of how sin is propagated throughout the race, the New Divinity generally defaulted to lines of reasoning laid down by Edwards. Consequential to Adam's transgression, the Holy Spirit vacated the

---

[50]H. E., "Observations on Being Made Sinners by Adam, and Righteous by Christ," *CEM* 5 (March 1805): 341.

[51]Hopkins, *System of Doctrines*, 1:218.

[52]Timothy Dwight, *Theology Explained and Defended in a Series of Sermons* (New Haven, CT: S. Converse, 1823), 1:480.

human race, leaving humankind subject to the principles of mere humanity, which were supposed to exist in harmony with the Spirit. As the race propagates, each individual inherits a Spirit-less temper that necessarily turns inward in selfishness and sin.[53] One writer for the *Connecticut Evangelical Magazine* summed it up this way: since Adam sinned, we come into existence with a "sinful temper, derived from him," and as such we "come into existence sinning." This is all "according to the universal course of divine providence." Though there is an intimate connection between Adam's transgression and his posterity, "still their own personal sin is the immediate cause or ground of their guilt and condemnation."[54]

This Edwardsean approach to imputation necessarily transformed the New Divinity understanding of the term *imputation*. Some, like John Smalley, attempted to abandon the term altogether and substitute it with the language of *derivation*. "Sin comes to all men from Adam by derivation, in the first place, and not by a previous imputation. All men are condemned as sinful themselves; and not antecedently to their being so, for the offense of another."[55] Most, however, retained the term but infused it with different meaning. Nathanael Emmons maintained that the imputation of Adam's sin is not to be understood as the "transfer" of guilt from one person to another. Rather, he points out that "according to scripture, the actions of one man are imputed to another, when one man receives benefit or suffers evil on account of another's conduct."[56] Thus, while God might "impute" the woeful consequences of fathers' sins to their children, as in the case of the rebellion of Korah, Dathan, and Abiram (Num 16), God does not transfer Korah's specific guilt to his children. The children suffer the evil consequences for their father's rebellion, but they are ultimately guilty for their own sin alone, not the sin of their father.

In sum, while many of the New Divinity denied the federal theory of imputation, they affirmed a substantial connection between Adam's sin and the sinning of the human race. Human beings sin necessarily at the first moment of their existence, and this sin is the direct consequence of Adam's transgression and the basis for their eternal condemnation. As such, many New Divinity revivalists, especially those from later generations, found no need to posit the theory of the

---

[53]Hopkins, *System of Doctrines*, 1:211-12; Edwards Jr., "Improvements Made by Edwards," 487.

[54]*CEM* 5 (March 1805): 343-44.

[55]Smalley, *Sermons*, 183.

[56]Emmons, "Original Sin," 489. See also Edwards Jr., "Improvements Made by Edwards," 486.

imputation of an alien guilt, a concept they believed was inherently unjust and ultimately unbiblical.

Atonement and justification. When the New Divinity came to apply Edwardsean insights to the doctrines of atonement and justification, the result was a stunning reformulation of the traditional Reformed position.[57] Similar to original sin, the main issue motivating their reformulation was their rejection of the traditional understanding of imputation, a rejection that stemmed from their adherence to the principle of personal merit. Merit and blameworthiness are personal virtues or vices that cannot be transferred from person to person. This idea had massive implications for their doctrines of atonement and justification, which led them to oppose views that most evangelicals have held in high regard. To the New Divinity, the atonement is not understood as the literal payment of sinners' moral debts. Rather, it is an act that secures the conditions where God can extend a pardon to sinners without neglecting sin. Similarly, justification is no longer viewed as the imputation of Christ's alien righteousness to a sinner's moral account; it is rather redefined as forgiveness or a divine legal acquittal that a sinner enjoys by virtue of faith. This section will draw out these ideas in detail.

In order to understand their positions on the atonement and justification, we must first appreciate their dissatisfaction with the traditional evangelical view commonly known as the penal substitutionary theory of the atonement. This view, the New Divinity noted, envisioned the atonement as the repayment of a moral debt: human sin incurs a moral debt that sinners can never repay. Out of grace, Christ died on the cross in the sinner's place as a penal substitute, embracing the full penalty due to sinners (he gave his life as a "ransom" for many; Mk 10:45). Through faith, the redeemed sinner is united to Christ, whereby there is two-way transfer (or imputation) of merits: the demerits of human sin are imputed to Christ, who fully pays the penalty, while the merits of Christ's active obedience (his holiness, righteousness, and positive standing before God) are imputed to sinners. The Christian stands before God clothed in Christ's righteousness, fully justified by faith alone. Because of the emphasis on Christ's work as paying a specific debt, traditional Calvinists regarded Christ's death as only atoning for the

---

[57]Because their views of the atonement and justification overlap considerably, we will treat them together in this section. For further works that explore these doctrines in greater detail, see Breitenbach, "Unregenerate Doings"; William Breitenbach, "The Consistent Calvinism of the New Divinity Movement," *The William and Mary Quarterly* 41, no. 2 (1984): 241-64; Dorus Paul Rudisill, *The Doctrine of the Atonement in Jonathan Edwards and His Successors* (New York: Poseidon Books, 1971).

sins of the elect. Christ's death, in other words, was intended to pay the debt only for those predestined for salvation; he did not die universally for every member of the human race. While the New Divinity deeply appreciated their Reformed predecessors in many ways, they respectfully disagreed with them on this understanding of the atonement for a number of reasons.

First, as noted above, the debt-payment theory entailed notions of imputation that directly contradict basic notions of justice and common sense. How is it possible, they asked, that personal virtue and/or vice be passed around from person to person? "Merit is personal," wrote John Smalley. "In the nature of things it cannot be otherwise. Another's having been righteous, doth not make me righteous, if I have not been so myself. . . . Debts may be discharged by an attorney. Damages of any kind may be repaired by a third person. But moral turpitude is not to be wiped away in this manner."[58]

Second, the debt-payment model led to a theological conundrum that the New Divinity found insurmountable. If Christ literally paid the full debt owed to God by the elect, then is God not *obligated* to save the elect? How is this consistent with *free* grace? "If our forgiveness be purchased and the price of it be already paid," Jonathan Edwards Jr. noted, "it seems to be a matter of debt, and not of grace."[59] Emmons agreed: "There is no grace in forgiving a debtor after his debt is paid, whether by himself or another."[60] For years, a small but vocal group of progressive antitrinitarians known as Socinians had been pointing out this apparent contradiction in the traditional Reformed view. Though no friends of Socinianism, the New Divinity apparently agreed with their critique of traditional Calvinism on this point.

Third, New Divinity writers constantly pointed out that limited atonement, which usually accompanied the debt-payment theory, contradicts Scripture. They countered that Christ died for the sins of the world universally, not some subset of it. Furthermore, they partially blamed the recent growth of Universalism to the debt-payment model. If the atonement pays a literal debt, and if the universal texts in Scripture, such as 1 John 2:2, are true, then it only makes sense that all are saved. Some Calvinists embraced this reasoning and converted to Universalism in the

---

[58]John Smalley, "Justification Through Christ, an Act of Free Grace," in *The Atonement: Discourses and Treatises*, ed. Edwards Amasa Park (Boston: Congregational Board of Publication, 1859), 57.

[59]Jonathan Edwards Jr., "Three Sermons on the Necessity of Atonement, and the Consistency Between That and Free Grace in Forgiveness," in Park, *Atonement*, 3.

[60]Nathanael Emmons, "Necessity of the Atonement," in Ide, *The Works of Nathanael Emmons, D.D.*, 5:26.

late eighteenth century. In sum, when the New Divinity stood back and assessed the entire situation, they did not have to look too far to diagnose the fundamental problem. As Jonathan Edwards Jr. noted with regard to Socinians, "The whole strength of [their objection] . . . in which [they] have so much triumphed [against Calvinists], . . . depends on the supposition that the atonement of Christ consists in *the literal payment of a debt which we owed to God*."[61] The problem, in other words, was the debt-payment model inherent in the penal substitutionary theory. To the New Divinity, the only way forward was to scrap this model and refashion the atonement in a completely new framework.

The new framework they forged was erected around the Edwardsean notion of God as a moral governor. This view finds its origins in God's desire to display his internal glory throughout the created order, a foundation point derived from Edwards's *Dissertation on the End for Which God Created the World*.[62] While God's glory is wonderfully displayed through the manifestation of his "natural attributes" (his creative power, wisdom, omnipresence, infinitude), his highest glories are revealed in the exhibition of his moral attributes, such as his holiness, justice, grace, and love. The moral law, as summarized by Jesus in the greatest commandment (Mt 22:37-40), reveals the center of gravity in the universal moral order. As God's moral attributes are discerned, known, and loved in creation, the universe increasingly shines with the reflected glory of God. Today evangelicals might call this manifestation of God in history the "kingdom of God"; the New Divinity preferred to call it God's "moral government."

The presence of sin, however, directly threatens God's moral government because it calls his holy character into question. Is God just, holy, and righteous, as he declares in his Word? Strict justice in the form of eternal punishment against all sinners would achieve the purpose of manifesting divine justice to creation. God's moral government would be upheld, as all would know that he is holy, righteous, and just. Yet God desires to lavish goodness and love on those who carry his image and not to cast every human being into hell. This, however, poses a problem. If God were to extend a pardon to sinners (something he could do), then it would appear that he is not just. God cannot contradict his holy, just nature.

---

[61]Edwards Jr., "Three Sermons," 27, emphasis added.
[62]See Stephen West, *Scripture Doctrine of Atonement: Proposed to Careful Examination*, 2nd ed. (Stockbridge, MA: Herald Office, 1809), 7-15, for this connection. For Edwards's work, see Jonathan Edwards, *Dissertation I. Concerning the End for Which God Created the World*, in *Ethical Writings*, ed. Paul Ramsey, WJE 8 (New Haven, CT: Yale University Press, 1989), 405-526.

Thus a great barrier stands in the way of humankind's salvation, one that finds its origins in the divine nature. "The great difficulty, therefore, in the way of man's salvation, was, to reconcile God's disposition to punish with his disposition to forgive; or in other words, to reconcile his justice with his mercy."[63]

Thankfully, God did find a way around this difficulty, the New Divinity affirmed. Through a work of atonement, God can uphold his justice (that is, his moral government) while at the same time extending pardon to sinners. This atonement, for the New Divinity, became something very different from what was understood by the broader evangelical community. It is not fundamentally about repaying a moral debt owed to God, but about honoring divine justice in the midst of forgiving sinners. The "nature and design of the atonement," Emmons summarized, is "to maintain and display the justice of God in the remission of sins."[64] Similarly, Stephen West wrote that the atonement "summarily consists in an *exhibition* of the righteous displeasure of God against sin, made in some other way than in the punishment of the sinner."[65]

How does this work? Through Christ's public suffering on the cross, he freely embraces the consequences of human sin. This act procured both subjective and objective results. Subjectively, Christ's suffering publically displays to the moral world God's infinite hatred of sin; all intelligent beings (human beings and angels) come to see subjectively the public sufferings of Christ. Objectively, Christ's suffering upheld, "honored," or "answered" God's holy law. The law is honored because God's justice is still manifested to the moral universe through the cross instead of universal eternal punishment. John Smalley offers a helpful illustration of this point.

> We are told of a certain ancient king (Zaleuchus, king of the Locrians) who, that he might effectually suppress adultery, which exceedingly prevailed among his subjects, enacted a law that the adulterer should be punished with the loss of both his eyes. His own son was convicted of this crime. The royal father, whose bowels yearned for him, and who could not bear to have one so dear to him forever deprived of the light of day, devised an expedient to soften, in that one instance, the rigor of his own law, and yet not abate its force in future. The king in a most public manner, before all the people, had one of his own eyes plucked out, that so one of

---

[63]Emmons, "Necessity of the Atonement," 20.
[64]Ibid., 23.
[65]West, *Scripture Doctrine of Atonement,* 117.

his son's eyes might be saved. By such a commutation as this, by deeming one eye for his son, at so costly a price as the loss of one of his own, he conceived the law would appear as awful, and be as great a terror to evil-doers, as if the letter of it had been executed.[66]

Strict justice, in this illustration, is not achieved, as both of the son's eyes were not put out. Yet a substitute punishment (the king sacrificing one of his own eyes) is accepted by the whole community, and the original law remains honored and feared by all. Christ's atonement operates in a similar way, the New Divinity held, by upholding God's moral government in the midst of forgiving sinners who exercise evangelical faith.

Several points need to be observed in order to get a fuller grasp on their view. First, one must note what is not included in this theory. Christ's atoning work does not include an exact one-to-one payment for humankind's sins. "The atonement," Jonathan Edwards Jr. wrote, "does not consist in the payment of a debt, properly so called. It consists rather in doing that, which, for the purpose of establishing the authority of the divine law, and of supporting in due tone the divine government, is equivalent to the punishment of the sinner according to the letter of the law."[67] If the law is upheld and God's moral government is supported through Christ's suffering, then that is all that is required for atonement. God is satisfied to accept Christ's temporal sufferings in the place of humankind's eternal punishment. To God, those sufferings were "equivalent in meaning to the punishment threatened in the moral law, and thus they satisfied Him who is determined to maintain the honor of this law."[68] Because God accepts Christ's voluntarily suffering in the place of humanity's, his atoning work can properly be called substitutionary. Yet because his suffering does not repay a moral debt by literally embracing their punishment, we can call this view a *nonpenal* substitutionary theory of the atonement.[69] Pardon, not payment of debt, is procured by an Edwardsean atonement.[70]

Second, because atonement is fundamentally about displaying God's hatred of sin and upholding the divine law, it is a work that has universal implications. All

---

[66]Smalley, "Justification Through Christ," 50.
[67]Edwards Jr., "Improvements Made by Edwards," 486.
[68]Edwards Amasa Park, "The Rise of the Edwardean Theory of the Atonement: An Introductory Essay," in Park, *Atonement*, x.
[69]Oliver D. Crisp, "Non-Penal Substitution," *International Journal of Systematic Theology* 9 (2007): 415-33.
[70]Nathanael Emmons, "The Purchase of Christ's Blood," in Ide, *The Works of Nathanael Emmons, D.D.,* 5:35.

humankind are benefactors of Christ's atoning work because the cross has displayed God's hatred of sin to all.

> If by the sufficiency of Christ's atonement, be meant such a manifestation of divine displeasure against the wickedness of men, as is enough to convince every candid spectator, that the disposition of the divine mind is perfectly conformable to the true spirit of God's written law; it may be truly said that there is sufficient atonement made for the sins of the whole world.[71]

Emmons agreed: "The atonement of Christ has the same favorable aspect upon the non-elect as upon the elect. It opens as wide a door of mercy to the one as to the other."[72] Consequently, New Divinity ministers were zealous to put this theology to work in their evangelistic endeavors. "Here there is a foundation laid, sufficiently broad, for the general invitations of the gospel; and for the joyful proclamation, that whoever will, may come and take of the waters of life freely."[73]

Third, their view of the atonement also affected the New Divinity doctrine of justification. Because they rejected the concept of imputation in general, they left this concept out of their understanding of justification. This led them to counter the common evangelical notion of being "clothed in Christ's righteousness" because they believed it harbored a deadly antinomian impetus (i.e., if I am clothed in Christ's righteousness, then I do not need to practice righteousness myself). When they did incorporate the language of being "clothed in Christ's righteousness," as Nathan Strong did, they qualified its true meaning. "Being cloathed [*sic*] with Christ's righteousness, is being forgiven and accepted by God, for the sake of what he hath done and suffered. But it does not mean, that the personal righteousness of Christ, is made our personal righteousness."[74] Positively, they defined justification as basically the forgiveness of sins. Justification "signifies no more nor less, than the pardon, or remission of sin," Emmons noted.[75] Like good Protestants, they were adamant that sinners are justified by faith alone, and they fiercely opposed works-righteousness.[76] Yet given the absence of imputation in

---

[71]West, *Scripture Doctrine of Atonement*, 139.
[72]Emmons, "Necessity of the Atonement," 23.
[73]West, *Scripture Doctrine of Atonement*, 140.
[74]Nathan Strong, *Sermons, on Various Subjects, Doctrinal, Experimental and Practical* (Hartford, CT: Hudson and Goodwin, 1798), 331; Smalley notes a problematic implication of such a position: "Were [believers] as righteous as Christ was,—had they, in any way, a perfect righteousness, properly their own, they would have no sins to confess; they would deserve no punishment, and need no pardon." Smalley, "Justification Through Christ," 56.
[75]Nathanael Emmons, "Justification of Believers," in Ide, *The Works of Nathanael Emmons, D.D.*, 5:44.
[76]Strong, *Sermons*, 312.

their doctrine, their discussion sometimes veered toward concepts of conditional justification that could be construed as works-righteousness. Emmons notes that "though [believers] are justified, and have received the Spirit of promise, which renders their salvation absolutely certain, yet they are still in a probationary state, because their salvation is suspended upon their fulfilling the conditions of their final and complete pardon." These conditions are "persevering in faith, and love, and every holy affection."[77] Statements like these and others demonstrate the New Divinity's commitment to a morally rigorous evangelical Christianity, and they reflect the close connection they discerned between justification and sanctification. Other evangelicals, especially among the Reformed, viewed such positions with a considerable amount of suspicion and wondered whether the New Divinity had not strayed from safe Protestant grounds.

SUMMARY

The revival theology that the New Divinity movement developed in the latter half of the eighteenth century was a unique mix of ideas that definitely reflected the influence of Jonathan Edwards's theology even if it did not exactly match his views. In most cases they did reproduce Edwards's strong doctrine of divine election. In other areas they modified his views. Specifically, the two features of Edwards's thought that we focused on in the previous chapter were taken up by the New Divinity and given unique expression in their writings.

First, Edwards's *disinterested spirituality* was transformed into a full-blown ethical theory known as *disinterested benevolence* in New Divinity teaching. This yielded the following results in their revival theology:

- It gave them an image of the ultimate goal of genuine Christian conversion. True Christians are those who delight in seeking the good of the universal order of being, often at great expense to themselves.

- It gave Bellamy a pointed criticism of free grace theology. True Christian spirituality does not originate in an assurance of God's love "for me" but emerges from a disinterested vision of God's moral beauty displayed in the gospel.

- It led Hopkins to posit that convicted sinners may come to a point in their preconversion struggles where they genuinely reach a stage of ultimate self-denial: willing to be damned for God's glory.

---

[77]Emmons, "Justification of Believers," 49-50.

Second, the *voluntarist accent* in Edwards's thought, most notably his understanding of natural ability, translated into the New Divinity's emphasis on *immediate repentance*. Hopkins's logic developed along the following lines:

- *The sinfulness of unregenerate doings.* If sinners do not have the Holy Spirit, then all of their actions are to be viewed as desperately wicked and sinful.

- *The sinful use of the means of grace.* Sinners who use the means of grace are using them selfishly and are actually compounding their guilt. The means of grace, in other words, do not positively tend to salvation but only render one's judgment greater if salvation is not found.

- *The gospel promises are intended only for the regenerate,* since only those who have been transformed by the Holy Spirit can selflessly receive the promises leading to true repentance and belief.

- In preaching and counseling those under conviction, ministers must not overemphasize the means of grace, though they must necessarily do so to a limited degree; they rather must emphasize the sinner's obligation to *repent immediately* since they have a natural ability to do so.

As the New Divinity tradition developed, its later leaders extended the voluntarist accent in Edwards's thought to revise other doctrines as well. Specifically, their affirmation of *the principle of personal merit* reveals this voluntarism and led to a significant transformation of the following doctrines:

- *Original sin.* Because merit is personal, there can be no transfer (or imputation) of guilt from Adam to his offspring. Sin infallibly results in every human being because of Adam, they argued, but we are not held responsible for his (or anybody else's) sin.

- *Atonement.* Because merit is personal, Christ's atoning work does not consist in paying for the sins of others. Rather, Christ's public suffering for sinners renders it possible for God to honor his holy law publicly while extending mercy to sinners who repent and believe Christ.

- *Justification.* Because merit is personal, Christ's righteousness is not imputed to us in justification. Justification is merely the extension of a divine pardon to the sinner who truly believes the gospel.

The contours of New Divinity revival theology might appear strange to many evangelicals today. What good, it may be asked, could come out of this movement?

While we cannot deny that there are considerable problems with their views, we must avoid the temptation to write off the movement completely as a sad detour in the history of American theology. As a matter of fact, New Divinity views attracted large numbers of adherents in the Second Great Awakening. As we will see in the next chapter, many prominent Congregationalists and Presbyterians embraced aspects of its vision of God, its evangelistic methods, and its Edwardsean spirituality as they heralded the gospel throughout the early decades of the United States.

CHAPTER FOUR

CONGREGATIONALIST AND NEW SCHOOL PRESBYTERIAN REVIVAL THEOLOGY IN THE SECOND GREAT AWAKENING

THE END OF THE EIGHTEENTH CENTURY WITNESSED an astounding transformation of America's religious landscape. The ferment associated with the Revolutionary War and the subsequent birth of the nation generated a complex environment that had a significant impact on revivals and revival theology. Some groups continued to advance the theologies we have already canvassed, while others made significant modifications to existing revival theologies. Still others struck out on a new course inspired by a mood that rejected Old World institutions and embraced the intense emotionalism that became characteristic of rural revivals on the frontier. Prominent denominations of the First Great Awakening, such as the Congregationalists and Presbyterians, were no longer the major forces of revival, as they came to be displaced by the surge of growth in Methodism and the Baptists, who both adapted quickly to the new American setting. In short, America's Second Great Awakening (1790–1840) was an incredibly complex event; no one revivalist, denomination, or theology captures its diversity.

In an effort to bring some order to this complexity, this chapter begins with a brief sketch of the Second Great Awakening. The goal here is to provide a historical framework for our subsequent discussions of the revival theologies treated in this chapter and throughout the rest of the book. After that we will narrow our focus on the Congregational revivals that surfaced in New England from the 1790s to the 1840s. These revivals were Edwardsean in character, drawing inspiration directly from the New Divinity revival theology of Bellamy, Hopkins, and Emmons. Attention will be given to how Congregationalists preached the gospel Edwardsean-style and also to how their message affected the spirituality of those who converted. Third, the chapter ends with a section detailing the further development of the voluntarist accent in the writings of Nathaniel William Taylor, the Congregational theologian from Yale, and Albert Barnes, the controversial New School Presbyterian minister from Philadelphia. Taylor's views developed the Edwardsean theme of the will to a point that many traditional Calvinists believed had transgressed the boundary of Calvinist orthodoxy. His views, however, gained traction among New School Presbyterians, a factor that contributed significantly to the great Presbyterian schism in 1837 between them and the more traditional Old School Presbyterians. Overall, these events detail how Edwardsean revival theology can generate both a robust evangelical spirituality and intense intradenominational division.

OVERVIEW OF THE SECOND GREAT AWAKENING

From the 1790s to the 1840s a seemingly continuous stream of revivals flowed across America's Protestant churches. Unlike the First Great Awakening, these post-Revolutionary revivals were not associated with one dynamic itinerant like a George Whitefield who caught everybody's attention.[1] Rather, they were more local in nature, involving leaders of different denominations who each left their particular stamp on the revivals they oversaw. Regional differences also contributed to diversity. New England revivals were more intellectual and emotionally "quiet" affairs conducted throughout the region's churches, while Methodist revivals in the South and West were often animated gatherings conducted

---

[1]Many associate the Second Great Awakening with the ministry of Charles Finney. There are at least two problems with this, however. First, the Second Great Awakening was characterized by much more diversity than the First Great Awakening, so much so that no one leader captured the spirit of the awakening in a way that Whitefield did in the early 1740s. Second, Finney was a latecomer to the Second Great Awakening; his ministry did not begin until the 1820s, thirty years after the first stirrings of revival began in the 1790s. It is perhaps better to view Finney as one who epitomized the theological trajectories of the age, rather than as the central figure who embodied the essence of the Second Great Awakening.

in outdoor camp meetings. This diversity makes it difficult for historians to specify the exact details of *the* awakening (beginning and ending points, main leaders, etc.). Consequently, the best way to summarize the Second Great Awakening is to examine it region by region for the purpose of comprehending the different phases and traditions present in the revivals of the period. Historians usually identify three different regions of the Second Great Awakening.[2]

The first region of the Second Great Awakening was New England, which was overseen by ministers in the New Divinity tradition, a narrative we will tell later in this chapter. The Edwardsean revivals that began in the region's Congregational churches in the early 1790s left an indelible imprint on northeastern evangelicalism well into the nineteenth century. As we will see below, the theology taught during these revivals was predominantly Edwardsean, derived from the New Divinity teachings of Bellamy and Hopkins. Leaders such as Edward Dorr Griffin, Asahel Nettleton, and Lyman Beecher presided over revivals that were both deeply emotional and yet calm and controlled in an effort to avoid enthusiasm. Revivals appeared at numerous schools, such as at Yale College under the presidency of Timothy Dwight in the 1790s as well as at Amherst, Dartmouth, Middlebury, and Williams colleges, each of which had Edwardseans on their faculties. Institutions such as Andover Seminary, the American Board of Commissioners for Foreign Missions, and many benevolence ministries flourished as thousands of laypersons gave their time and money to extend the gospel's influence. Clearly a massive effort was under way to evangelize the nation and the world. This phase of the awakening demonstrated the significant penetration of Edwardseanism into New England culture, as it involved the combined efforts of churches, colleges, seminaries, publishing enterprises, missions, and benevolent societies. To speak of an "Edwardsean enculturation" of Calvinist New England, as one scholar has suggested, is not far off the mark.[3]

The second region of the Second Great Awakening was the western frontier, beginning in the 1790s, when many Americans left the crowded coastal states for the continental interior. The frontier societies in the new states of Ohio, Kentucky,

---

[2]For general overviews of the Second Great Awakening, see Daniel Walker Howe, *What Hath God Wrought: The Transformation of America, 1815–1848* (New York: Oxford University Press, 2009), 164–202; Barry Hankins, *The Second Great Awakening and the Transcendentalists* (Westport, CT: Greenwood Press, 2004); Richard Carwardine, *Transatlantic Revivalism: Popular Evangelicalism in Britain and America, 1790–1865* (Westport CT: Greenwood Press, 1978); Sydney E. Ahlstrom, *A Religious History of the American People*, 2nd ed. (New Haven, CT: Yale University Press, 2004), 415-71.

[3]Douglas A. Sweeney, *Nathaniel Taylor, New Haven Theology, and the Legacy of Jonathan Edwards* (New York: Oxford University Press, 2002), 40.

and Tennessee were, to a large degree, sparsely populated, mobile, and lawless. Individualism characterized the populace as the austerities of daily life exalted pragmatism over tradition, common sense over education, and democratic forms of social organization over hierarchical ones. These sentiments spilled over into individuals' denominational preferences, as many came to reject the formalism and hierarchy of traditional churches. Reaching the lost in this context required different evangelistic strategies, and the Presbyterian, Methodist, and Baptist ministers who arrived in the region in the 1790s developed several innovative methods for the purposes of saving souls.

First, they employed the *camp meeting* as the primary venue for evangelistic preaching. Families would travel long distances, set up camp, and attend a series of preaching services that culminated in a celebration of the Lord's Supper at the end of the event.[4] In July 1800, Presbyterian James McGready noted how the news of revival attracted families from great distances: "Multitudes crowded [in the Gasper River Congregation in southern Kentucky] from all parts of the country to see a strange work, from the distance of forty, fifty, and even a hundred miles away; whole families came in their wagons."[5] Sometimes these events grew rather large and became interdenominational meetings:

> The roads were literally crowded with wagons, carriages, horsemen, and footmen, moving to the solemn camp. The sight was affecting. It was judged, by military men on the ground, that there were between twenty and thirty thousand collected. Four or five preachers were frequently speaking at the same time, in different parts of the encampment, without confusion. The Methodist and Baptist preachers aided in the work, and all appeared cordially united in it—of one mind and one soul, and the salvation of sinners seemed to be the great object of all.[6]

The great Cane Ridge Revival led by Barton Stone in August 1801 is said to have hosted close to twenty-five thousand attendees. The fame of these events, coupled by the great numbers of conversions, ensured that the camp-meeting format would become an extremely popular tool for revivalists for decades to come.

---

[4]For an excellent introduction to these revivals, see John B. Boles, *The Great Revival, 1787–1805: The Origins of the Southern Evangelical Mind* (Lexington: University Press of Kentucky, 1972), 36-69.

[5]James McGready, *The Posthumous Works of the Reverend and Pious James M'Gready* (Louisville: W. W. Worsley, 1831), 1:xiii.

[6]Barton W. Stone, *The Biography of Eld. Barton Warren Stone* (Cincinnati: J. A. & U. P. James, 1847), 37-38; Peter Cartwright, *Autobiography of Peter Cartwright: The Backwoods Preacher* (New York: Carlton & Porter, 1857), 30-31.

Second, many Second Great Awakening revivalists presided over *deeply emotional revival services* that featured intensely affective preaching. It was maintained that such preaching was used by the Holy Spirit to generate such a great deal of conviction that it resulted in visible, physical phenomena in the crowds, such as sobbing, nervous shaking, and people crying out loud for divine mercy. These manifestations, which were known in the First Great Awakening, were accompanied by even more dramatic physical effects, such as being "struck down," in which an individual fell over, or experiencing "the jerks," where an individual's head or torso would jerk back and forth in a rhythmic motion. Regarding the latter, Stone relates that "I have seen the person stand in one place and jerk backward and forward in quick succession, their head nearly touch the floor behind and before."[7] When asked, persons claimed it was an involuntary motion that could not be helped. "No matter whether they were saints or sinners," observed Methodist Peter Cartwright, "they would be taken under a warm song or sermon, and seized with a convulsive jerking all over, which they could not by any possibility avoid, and the more they resisted the more they jerked."[8] Extraordinary phenomena such as these inspired awe, religious zeal, and intense interest in frontier revivals.

Third, frontier revivalists employed the *altar call* as another innovative method for evangelism. Simply stated, in an altar call the minister calls the sinner to respond to the gospel message at the end of the sermon by publicly moving forward to a designated area (usually near the pulpit) where he or she can find spiritual counsel that hopefully concludes with the individual's repentance and faith. The origins of this practice are difficult to determine. Calling sinners to faith and repentance has always been a central feature of evangelical preaching. Associating this spiritual response with a visible act of getting up at the preacher's bidding and moving forward toward a consultation area—whether to an "altar," a fenced enclosure, a "mourner's bench," an "anxious bench," or a "praying pen"—was a new development subsequent to the First Great Awakening. The best research has concluded that the practice most likely originated among Methodist or Separate Baptist revivals in the 1780s and 1790s.[9] By 1820 the practice was known and utilized widely, but it was by no means universal, nor was it considered necessary.[10]

---

[7]Stone, *Biography*, 40.
[8]Cartwright, *Autobiography of Peter Cartwright*, 48.
[9]David Bennett, *The Altar Call: Its Origins and Present Usage* (Lanham, MD: University Press of America, 2000), 29-47.
[10]Ibid., 64-71.

In sum, the western frontier revivals were intensely animated events led by revivalists who were not afraid to experiment with new methods for spreading the gospel. Camp meetings, openness to extraordinary manifestations of the Holy Spirit, and a primitive version of the altar call became common features of these revivals. In time, these new methods ebbed eastward, where they generated intense controversy among churches that were accustomed to a different kind of revival fervor.

The third region of the Second Great Awakening we shall examine lies in the upstate region of New York and is associated with the spectacular ministry of Charles Finney. Finney's career as a revivalist began in the 1820s, well after the advent of the Second Great Awakening, and extended into the 1830s, during which he labored throughout the Northeast, predominantly New York state. The revivals sparked under his ministry were so massive that the region became known as the "burnt over district." Finney was not so much an innovator but a masterful repackager. Essentially, he embraced some of the new methods developed in frontier revivalism, toned them down, and vigorously promoted them on the East Coast. His repackaging effort extended to theology as well, where he developed an extreme—some would say unrecognizable—version of Edwardsean revival theology. This combination of Edwardsean theology coupled with the popular revival techniques borrowed from the frontier proved to be a potent mixture that ignited both revivals and theological controversy.

In the upcoming chapters we will examine the revival theologies held by the revivalists in these various settings. Congregationalists and New School Presbyterians advocated Edwardsean revival theology throughout New England as well as in New York, Pennsylvania, and Ohio. Methodists preached their Wesleyan revival theology in both the western frontier and throughout the rural South, a narrative we shall explore in the next chapter. In chapter six we will canvass the diversity of revival theologies held by Baptists who ministered throughout the United States, and chapter seven will be devoted to the new measures revival theology of Charles Finney.

EDWARDSEAN REVIVALS AMONG THE CONGREGATIONALISTS IN NEW ENGLAND

Toward the end of the eighteenth century, New Divinity ministers began seeing the fruit of decades of labor. Beginning in the early 1790s and extending into the next several decades, we find a surge of revivals dotting the landscape of New England

Congregationalism. Most of these revivals were led by ministers who were thoroughly trained by New Divinity leaders. The personal conversion experiences and corporate revivals resulting from their work reflect the Edwardsean themes analyzed in the last chapter, a point that demonstrates that New Divinity theology trickled down to the religious lives of many New Englanders. This section will illustrate this by first examining the ministries and methods of these Edwardsean ministers. From there we will examine the Edwardsean conversion and revival narratives they published.

New Divinity ministers. The Edwardsean leaders of these New England revivals were united by bonds forged primarily by a ministerial educational system they developed known as the schools of the prophets.[11] During the First Great Awakening, Jonathan Edwards began receiving newly minted ministerial graduates into his home for specialized training in theology and pastoral ministry. Both Bellamy and Hopkins were the benefactors of this system, receiving hands-on training in pastoral duties and preaching as well as intense theological mentoring. Bellamy and, to a lesser degree, Hopkins reproduced this pattern in their own ministries, which was then reproduced by many of the five-dozen ministers they trained. Hopkins trained Jonathan Edwards Jr., who in turn trained Timothy Dwight, president of Yale from 1795 to 1817. Bellamy trained close to sixty students over his long ministry, including John Smalley (who trained Nathanael Emmons), Adoniram Judson Sr. (father of the famed missionary), and Samuel Mills Sr. (father of the other famed missionary). By the turn of the century a significant New Divinity movement was afoot among New England Congregationalism, a point that did not go unnoticed. Toward the end of his life Samuel Hopkins observed that New Divinity theology was "fast increasing" among regional Congregationalists: "There are now more than one hundred in the ministry who espouse the same sentiments in the United States of America."[12] William Bentley, a liberal from Salem, noted in 1813 that Hopkins's "System of Divinity is the basis of the popular theology in New England."[13] The schools of the prophets provided a near-perfect vehicle for the transmission and dissemination of their

---

[11]D. W. Kling, "New Divinity Schools of the Prophets, 1750–1825: A Case Study in Ministerial Education," *History of Education Quarterly* 37, no. 2 (1997): 185-206.

[12]Samuel Hopkins, *Sketches of the Life of the Late Rev. Samuel Hopkins, D.D., Pastor of the First Congregational Church in Newport* (Hartford, CT: Hudson and Goodwin, 1805), 103; Joseph A. Conforti, *Samuel Hopkins and the New Divinity Movement: Calvinism, the Congregational Ministry, and Reform in New England Between the Great Awakenings* (Grand Rapids: Christian University Press, 1981), 4-5.

[13]William Bentley, *The Diary of William Bentley, D.D., Pastor of the East Church, Salem, Massachusetts: 1811–1819* (Salem, MA: Essex Institute, 1914), 4:302, as cited in Conforti, *Samuel Hopkins and the New Divinity*, 5.

revival theology. By 1800, a quarter of New England Congregational churches were led by Edwardsean ministers, and this number was growing as the revivals they saw in the 1790s continued well into the nineteenth century.[14]

A thorough analysis of their evangelistic and homiletical strategies is beyond the scope of this work.[15] We can catch a glimpse of their approach to revivals by briefly examining Edward Dorr Griffin, one of their best preachers.[16] Born in 1770 to a wealthy farming family in East Haddam, Connecticut, Griffin distinguished himself as an excellent student, graduating from Yale in 1790. After an illness he was converted in 1791, left his pursuit of law, and studied theology with Jonathan Edwards Jr. In the 1790s he rose to prominence among the New Divinity as a powerful preacher who presided over numerous revivals. Over the next four decades he became one of the central leaders of New England Calvinism. He held pastorates at New Salem and New Hartford, Connecticut, and Newark, New Jersey, and was the founding pastor of Boston's historic Park Street Congregational Church. In addition to pastoral ministry, Griffin served as professor of pulpit eloquence at the newly founded Andover Seminary, helped establish the American Board of Commissioners for Foreign Missions, and presided over Williams College as its president from 1821 to 1836, the year before his death.

Griffin's published works, mostly sermons, are packed with Edwardsean theology and reflect the unique features of the New Divinity's "Consistent" Calvinism. He was a staunch defender of a Calvinist understanding of election, a point he felt was essential to preaching true revival. "If God ever gives you a new heart," he preached, "it will not be for one exertion you ever made, or in answer to a single prayer you ever offered. . . . You are altogether in his hands. Your last hope hangs on his sovereign will. You lie wholly at the mercy of him whom you have made your enemy by wicked works. If he frown[s] you die. Fall down at his feet till he shall raise and heal and bid you live."[17]

---

[14]For a thorough study on New Divinity revivals from this period, see David William Kling, *A Field of Divine Wonders: The New Divinity and Village Revivals in Northwestern Connecticut, 1792–1822* (University Park: Pennsylvania State University Press, 1993). The following narrative relies significantly on Kling's work.

[15]For a lengthy study on New Divinity preaching, see ibid., 110-43.

[16]For works on Griffin, see Edward Dorr Griffin, *Sermons by the Late Rev. Edward D. Griffin, D.D.*, ed. William B. Sprague (New York: John S. Taylor, 1839), 1:1-270; Kling, *Field of Divine Wonders*, 126-37; Mark Rogers, "Edward Dorr Griffin and the Edwardsian Second Great Awakening" (PhD diss., Trinity Evangelical Divinity School, 2012).

[17]Edward Dorr Griffin, "Taking the Kingdom by Violence," in Sprague, *Sermons by the Late Rev. Edward D. Griffin*, 1:400; Rogers, "Griffin and the Edwardsian Awakening," 92.

Within this commitment to divine sovereignty Griffin employed the full arsenal of the Edwardsean themes we have explored in previous chapters. Human
beings inhabit a universe in which God displays his divine perfections, which
ought to be seen and admired by all his subjects.

> When [the Christian] looks abroad into the works of God his eye is filled with
> grateful tears. He is assured that a wise and faithful providence governs all. He sees
> that every thing valuable to himself and to the universe is safe under the shadow of
> the divine throne.... When he plunges into the ocean of the divine perfections and
> loses himself in the immensity and eternity of God; and when he is conscious of
> being embraced by the everlasting covenant, and of having God for an eternal
> portion, he is entranced and feels immortality growing up within him.[18]

Though God's glory abounds throughout creation, the ungodly are blind to it
and pursue a love of the world. "Who are the ungodly?" Griffin asks. "They who
do not *love* God, who do not love *all* his perfections, who do not love his holiness
and justice; they who do not love his government, his sovereignty,—[and] love
to find themselves and all creatures in his hands and at his disposal."[19] While
nonbelievers may possess a genuine love for others, their affections fall far short
of the universal, disinterested benevolence that God requires. The

> grand defect [of their affections] is that they are *limited in their very nature to a
> contracted circle*. They do not go up to God, and breathe through Him good wishes
> to the whole intellectual system. They brood exclusively over a private interest, and
> unless bound by a better principle, are ready to fly in the face of the whole universe
> that comes to disturb that. In their greatest enlargement they still exclude the
> Creator. They stop at the threshold of being. They fix on a drop of the ocean.... A
> limited affection ... necessarily includes, as it stands alone, a principle of hostility
> to the universe.[20]

Griffin's portrayal of the human condition resounds with the New Divinity theme
of God-centered virtue found in Bellamy and Hopkins. Lacking a principle of
disinterested benevolence, nonbelievers necessarily fall into loving the limited
sphere of their own little worlds. Without a sight of the divine glory in the gospel,

---

[18]Edward Dorr Griffin, *Sermons, Not Before Published, on Various Practical Subjects* (New York: M. W. Dodd,
1844), 150.

[19]Ibid., 60-61.

[20]Edward Dorr Griffin, *A Series of Lectures, Delivered in Park Street Church, Boston, on Sabbath Evening* (Boston:
Nathaniel Willis, 1813), 85-86.

they are bound to follow their hearts in ascribing glory to created things rather than to the infinite God.

This "binding" does not undermine their responsibility. On the contrary, Griffin affirmed the basic tenets of Edwardsean anthropology, specifically the distinction between sinners' natural ability to love God and their moral inability from doing the same. Devoid of the Holy Spirit, human beings possess a moral inability that prevents them from appreciating the glory of God in the gospel. Yet this inability amounts merely to a stubbornness that refuses Christ, a posture of the soul that, though necessary, is fully blameworthy. In reality, sinners do indeed have natural capacities for loving God and thus have a natural ability, a theoretical "power" to comply cordially with the claims of the gospel. "As they possess understanding, will, and affections and are capable of loving and hating, it will be allowed that nothing prevents [them from loving God] but a wrong temper of heart—nothing, . . . but supreme selfishness, producing an implacable opposition, too deep and powerful to be overcome but by the Spirit of God."[21]

Griffin's evangelistic preaching thus simultaneously followed two tracks corresponding with this distinction. On the one hand, because of nonbelievers' moral inability, the preacher is to hammer the point that there is nothing they can do to effect their salvation. They can employ the means of grace, but even these have no real sway in the heart prior to God's work of regeneration.[22] Their only course of action is to bow humbly before God's sovereign will and plead with him for a new heart. On the other hand, because of their natural ability, the preacher must press home the reality that all that is required is their cordial consent to the claims of the gospel, a choice they theoretically *can* make now because they possess a natural ability to love God. Griffin spun this half of the ability/inability distinction positively: "If there is no natural *inability*, there is natural *power*," he maintained. "Sinners have as much power to *change their hearts* as they have to alter at once any of their worldly or social dispositions."[23] Based on this theoretical power, Griffin challenged sinners to repent immediately. After delineating all the frivolous excuses sinners make in refusing the gospel, he ended a sermon titled "Excuses" with an appeal to immediate repentance.

---

[21]Ibid., 247-48.
[22]Ibid., 179. Here Griffin follows Hopkins on the means of grace.
[23]Ibid., 246.

Here then you stand without one excuse for rejecting the Gospel another moment. Why then will you not accept it at once? Do you begin to name a reason? But that is taken from you. You have *none left*. Do you say, your wicked *heart* will not consent? But my business is *with that wicked heart*. Why will not you, O stubborn heart, now submit? Hardened rebel, why will not *you* lay down your arms? . . . Remember the rebels in the wilderness. You are now brought to the border of the promised land. Refuse now and you die; accept now and you live forever. Amen.[24]

These snapshots of Griffin's preaching briefly demonstrate his adherence to the fundamental outlines of New Divinity revival theology. It was sermons like these that rang forth from New Divinity pulpits in the late eighteenth and early nineteenth centuries.

New Divinity revivals. In the 1790s revivals became a frequent occurrence in New England's New Divinity churches. Reflecting on his own region of northwest Connecticut, Griffin marveled that "in 1799, I could stand at my doorstep in New Hartford, Litchfield county, and number fifty or sixty congregations laid down in one field of divine wonders."[25] Soon, Congregational associations began publishing religious periodicals, such as the *Connecticut Evangelical Magazine* and the *Massachusetts Missionary Magazine*, which were founded with the express purpose to build up the evangelical churches of the region with "essays on the doctrines of Christianity, and on religious, experimental and moral subjects." These subjects were to include "religious intelligence concerning the state of Christ's kingdom, throughout the Christian world . . . , Information respecting Missions to the new settlements in the United States and among the Heathen nations:—[and] Narratives of revivals of religion in particular places together with the distinguishing marks of true and false religion."[26] The numerous sections devoted to revival and conversion narratives in these magazines reveal how pervasive New Divinity revival theology was in the lives of churches and individuals throughout the region.

The revival narratives reveal no commonality as to exactly why revival began at one point in time versus another. Often some not-so-extraordinary event—a death in the community, the preaching of a visiting minister, the news of revival in a neighboring town—triggered a domino effect of conviction. When this happened,

---

[24]Edward Dorr Griffin, "Excuses," in Sprague, *Sermons by the Late Rev. Edward D. Griffin*, 1:547.
[25]Edward Dorr Griffin, "A Letter to the Rev. Dr. William Sprague," in *Lectures on Revivals of Religion*, by William B. Sprague, 2nd ed. (New York: Appleton, 1833), 359, as cited in Kling, *Field of Divine Wonders*, 3.
[26]*CEM* 1 (July 1800): 3.

ministers saw it as a sudden, often surprising, awakening of religious concern. Jeremiah Hallock of West Simsbury, Connecticut, is representative of this. The "sudden" and "unexpected" revival in his town in October 1799 began after a very ordinary pulpit exchange one Lord's Day. "On my return the next evening, I found a young woman under deep impressions of mind. She told me, that she was a poor sinner, going down to hell."[27] Though she tried to avoid it, "she could no longer keep [her deep concern a] secret," and over the course of the next several days others came under deep concern over the state of their souls. Soon "fourteen children and youth[s] were found whose minds appeared to be impressed." Extra midweek services were held. Over the course of several weeks, Hallock details the surprising spread of concern to adults, the elderly, and folks who were completely immersed in the world. The religious concern in West Simsbury was intense but did not tend to enthusiasm:

> The things which took hold of the mind were plain gospel truths, with which the people had long been acquainted. . . . The work was by no means noisy, but rational, deep and still. The rational faculties of the soul were touched, and poor sinners began to see, that everything in the bible was true; that God was in earnest in his precepts, and threatening; that they were wholly sinful and in the hand of a sovereign God.[28]

This theme of the "still" revivals they reported was at once an attempt to avoid the radical revivalism of the First Great Awakening and an implicit polemic against the more animated revivals that were making waves on America's frontier.

Hallock's narrative of the sudden conviction in his town is populated with the conversion stories of individuals he counseled. Indeed, it is in these stories that the particularities of New Divinity revival theology emerge. Several themes found in these stories show a great deal of continuity with those we surveyed in the First Great Awakening. First, a period of deep conviction of sin, oftentimes lengthy, was accompanied with a great wrestling over the various doctrines of the gospel. In wrestling with the guilt of their sinfulness, many employed vivid language of sinking into hell. "I was in very great distress," one young woman relayed. "I felt so loaded with sin that it seemed as if I could not bear up under it. I felt as if I should sink into hell, and that it would be just if I should sink there."[29] While

---

[27]*CEM* 1 (October 1800): 137.
[28]Ibid., 139.
[29]*MMM* 2 (June 1804): 28.

talking with her mother, another young woman exclaimed, "'It appears to me, I am sinking into hell!' As I turned and came into the house it seemed as if God was showering down his vengeance upon me; that he had set me up for his mark, and his arrows were drinking up my spirits! These words seemed to ring in my ears, 'No peace to the wicked! No peace to the wicked!'"[30]

Second, the knowledge of God contained in Scripture became odious in the sight of many. "My heart rose against the Bible," one youth related in a letter to her pastor. "I could find nothing in it but what was against me, and for that reason I dreaded to read it."[31] Prior to his conversion, Asahel Nettleton observed a similar regard: "I searched the scriptures daily, hoping to find inconsistencies in them, to condemn the Bible because it was against me; and while I was diligently pursuing, every thing I read, and every sermon I heard, condemned me."[32]

Third, the doctrine of God's sovereignty in salvation was particularly grievous to many would-be converts. One woman reported that for "more than three months" she was led to believe that she "was made for the very purpose of being miserable, and that it was decreed from all eternity that I should perish forever."[33] Samuel J. Mills Jr., the future missionary, similarly wrestled with divine sovereignty as he harbored jealousy toward family members who were converted "while he himself was apparently left to obduracy and ruin."[34]

These features demonstrate continuity with conversion narratives found in the First Great Awakening. The unique Edwardsean features in these conversion narratives emerge when we examine the nature of the conviction process. First, in New Divinity theology the nature of the conviction process must be characterized by a conscious awareness of one's own hatred of God and of divine things. As noted in the previous chapter, Hopkins underscored that nonbelievers do not love divine things nor the universal system of being. Lacking disinterested benevolence, self-love predominates, resulting in a disposition that objectively opposes God and all he stands for. New Divinity preaching and pastoral counsel sought as a goal to bring sinners to a deep awareness of their animosity toward God, his word, his ways, and even heaven.

---

[30]*MMM* 2 (November 1804): 226.

[31]*CEM* 1 (July 1800): 32.

[32]*CEM* 5 (July 1804): 34. Nettleton is identified as the author of this narrative in Bennet Tyler, *Nettleton and His Labours: Being the Memoir of Dr. Nettleton* (Edinburgh: T&T Clark, 1854), 19-21.

[33]*CEM* 1 (July 1800): 32.

[34]Gardiner Spring, *Memoir of Samuel John Mills* (Boston: Perkins & Marvin, 1829), 4. See p. 7 for his former "opposition to divine sovereignty."

"I began to murmur and repine, and accused God of the greatest injustice," Nettleton noted. "I wished that he might not be, and began really to doubt the truths of his holy word, and to disbelieve his existence, for if there were a God, I perfectly hated him."[35] Hatred for God also translated into hatred for his ultimate blessings, as one young lady noted regarding heaven. "Entirely opposed to God and the way of salvation, I thought if it were possible for me to be placed in heaven among the blessed with the same heart I then had, I should be in complete misery."[36] These experiences derived from the sharp distinction the New Divinity made between believers, who love all things distinterestedly, and the wicked, who truly hate God out of a self-love for their own little portion of the world.

A second Edwardsean feature found in these conversion narratives relates to the spiritual resignation that often followed one's willingness to be damned. One of the most common elements in these conviction narratives is that virtually all of them contain a statement of *resignation to the divine will*, usually in the form of an acknowledging that God is just in one's own personal damnation. Reflecting on the 1798 revival in Torringford, Connecticut, Samuel J. Mills Sr. noted that many were "led to a discovery of the justice of God in their condemnation—to see and to feel that the law was right and holy, and hell their proper place, than they found their mouths shut, and their complaints at an end. They have readily acknowledged that God would be glorious in executing sentence against them."[37] One young woman noted that "I saw that God had an absolute right to do with me just as he pleased, and if he should send me to hell I felt as though I should not complain. I thought I would love him if he should make me miserable."[38] Expressions like these are none other than Hopkins's doctrine of a "willingness to be damned" dressed in the language of spiritual resignation. In the course of conviction, sinners must come to a place where they see and even delight in the justice of God's law as well as its just verdict directed toward the self.

Many New Divinity ministers interpreted this point of spiritual resignation to be a vital turning point in the soul's journey. It signified the end of a struggle for self-control and openness to be placed completely in the hands of God. Many reported a sense of calmness after resigning to the divine will. Peter Starr of

---

[35]*CEM* 5 (July 1804): 34.
[36]*MMM* 2 (July 1804): 62-63.
[37]*CEM* 1 (July 1800): 28.
[38]Ibid., 34.

Warren, Connecticut, observed that once folks in his congregation came to "a willingness to be in [God's] hands, and at his disposal; being satisfied that he would be just, should he cast them of forever," they experienced a "serenity of mind, which they never enjoyed before; and from this period, they date their hopes, of having experienced a saving conversion."[39] Another convert from West Britain, Connecticut, noted the same thing in his confession: "I got no relief, until feeling my absolute dependence on the sovereign will of God, to dispose of me as he should see fit, I resigned myself into his hands, sensible, that if he should renew me, I should be saved; but if not, and if he should send me to hell, he would be perfectly just, and I should see it and know it forever."[40] At the end of her conviction process, one teenager reported that "it seemed to me I was willing to give up to God, and let him do as he pleased with me. This thought passed my mind, 'Lord, not my will, but thine be done.' Directly it seemed to me, that God appeared for my help, and Christ took off all my load, removed my distress, and filled my soul with such joy, that I could not contain myself."[41]

From this point of spiritual calmness, many relayed that they experienced a new set of convictions, perceptions, and desires that they had not had before. Biblical doctrine and the Bible itself become objects of great regard. "The Bible appeared to me entirely new. It appeared strange that I had lived to such an age, and read the Bible so much as I had, and never before discovered the beauty, the glory, and the excellency, which were contained in it. I discovered more in one verse, than ever I did before in the whole Bible."[42] For Asahel Nettleton, the doctrines that he had formerly hated—the character of God and the doctrines of election and free grace—appeared "delightful" shortly after an "unusual calmness pervaded my soul."[43] Jonathan Miller, pastor of West Britain, Connecticut, similarly noted how these new perceptions extended to the created order. "Some have been immediately filled with great joy, and admiring views of the excellencies and perfections of God; every thing about them, even the natural creation has appeared new."[44] This point is illustrated by a twelve-year-old boy who noted that after a difficult period of conviction and prayer that "everything looked new.

---

[39]*CEM* 1 (September 1800): 101.
[40]*CEM* 1 (July 1800): 25.
[41]*MMM* 2 (June 1804): 29.
[42]*MMM* 2 (July 1804): 63.
[43]*CEM* 5 (July 1804): 34.
[44]*CEM* 1 (July 1800): 24.

When I looked out of the window, things seemed to look of a different colour. I felt full of joy, for it seemed to me, that the righteous God had come and delivered me from my sins."[45] Statements like these most likely derive from the visual orientation of Edwardsean spirituality. As God manifests his excellencies throughout the created order, new converts "see" divine glory not only in scriptural meditations on God but in nature as well.

A third signature experience of a New Divinity conversion is the frequent reference to persons not being aware that they are converted. "It has been no uncommon thing," Samuel Mills Sr. notes,

> for the subjects of the work, whose chief distress and anxiety antecedently arose from a sense of their being in the hands of God, unexpectedly to find themselves rejoicing in that very consideration—contemplating the glory, and happiness of God, as an object of higher consequence, and more precious than their own personal salvation, and all this, while as yet, they have had no idea of having experienced any saving change of heart.[46]

This feature is related to the doctrine of disinterested benevolence. Disinterestedness so transfixes the soul on the delight of divine beauty that it takes little notice of the self's interests, including its relation to eternal salvation. Only when converts later begin to reflect on how new affections have possessed the heart do they realize that they have experienced the new birth. Thus *not* being concerned about one's own salvation out of an overwhelming delight in divine things was, for many New Divinity pastors and parishioners, a reliable sign of true conversion.[47]

Last, the New Divinity's unique interpretation of the atonement sometimes surfaces in these conversion narratives. We see this in several places in Ann Hasseltine's diary. As noted in the introduction to this book, Hasseltine, who later became the wife of Adoniram Judson, came under conviction in 1807 during a revival in her church in Bradford, Massachusetts. The reflections she left behind in her journal reveal themes typical of an Edwardsean conversion: an initial hatred of divine sovereignty; a realization that she would hate heaven if allowed to go there with her current heart; a desire for annihilation, followed by a new sense of

---

[45]*MMM* 2 (June 1804): 30.
[46]*CEM* 1 (July 1800): 29.
[47]This was also a sign that distinguished Edwardsean conversion from a free grace version of conversion such as Croswell's, which emphasized the certain knowledge of one's salvation as being a sign of being converted.

the beauty of Christ and the way of salvation; and a new desire to love people with an undying love. She read spiritual literature throughout this period, including works by Edwards and Doddridge as well as Bellamy's *True Religion Delineated* and a biography of Samuel Hopkins. Peppered throughout are statements revealing her fascination and wonder at Christ's atoning work. In early November, she took courage in the fact that she could "see a beauty in the character of Christ, that makes me ardently desire to be like him." She continued, "O how deplorable would be my situation, thus covered with sin, was it not for the atonement Christ has made. But he is my Mediator with the Father. He has magnified the law and made it honorable. He can save sinners, consistently with the divine glory. God can now be just, and the justifier of those who believe in his Son."[48]

This concern for God's law being "magnified" and "honored" in Christ's atoning work is echoed several months later in an entry from July 1808.

> But though my heart is treacherous, I trust that I have some evidence of being a true Christian; for when contemplating the moral perfections of God, my heart is pleased with, and approves of, just such a Being. His law, which once appeared unjust and severe, now appears to be holy, just, and good. His justice appears equally glorious as his mercy, and illustrative of the same love to universal happiness. The way of salvation by Christ appears glorious, because herein God can be just, and yet display his mercy to the penitent sinner.[49]

We might recall that the greatest problem the New Divinity discerned in the work of atonement had to do with the reconciliation of divine justice and mercy. How can the divine law be honored in the act of pardoning rebellious sinners? Hasseltine's casual reflections on the atonement here reflect this exact concern. Her conversion experience demonstrates many of the unique features found in the New Divinity's revival theology.

Hasseltine's heroic work as a missionary in Southeast Asia reveals the self-denying ethic that pervaded committed New Divinity laborers for the gospel. Their doctrine of disinterested benevolence no doubt factored into this self-denial. Scholars have recently noted the connection between this Edwardsean theological ideal and the New Divinity activism that touched both educational institutions and missions. Many of New England's regional colleges, such as Williams,

---

[48]James D. Knowles, *Memoir of Mrs. Ann H. Judson, Late Missionary to Burmah*, 3rd ed. (Boston: Lincoln & Edmands, 1829), 23.

[49]Ibid., 30.

Dartmouth, Union, Amherst, and Middlebury, had many Edwardsean faculty members early in the nineteenth century.[50] Andover Seminary, the first Protestant seminary in North America, was founded in 1808 largely as an Edwardsean institution. The famed Haystack Prayer Meeting, which is often credited as inspiring the modern missions movement in America, was held at Williams College, a school heavily influenced by Edwardsean theology and by students who had deep ties to the New Divinity ministerial network.[51] Some of these students later attended Andover and were instrumental in founding the American Board of Commissioners for Foreign Missions, which had a significantly Edwardsean orientation in its early years.[52] These historical trajectories, which are beyond the scope of this work, reveal that the turn-of-the-century Edwardsean revivals did not just transform hearts but touched the world as well.

In summary, Edwardsean revival theology shaped many of the revivals in Congregationalist New England. As revivalists preached the gospel, they highlighted many of the features of the New Divinity: an emphasis on the sovereignty of God in election, the notion that the moral ideal is shaped by the selfless ethic of disinterested benevolence, and the seemingly paradoxical message that sinners are under the responsibility to repent immediately (natural ability) even though their hearts necessarily incline them to hate God (moral inability). Portions of this message trickled down into the spirituality of those being converted, as would-be converts came to experience their hatred for God, spiritual resignation to his will (even if it meant damnation), and the awakening of new affections for divine things that so attracted the gaze of the soul to God that new converts were unaware that they had been born again. These were the central characteristics of New Divinity revival theology. As the theological tradition matured and developed, a newer, progressive version of it appeared in the 1820s with the formation of Yale Divinity School and its first professor of theology, Nathaniel William Taylor. Taylor intended his New Haven Theology to bring further consistency to advances made by Edwardsean Calvinists, but it drew harsh criticism not only from conservative Calvinists of Old School Presbyterianism but also from the voices within the Edwardsean household itself.

---

[50]D. W. Kling, "The New Divinity and Williams College, 1793–1836," *Religion and American Culture: A Journal of Interpretation* 6, no. 2 (1996): 195-97.

[51]Samuel Mills Jr. was the son of Samuel Mills Sr. of Torringford, Connecticut. Both Gordon Hall and Harvey Loomis received part of their theological training in the New Divinity schools of the prophets.

[52]David W. Kling, "The New Divinity and the Origins of the American Board of Commissioners for Foreign Missions," *Church History* 72, no. 4 (December 1, 2003): 791-819.

FURTHER DEVELOPMENTS IN NEW DIVINITY THEOLOGY: TAYLORISM AND NEW SCHOOL PRESBYTERIANISM

By 1820 Nathaniel William Taylor (1786–1858) had come to the conclusion that New Divinity theology needed a serious face-lift. For some time, Unitarians and traditional Calvinists had been criticizing Edwardsean theology, and Taylor believed a new response was needed. Yale Divinity School was founded in 1822 with the vision of rising to these challenges, and Taylor was called to be its first professor of theology, a position he held until his death in 1858. Previously, Taylor worked closely with Yale president Timothy Dwight, and for ten years (1812–1822) he was a successful pastor at New Haven's First Church, where he led the congregation through three periods of revival. His transition to Yale marked the beginning of a new version of Edwardsean theology known as the New Haven Theology.

Taylor's theology reproduced many of the same features we have seen in New Divinity revival theology. He affirmed similar views on doctrines related to sin, which was defined exclusively with regard to voluntary actions (sin is "in the sinning"). Taylor affirmed original sin in the primitivist sense that the New Divinity had affirmed for decades: humanity is sinful not because there exist sinful natures causing wills to sin, but because in the present postlapsarian circumstances human nature lacks the possession of the Holy Spirit. Without the Spirit, human beings will naturally turn inward and seek their own selfish ends as soon as they begin to be moral agents.[53] Such is human nature, Taylor wrote, that human beings *"will sin and only sin in all the appropriate circumstances of their being."*[54] Last, Taylor agreed with his New Divinity predecessors in their rejection of the doctrine of the imputation of Adam's sin to his posterity. If sin is voluntary, and if the absence of the Holy Spirit is all that is needed to postulate the inevitability of sin, then there is no need to posit that the human race is held guilty for Adam's specific transgression. Human beings sin "in Adam" because the consequences of his act brought about circumstances (the withdrawal of the Holy Spirit) that make it certain that they will freely sin from the moment they begin to act, not because they somehow are morally involved in his transgression via imputation. Thus everyone needs the regenerating influences of the Holy

---

[53]Sweeney, *Nathaniel Taylor*, 80-81. The following summary of Taylor's views relies significantly on Sweeney's interpretation.

[54]Nathaniel W. Taylor, *Concio ad Clerum: A Sermon Delivered in the Chapel of Yale College, September 10, 1828* (New Haven, CT: A. H. Maltby and Homan Hallock, 1842), 13.

Spirit: "To become a human being, is to come under the necessity of being born again of the Spirit."[55]

Taylor's innovations to New Divinity theology centered on his understanding of the preregenerate capacities of the will. First, Taylor sought to readjust the popular Edwardsean vocabulary of the sinner's "moral inability" and "natural ability." In his mind the language of *inability* had run its course, as it was too constraining. His solution was to speak of the sinner's "certainty" of sinning "without necessity."[56] In other words, while it is certain that human beings will sin, there is no philosophical necessity in this, because no one or nothing is coercing them to sin; they sin freely. Conversely, there is also no necessity preventing sinners from repentance and faith in Christ, since they naturally have the capacity required to submit to the terms of the gospel. Taylor is essentially turning the Edwardsean logic around to privilege the sinner's theoretical ability. "But we have shown," Taylor preached, "that man has ample power, even the power of a perfect moral agent; we have shown that it is right in itself, that he should make himself a new heart without any divine influence."[57] Elsewhere he noted that "as a moral agent, man is *qualified* in respect to constitutional powers and properties, to perform without divine grace, what God requires of him."[58] Taylor's alteration of Edwardsean vocabulary was consistent with more optimistic language regarding the sinner's capacity to follow Christ. While traditional Edwardseans employed the natural ability/moral inability distinction to emphasize God's sovereignty in regeneration, Taylor's updated formula appeared to underscore the sinner's potential for making themselves a new heart.

This optimism is seen more starkly in Taylor's interpretation of the doctrine of regeneration. Similar to traditional Edwardseans, Taylor believed that regeneration is essentially a work of the Spirit that involves human beings choosing God rather than the world as their supreme happiness. However, he went on to argue that prior to the moment of regeneration sinners are brought to a point in their use of the means of grace where *the principle of selfishness is actually suspended* and they employ the means without sin. He described how this works in several places

---

[55]Ibid., 19.

[56]Sweeney, *Nathaniel Taylor*, 75-76.

[57]Nathaniel W. Taylor, "The Sinner's Duty to Make Himself a New Heart," in *Practical Sermons* (New York: Clark, Austin, and Smith, 1858), 409.

[58]Nathaniel W. Taylor, *Essays on the Means of Regeneration* (New Haven, CT: Baldwin and Treadway, 1829), 223.

but most extensively in *Essays on the Means of Regeneration* (1829). He begins by reaffirming Edwards's distinction between the principles of self-love and self-ishness. Self-love is a neutral principle (it is neither holy nor evil) woven into our souls that leads us to seek happiness, self-preservation, and enjoyment of the good. Selfishness, by contrast, is a distortion of the principle of self-love in which individuals devoid of the Holy Spirit seek happiness in worldly things to the exclusion of God. Though clearly related, these two principles are distinct: the desire for happiness (self-love) is not sinful; actively seeking that happiness in the world (selfishness) is.

Taylor applied this distinction to his theology of conviction. He argued that when sinners come under conviction of sin and begin to use the means of grace, the selfish principle can actually be weakened because the means of grace have a positive effect on sinful souls; the means "must either have some *tendency* to produce regeneration; or some necessary or real *connection* with it."[59] This tendency can be so strong that it momentarily suspends the principle of selfishness, leaving only the original principle of self-love to operate as the dominant principle of the heart. This, in turn, enables the mind to deliberate sinlessly whether God or the world is the greater good of the soul. All of this, Taylor indicated, takes place prior to that "interposition of the Holy Spirit" associated with the work of regeneration.[60] Critics noted that this argument gives the impression that all that is required for salvation is a simple use of the means of grace and the act of choosing God as one's greatest good. Taylor, of course, responded that the Holy Spirit's supernatural agency is necessary for regeneration and conversion, and he went to great lengths to detail his views. But many suspected that Pelagianism lurked beneath Taylor's complex and subtle responses.

Taylor's New Haven Theology generated a great deal of heat both inside and outside New England Congregationalism. Edward Dorr Griffin sharply criticized Taylor's views in print,[61] while Bennet Tyler (1783–1858), a conservative Edwardsean Congregationalist and president of Dartmouth College, argued that Taylor's system was essentially Pelagian.[62] In the 1830s Tyler extensively engaged

---

[59]Ibid., 22-23. In this point, Taylor directly counters Hopkins's doctrine of the sinfulness of unregenerate doings.

[60]Ibid., 19.

[61]Edward D. Griffin, *The Doctrine of Divine Efficiency, Defended Against Certain Modern Speculations* (New York: Jonathan Leavitt, 1833).

[62]Bennet Tyler, *Letter on the Origin and Progress of the New Haven Theology* (New York: Robert Carter and

Taylor in a paper war known as the Tyler-Taylor controversy, and he eventually founded what would later become Hartford Theological Seminary in an effort to stave off the growing influence of Taylorism among Congregationalists.

The fireworks were even greater among the Presbyterians. To appreciate this, we must trace some of the backgrounds leading up to the great controversy in the 1830s that effected a split in American Presbyterianism. For decades Presbyterian missionaries and revivalists in the West were some of the biggest fans of New Divinity Calvinism. The popularity was due not only to Edwards's celebrity and the evangelistic potential of New Divinity theology; it also derived from a surge of Congregationalists transferring their allegiances to Presbyterianism in the period. The early nineteenth century witnessed the migration of many New Englanders westward. Many of these individuals hailed from Edwardsean congregations or were familiar with Edwardsean theology. In 1801, Congregationalists and Presbyterians joined forces in an agreement known as the Plan of Union to combine their resources in evangelizing the new areas, which stretched from western New York southwest toward Tennessee. The agreement included the stipulation that each newly planted church retained the right to affiliate with either denomination. The deal wound up favoring the Presbyterians, since many of the new churches found the network of presbyteries more appealing than the Congregationalist ideal of church autonomy in the sparsely populated frontier. Sometimes whole Congregationalist associations converted over to Presbyterianism.[63] By 1830 these revival-oriented western Presbyterian churches had come to be known as New School Presbyterians, largely because they espoused the newer Edwardsean Calvinism of the New Divinity. They were opposed by "Old School" conservatives, who saw New School theology as a threat to Westminster Calvinism and traditional Presbyterian polity.

At the time, some of the best-known clergymen in the country were New School Presbyterians. Lyman Beecher (1775–1863), pastor, revivalist, and moral reformer, was reared in the Connecticut New Divinity tradition and ministered in both Congregationalist and Presbyterian congregations throughout the Northeast before becoming president of Lane Theological Seminary in 1832, a New School Presbyterian institution in Cincinnati. Beecher is well-known for his

---

Ezra Collier, 1837), 171.

[63]George Marsden, *The Evangelical Mind and the New School Presbyterian Experience: A Case Study of Thought and Theology in Nineteenth-Century America* (New Haven, CT: Yale University Press, 1970), 11.

moral crusades against dueling and alcohol as well as for being the father of Harriet Beecher Stowe and Henry Ward Beecher. His close friendship with Taylor ensured that Taylorism would have a broad audience.

Albert Barnes (1798–1870) was another popular New School Presbyterian. Still known today for his popular *Notes on the Old and New Testament,* Barnes came to prominence with the publication of his sermon "The Way of Salvation" in 1829. The text is remarkable for the way it translates the complexities of Edwardsean theology into a clear and simple presentation of the message of salvation. A brief survey of it is necessary to illustrate Barnes's practical evangelistic strategy emerging from his New School theology.

Six points unfold in its pages. First, the human race is "destitute of holiness." No one follows the law, which requires "love to God, supreme and unqualified." Though all have sinned, no one is held responsible for Adam's sin, but we each, when we reach our first act of moral agency, sin and will continue to do so unless renewed by grace.[64] Second, God's plan of mercy involved sending his beloved son Jesus Christ into the world to become the mediator between God and humankind. In his death, he did not endure the penalty of the law, but rather suffered in a way that "evinced the hatred of God against sin," thus making it fitting that he should accept his Son's suffering in the place of sinners' eternal torment and offer pardon to a rebellious world. The atonement is thus for all, offered to all humankind in "perfect sincerity."[65] Barnes's entire theology revolves around this central point:

> I assume the free and full offer of the Gospel to all men, to be one of those cardinal points of the system by which I *gauge* all my other views of truth. It is, in my view, a corner-stone of the whole edifice; that which makes it so glorious to God, and so full of good-will to men. I hold no doctrines . . . which will be in *my* views inconsistent with the free and full offer of the Gospel to all men.[66]

Third, Barnes noted that human beings reject the gospel not because of God's decree but because "they *will* not submit to him" out of their hardness of heart.[67] Fourth, the Holy Spirit is the necessary agent of salvation, who was sent by God to arrest our attention and get us to see our dire plight. "He goes *before* the

---

[64]Albert Barnes, *The Way of Salvation,* 7th ed. (New York: Leavitt, Lord, 1836), 14-16.
[65]Ibid., 19-22.
[66]Ibid., 22.
[67]Ibid., 25.

convicted sinner to remove obstacles; he pours light into the mind; he impresses truth; he urges duty." While his work in our hearts is necessary, it is not by compulsion, but is fully consistent with human willing. "The work of salvation, and the work of damnation, are the two most deliberate and solemn acts *of choosing,* that mortal men ever perform."[68] Fifth, the change that God works in conversion centers on the transformation of human affections:

> He that [formerly] sought only to live and enjoy himself here, now rises to higher objects, begins to feel that he is in the infancy of his being, and casts an eye of desire to the green fields in the skies, where he may for ever sweep the lyre in the praise of the Son of God, and unite with angels and archangels in lauding him that sitteth on the throne for ever and ever.[69]

Finally, Barnes finished with a robust and assuring statement of perseverance. "God will watch over each renewed spirit till the day of judgment, and bring it infallibly to his kingdom."[70] Though the earmarks of Edwardsean theology are visible throughout the sermon, the most memorable point is where he solemnly impresses sinners with their duty to repent and the unavoidable conclusion that, if they do nothing, it is their own fault.

> You *know* your duty, and your doom, if you do it not.... If you *will perish*, I must sit down and weep as I see you glide to the lake of death. Yet I cannot see you take that dread[ed] plunge—see you die, die for ever, without once more assuring you that the offer of the gospel is freely made to you. While you linger this side the fatal verge, that shall close life, and hope, and happiness, I would once more lift up my voice and say, See, sinner, see a God of love. He comes to you.... To him I commend you, with the deep feeling in my own bosom, that you are in his hands; that you are solemnly bound to repent *to-day,* and believe the gospel, and that if you perish, you only will be to blame.[71]

In short, Barnes's message was "repent, believe! If you die, it is your own fault; there are no excuses." Such was the essence of much New School evangelism.

The most famous New School Presbyterian was Charles Finney (1792–1875). For almost a decade, Finney blazed a trail through the Northeast as Presbyterianism's most famous New School revivalist. Though he is often regarded as a highly

---

[68]Ibid., 27-28.
[69]Ibid., 33-34.
[70]Ibid., 36.
[71]Ibid., 45-46.

original maverick of nineteenth-century revivalism, Finney actually borrowed liberally from Taylor's thought. We will explore this thesis at length in chapter seven.

The combined effect of the rise of New School theology caused great alarm among conservative Presbyterians in the 1830s, especially after Barnes was invited to be the pastor at Philadelphia's First Presbyterian Church located right in the heart of Old School territory. Old Schoolers charged Taylorism with heresy and vigorously campaigned to rid their denomination of its impurities. New School leaders such as Beecher and Barnes were officially charged with heresy, only to be acquitted by synods who were sympathetic to New School theology. It was only when Old School leaders gained a majority of the denomination's General Assembly in 1837 that they achieved victory. There they managed to dissolve the Plan of Union, a move that effectively excised four New School synods from their national fellowship, one-fifth of the entire denomination. The action effectively split American Presbyterianism into two denominational entities, a breach that would not be healed until 1869.[72] Clearly, while Taylorism was thought to bless many Presbyterian churches, it proved to be highly divisive, as conservative Presbyterian Calvinists could not stomach what they viewed as its unrecognizable version of Calvinism.

SUMMARY

New Divinity revival theology lived well into the nineteenth century among the Congregationalist revivals in the Northeast. The preaching and conversion experiences of those who participated in these revivals reflect its common features:

- preaching that stressed God's sovereignty in salvation, sinners' total selfishness in the love of their own private interests, and their moral inability to save themselves

- the call to immediate repentance based on the doctrine of natural ability

- experiences of conviction that often included a deep awareness of one's own hatred for God, his word, and heaven

- the experience of complete resignation to God's will (even if it meant personal damnation), and a subsequent and unexpected calm, followed by the dawning of a new awareness of the gospel, Christ, and the glory of God

---

[72]For details on this controversy, see Marsden, *Evangelical Mind*, 59-87.

In the 1820s Edwardsean theology developed further in the hands of Nathaniel William Taylor, who introduced two significant alterations:

- new labels for the Edwardsean "natural ability/moral inability" distinction, which rhetorically minimized the language of inability and effectively privileged the sinner's theoretical ability to make themself a new heart

- the supposition that the means of grace can actually lead to the suspension of sinners' selfish principles, which enables them to consider the gospel claims in a sinless state

Taylor's views, which came to be called New Haven Theology, spread among many Congregationalists and New School Presbyterians. Traditional New England theologians and Old School Calvinists sharply criticized what they considered this new Pelagian version of Edwardsean theology, a point that led to division among New England Congregationalism and American Presbyterianism.

While Taylor and New School Presbyterians took offense at the charge that they were Arminians, there were those who proudly wore that label. American Methodists had been ministering in North America since the mid-1700s and were exploding in numbers by the turn of the century. They championed an Arminian revival theology derived largely from John Wesley's writings and adapted to the highly emotional revivals they presided over. In the next chapter we will turn our attention to their views, which helped them grow from humble beginnings to become the largest Protestant denomination in America by 1860.

CHAPTER FIVE

METHODIST REVIVAL THEOLOGY IN THE SECOND GREAT AWAKENING

IN 1785 AMERICAN METHODISTS published an overview of their organization that outlined points of their ecclesiastical polity.[1] In it they reproduced a succinct summary of Methodism's origins penned by John and Charles Wesley.

> In 1729, two young men, reading the Bible, saw they could not be saved without holiness, followed after it, and incited others so to do. In 1737 they saw [that] holiness comes by faith. They saw likewise, that men are justified before they are sanctified: but still holiness was their point. God then thrust them out, utterly against their will, to raise a holy people. When Satan could no otherwise hinder this, he threw *Calvinism* in the way; and then *Antinomianism*, which strikes directly at the root of all holiness.[2]

In this quote we find the central elements of Methodist theology. The Wesley brothers' ultimate vision centered on *holiness*, which they saw as necessary to salvation (Heb 12:14) and which they developed into a controversial doctrine known as Christian perfection. To this they added the evangelical essentials of

---

[1]Methodist Episcopal Church, Thomas Coke, and Francis Asbury, *Minutes of Several Conversations Between the Rev. Thomas Coke, LL. D., the Rev. Francis Asbury and Others* (Philadelphia: Charles Cist, 1785).
[2]Ibid., 4.

justification by faith and *the new birth.* These truths not only transformed their own lives but also "thrust them out . . . to raise a holy people" through *vigorous evangelistic preaching* that stressed *the universal offer of the gospel.* Their evangelistic labors aligned them with the growing revival movements of the period. It also drew them into heated conflict with Calvinist leaders, who found many points in Methodist teaching to be deeply disturbing.[3] Together these points—the centrality of personal holiness, Christian perfection, justification, the universal offer of the gospel, the evangelical revival setting, and heated debate with Calvinists—coalesced in John Wesley's mind to forge a revival theology unique to the English-speaking world of the eighteenth century.

American Methodist pioneers, many trained by Wesley himself, brought with them the fundamental features of Methodism when they arrived in the American colonies in the 1760s and 1770s.[4] They reproduced Wesley's organized network of small groups known as classes and bands, which served as spiritual incubators for new believers as well as training grounds for young ministers. They also reproduced Wesley's ministry methods. Newly identified leaders were appointed to take preaching circuits over extensive geographical areas, in which, over a period of several weeks, they would minister at each station on their circuits, preaching outdoors, organizing new believers, and training new leaders. Unlike a settled minister, who is tied to one church in one town, these Methodist circuit riders, as they became known, were able to fan out over large regions and quickly adapt to changes in the population patterns.[5] The formula fostered explosive growth in the new movement.

Another factor that contributed to their growth was effective leadership. When Wesley sent Francis Asbury (1745–1816) to America in 1771, he probably was not aware of the great gift he was giving to future American Methodists. Single-minded and indefatigable, Asbury had a gift for organization, networking, and adapting Methodism to the American setting. Though a powerful leader—by Christmas 1784 he had become Methodism's first American bishop—it was

---

[3]For on overview of the English Methodist-Calvinist controversy in the 1770s, see Henry D. Rack, *Reasonable Enthusiast: John Wesley and the Rise of Methodism*, 3rd ed. (London: Epworth, 2002), 450-61.

[4]On the history of early American Methodism, see David Hempton, *Methodism: Empire of the Spirit* (New Haven, CT: Yale University Press, 2005); Russell E. Richey, *Methodism in the American Forest* (New York: Oxford University Press, 2015); Jeanne Miller Schmidt, Russell E. Richey, and Kenneth E. Rowe, *American Methodism: A Compact History* (Nashville: Abingdon, 2012); and John H. Wigger, *American Saint: Francis Asbury and the Methodists* (New York: Oxford University Press, 2009).

[5]For a description of the American circuit-riding system, see Wigger, *American Saint*, 8-9.

his sacrificial example that inspired awe and engendered loyalty to the Methodist cause. In his forty-five years in America, he traveled more than three hundred thousand miles on horseback, delivering more than sixteen thousand sermons, all the while never earning more than sixty-four dollars a year. Under his leadership a cadre of selfless young itinerants—who forsook marriage, property, wealth, status, and settled ministries—fanned out across America. When Asbury came to America, the Methodist faith numbered a meager five thousand. Shortly after his death in 1816, there were a quarter-million American Methodists. By the eve of the Civil War, Methodism had exploded to become the largest Protestant denomination in the United States, numbering 1.7 million.[6] As one historian put it, they were "a vast engine of salvation."[7]

The revival theology that Asbury and other early American Methodists taught was basically a reproduction of Wesley's views. Because they were practitioners deeply involved in the throes of itinerant ministry, they did not produce many treatises, theological discourses, or even published sermons. This does not mean they were nontheological. In 1789–1790 they published a religious periodical titled *The Arminian Magazine*, which contained significant theological excerpts.[8] More importantly, many circuit riders, like Asbury and Freeborn Garrettson (1752–1827), kept private journals, in which we see them deeply immersed in Scripture (meditating on horseback during their travels), in sermon preparation (most of which was delivered extemporaneously), and in religious reading (Asbury was constantly reading theology, history, and Christian biography). These journals also record the contents of sermons preached, theological discussions with laypersons, and various debates, giving us a rough outline of their theological views. Later, in the early nineteenth century, we see the advent of American Methodist theological literature in works by Nathan Bangs, Asa Shinn, Timothy Merritt, Wilbur Fisk, and Thomas Ralston. Methodist leaders were vigorously theological, but their sights were set more on the conversion of souls than on the making of many books.

---

[6]Mark A. Noll, *America's God: From Jonathan Edwards to Abraham Lincoln* (New York: Oxford University Press, 2002), 169. For further analysis and statistics of American Methodist growth at the end of the eighteenth century and into the nineteenth, see John H. Wigger, *Taking Heaven by Storm: Methodism and the Rise of Popular Christianity in America* (New York: Oxford University Press, 1998), 3-7.

[7]Noll, *America's God*, 330.

[8]Methodist Episcopal Church, *The Arminian Magazine: Consisting of Extracts and Original Treatises on General Redemption*, 2 vols. (Philadelphia: Prichard and Hall, 1789).

Our examination of Methodist revival theology in America will concentrate on the journals of the first-generation pioneers, such as Asbury and Garrettson, as well as the theological treatises of the first third of the nineteenth century. These works were written by ministers who had experience with revivals. The positions they advanced were fairly consistent. The revival theology inherent in them is basically a Wesleyan or evangelical version of Arminianism. Its central features, drawn from their reading of Scripture and forged in the intense piety of revivalism, may be summed up in three theological instincts: (1) a view of God that underscores his loving and just interaction with human free agents, (2) an emphasis on the universal offer of the gospel to every human being, and (3) the serious call to holiness and Christian perfection. We will examine each of these three positions separately.

THE GOD OF LOVE: THE FOUNDATION OF METHODIST REVIVAL THEOLOGY

Though it is possible to base Methodist revival theology in the concept of the universal offer of the gospel, we must dig deeper to an even more fundamental starting point: the doctrine of God's divine goodness, wisdom, and love. Early American Methodists anchored their revival theology in a vision of God's stance toward the world that underscored benevolence, kindness, and goodwill. "Divine goodness," Asa Shinn writes, "is the leading principle of [God's] conduct toward his creatures."[9] A creation devoid of a good and loving God at its helm would never draw any loving followers. Consequently, they cast God's sovereignty in terms that highlighted his wise administration of creation and just interaction with the moral order rather than in terms of boundless power, unconditionality, and decree. We see these positions most prominently in their polemical statements against Calvinist views, which they understood to ascribe evil to God. "If every event which comes to pass, is brought to pass by God's plan . . . as an effect of his decree," Nathan Bangs wrote in a letter against a Hopkinsian minister, "then there can be no event, however trivial in itself, however wicked, foolish, and inconsistent, but what is included in this plan which you ascribe to God, and which according to your statement, is the effect of his uncontrollable decree."[10] Similarly, Bangs later asserted that to affirm that God chose Jacob over Esau "without any respect to their moral characters" is perhaps to "advance one of the most shocking ideas

---

[9]Asa Shinn, *An Essay on the Plan of Salvation* (Baltimore: Neal, Wills and Cole, 1813), 240.
[10]Nathan Bangs, *The Errors of Hopkinsianism Detected and Refuted* (New York: John C. Totten, 1815), 15.

which can enter into the heart of man." The reason for this shock is that such a position brings injustice into the heart of God. "[When I read this] I was ready to cry out, Good Lord, is this thy character? It cannot be—it is utterly impossible for the *God of love*, of justice and goodness, to form such determination. It is the blackest impeachment imaginable of his *holy* and *merciful* character!"[11] Statements like these are common throughout American Methodist writings and reveal a fundamental theological instinct they shared: that divine love, goodness, and justice cannot possibly be reconciled with the sovereign deity promoted by the Calvinists.

A close corollary to the centrality of divine love, linked ever so tightly in the Methodist mind, is the prominence they gave in their revival theology to the concept of human freedom. God's love *cannot be*, they maintained, without space given to the reality of human freedom, responsibility, and genuine culpability. There is "no fact more certain," Bangs writes, "then our free agency."[12] In contrast to the traditional Calvinist view, which emphasized God's decree over every event, including human beings' moral choices, Methodists affirmed that God made humans free moral agents and subsequently interacts with them in freedom and love and for their good. Such a position portrays divine-human interaction in terms more recognizable of a genuine relationship, and it also removes the injustice they perceived in the Calvinist God, who oddly punishes the unrighteous for wicked choices they were destined to commit. God "does not unconditionally decree anything," Freeborn Garrettson writes; rather, he "leaves his rational creatures to act freely."[13] Any intermingling of human volition with divine decreeing would inevitably draw God into moral evil. Thus, according to Asa Shinn, there are only two theological options: "Either to believe that our creator is essentially wicked or that his creatures were made free, and introduced evil by an abuse of their liberty."[14] Shinn and other American Methodists opted for the latter option: God is so committed to preserving human freedom that he did not restrain Adam from sinning in Eden. The "reason why God did not hinder the introduction of moral evil, by making it *impossible* for his creatures to sin, was because it could not be done without making it impossible for any creature to enjoy *holiness* or *moral happiness*. God left his creatures free, because *God is love*."[15]

---

[11]Ibid., 105.

[12]Ibid., vii.

[13]Freeborn Garrettson, *American Methodist Pioneer: The Life and Journals of the Rev. Freeborn Garrettson, 1752–1827*, ed. Robert Drew Simpson (Rutland, VT: Academy Books, 1984), 278.

[14]Shinn, *Plan of Salvation*, 212.

[15]Ibid., 214-15.

Several implications arise from this combined emphasis on divine love and human freedom. First, God genuinely desires the salvation of all humankind. We do not find in their writings the complex Calvinist discussions attempting to reconcile God's universal desire that all be saved with his actual electing of a chosen few. When the Bible indicates that God desires everyone's salvation (1 Tim 2:4; 2 Pet 3:9), Methodists took this at face value. Francis Asbury notes this in his sermon outline of 2 Corinthians 5. "The Gospel is a universal ministration of grace and truth: 'we persuade men'—all men, everywhere. This position is proved by the general love of God; the general commission giving the ambassadors of Christ; the general atonement; general offers of grace; [and] the general judgment."[16] Jesse Lee agrees: "God had taken his oath against Calvinism, because he had declared by the mouth of his holy prophet, 'As I live saith the Lord God, I have no pleasure in the death of the wicked, but that the wicked might turn from his way and live.'"[17]

Second, American Methodist writers were careful to speak of divine providence in terms that highlighted God's wise interaction with human free agents rather than in terms of sovereign power over human wills. "God governs the world in wisdom," Bangs writes. "He rules mankind as free, responsible agents, and not by a dire necessity."[18] While divine providence "extends to all causes and events," it does so in such a way that it "checks and restrains the evil designs of the wicked" rather than actively decreeing any such things. Providence thus understood portrays God more as a divine intervener who, with infinite wisdom, genuinely responds and graciously interacts with human free agents. "So that although he did not decree that mankind should sin, yet out of tender compassion to them, he has provided a sovereign remedy for all their malidies [sic]; and mercifully assists those who are willing to accept of its healing influence, in making a saving application of it their souls."[19] This in turn led them to affirm the traditional Arminian understanding of election, which stressed divine foreknowledge as the basis for God's predestination. God, in other words, elects individuals to salvation on the basis of a faith that he foresaw them embrace in their freedom.[20] The Calvinist

---

[16]Francis Asbury, *Journal of Rev. Francis Asbury: Bishop of the Methodist Episcopal Church* (New York: Lane & Scott, 1852), 3:146.

[17]Jesse Lee, *Memoir of the Rev. Jesse Lee*, ed. Minton Thrift (New York: Meyers & Smith, 1823), 102-3.

[18]Bangs, *Errors of Hopkinsianism*, 55.

[19]Ibid., 56.

[20]Ibid., 123; Thomas Neely Ralston, *Elements of Divinity* (Louisville: Morton & Griswold, 1847), 193-207.

view of unconditional election, in which God elects some to salvation on the basis of his own pleasure, was roundly rejected by Methodists because it countered their view of God. If unconditional election is true, then unconditional reprobation is, and if so, "what shall we do with [God's] holiness, wisdom and mercy?"[21]

The combined effect of these observations was meant to commend to the world a God who is rich in mercy, abundant in grace, and open to all who would come to him. It is hard to avoid the immense broadness they discerned in divine mercy pulsating throughout their writings.

> How sublime, and how glorious does the predestination of God appear, when viewed in this point of light! No lowering clouds of eternal wrath against reprobated millions, appear to darken the sky of Gospel truth. No *narrow rivulet* of electing love runs through the plain of human misery, merely to quench the thirst of a *few* favoured souls. But the luminous rays of divine light from the *Sun of righteousness*, are widely diffused throughout the horizon of the moral world; and the *broad river* of redeeming love, widening as it majestically flows along, is sufficiently capacious to satisfy the "raging thirst" of all the perishing sons of fallen man. How delightful to behold a smiling God in the face of Jesus Christ, with arms of benevolence extended to all the human race, ready to infold them with paternal love![22]

Such statements found fertile soil in the theological minds of thousands of Methodists, who yearned to see the gospel offered to all.

THE UNIVERSAL OFFER OF THE GOSPEL IN METHODIST REVIVAL THEOLOGY

The benevolent stance God displays toward the fallen world in Christ, discussed above, translated into doctrines that supported the universal offer of the gospel. Though pro-revival Calvinists had proclaimed the good news indiscriminately to all, a significant asterisk, one that was a product of their predestinarian theology, surfaced in their minds as they preached. "Yes, you are all called to faith in Christ, but only a few of you shall be divinely gifted to repent and believe." Methodist revivalists found this sentiment to be inherently contradictory and never tired of exposing what they believed to be its numerous inconsistencies. Even the New Divinity brand of Calvinism, which was designed to give sinners more hope ("You have a natural ability; repent and believe now!"), came under Methodist scrutiny.

---

[21]Garrettson, *American Methodist Pioneer*, 295.
[22]Bangs, *Errors of Hopkinsianism*, 299-300.

Bangs found this famous New Divinity distinction to be inherently fraught with logical fallacies. If the reprobate have a natural ability, then they "*can* love [God], independent of redeeming grace," a point that renders the decree of reprobation resistible and null. If moral inability is true, then it undermines natural ability; both cannot be true. The only way out of this forest of fallacies is to scrap the entire system and opt for a view that, they argued, is more faithful to Scripture, the universal love of God, and common sense. "The fact is, [these doctrines] are *both erroneous.—Christ died for all men.* All *may* and *can* repent and love God, if they will, and be saved with everlasting life, through the *merits of Christ* and the agency of the *Holy Spirit*."[23]

How did Methodists work out these insights into a mature revival theology that avoided the conundrums of Calvinism? They basically began where the Calvinists did: with a strong affirmation of total depravity; "none hold to human depravity stronger than we do," Bangs asserted.[24] "The condition of man after the fall of Adam is such," reads their Articles of Religion, "that he cannot turn and prepare himself, by his own natural strength and works, to faith and calling upon God."[25] Human inability derives from original sin, which they argued consists in the inheritance of a corrupt nature from Adam that is continually inclined to evil.[26] Generally, they affirmed that Adam was the covenantal representative of the entire human race, who, on sinning, made it certain that his posterity would suffer the consequences of his sin by inheriting a corrupt nature.[27] A corrupt nature, however, is all that one inherits from Adam; one does not inherit Adam's guilt as a result of being born into the human race. "The bible no where says that Adam's sin was imputed to his posterity," Asa Shinn asserted.[28] Rather, in theological patterns reminiscent of the New Divinity, they maintained that each individual is held guilty for their own sin. In short, while all are corrupt because of Adam, all stand guilty individually for their own personal sins.

It is here where any similarities between their views and others' end. While Methodists affirmed total depravity, they maintained that its effects have been

---

[23]Ibid., 287.
[24]Ibid., 67.
[25]"Articles of Religion," VIII, in Methodist Episcopal Church, *The Doctrines and Discipline of the Methodist Episcopal Church* (New York: B. Waugh and T. Mason, 1832), 10-11.
[26]Ibid., VII, 10.
[27]Shinn, *Plan of Salvation*, 294-98.
[28]Ibid., 301.

universally undone through the atoning work of Jesus Christ. God, mindful of Christ's atonement, has supernaturally restored to every person spiritual abilities to perceive the truths of the gospel and freely respond to its universal call. This, in a nutshell, is the classic Wesleyan understanding of God's prevenient grace. "In the first Adam we lost our will and power to do good," writes Freeborn Garrettson. "In Christ, the second Adam, we are graciously restored both to a will and power; and with a great degree of propriety, the Lord may say, *choose life, that you may live.*"[29] More specifically, Bangs notes that, because Christ bore the penalty of the Adamic law, all humanity is now viewed in relation to the covenant of grace. Since the promise of Christ was announced early (Gen 3:15), God regards the entire span of human history in relation to the new covenant. "All are born into the world under the privileges of the new covenant of redemption," he notes, "and therefore none now, are in the same state that Adam was, previous to the grand promise of redemption."[30] Being in the new covenant does not automatically entitle one to salvation, for that would bypass individual freedom. It does, however, graciously grant every person spiritual light, grace, and a power to repent and believe Christ "at some period of [one's] life."[31]

It is important to note that for Methodists this ability is the result of God's *gracious supernatural* activity in the human race. Human beings, they affirmed, cannot come to Christ on their own natural power; sin has totally robbed them of that. Neither do they have a theoretical natural ability, as the New Divinity affirmed. Their ability arises from supernatural grace that extends indiscriminately to all, the result of Christ's atoning work. In this system, grace—supernatural *saving* grace that *can* bring salvation—touches every human being, yet in such a way that it renders ultimate salvation possible, not efficacious or necessary. The door to eternal life is opened to all, yet in order to partake of its blessings one must walk through it exercising one's free will. By extending God's saving grace to all, Methodists were obliged to dilute, to some degree, their understanding of the nature of grace, since grace was made contingent on the response of human choice and could be undone by it through apostasy, as we shall see in the next section. For the Calvinist, by contrast, grace comes powerfully to the prechosen few, bringing with it the entire package of redemption's blessings (regeneration, faith,

---

[29]Garrettson, *American Methodist Pioneer*, 144.
[30]Bangs, *Errors of Hopkinsianism*, 69.
[31]Ibid., 93.

repentance, justification, sanctification, perseverance, and glorification). The price they had to pay for their powerful portrayal of grace was to limit it to the elect, leaving the rest graceless and certain of eternal damnation. In the eyes of America's early Methodists, such a limitation could not be tolerated, not when Scripture appears to portray God's love to the world as universal in scope. The sermonic implications of such doctrine did not go unnoticed by their circuit-riding revivalists, such as Garrettson.

> Sinner, hear the voice of the eternal God, and lay aside your vain excuses. No longer cry out, I can do no-thing. For if you are not careful, you will do enough to damn your precious soul. We offer Christ to all upon earth, who have not sinned away their day of grace. Why, O! why should people be angry with us for preaching deliverance to poor captive souls—souls that are fallen—souls for whom Christ died—souls that must perish everlastingly without a change—Christ has merited every thing we need—Oh! then, dear souls, comply with his conditions—repent, believe, obey, and you shall live.[32]

The basis for the universal offer of the gospel and the universal reach of prevenient grace lies in their doctrine of the atonement. Methodists underscored the New Testament's universal texts with regard to the extent of the atonement: Christ died as a propitiation, not only for believers' sins, but for those of the whole world (1 Jn 2:2); the Lord "bought" even heretical teachers, who "bring upon themselves swift destruction" (2 Pet 2:1); and John the Baptist testifies that Jesus Christ is the Lamb of God, who takes away the sin of the world (Jn 1:29). Generally, they were content to reproduce these texts in support of their view that Christ's atoning work has universal implications. When they did explore the technicalities of the doctrine, they usually employed language that was consistent with the moral government theory. The atonement is not to be understood as a "commercial transaction," Thomas Ralston notes, but a "governmental arrangement" in which God "removes the difficulties which stood in the way of man's salvation."[33] Asa Shinn agreed: "Christ rendered such satisfaction as made it just for God to pardon any sinner in the world, on condition of repentance and faith in the Lord Jesus Christ."[34] These quotes cohere with the view that the atonement is essentially designed to demonstrate how God can remain just in pardoning sinners.

---

[32]Garrettson, *American Methodist Pioneer*, 144.
[33]Ralston, *Elements of Divinity*, 168.
[34]Shinn, *Plan of Salvation*, 177.

Sins are not literally "paid for" but rather upheld to be heinous before the world. "Christ did not properly or legally discharge our debt, either by obedience or suffering," Shinn notes. Rather, he "made it *just* for God to grant sinners a *gracious pardon, on certain conditions.*"[35] Once the conditions of repentance and faith are met, God can justly pardon in a way that simultaneously demonstrates his hatred of sin and his love for sinners.

This formulation of the atonement affected Methodists' understanding of justification. Without a substitutionary understanding of the atonement, the doctrine of justification is defined only in terms of forgiveness and remission of sin, without reference to the imputation of Christ's righteousness. Bangs defined justification as "*a free pardon of all actual sin, and a restoration to the favor of God.*"[36] Shinn found the notion of the imputation of Christ's righteousness to be a "mysterious" doctrine that drew its adherents toward moral laxness and antinomianism. "If the merits and righteousness of Christ be actually transferred to us by imputation, we are all as completely righteous and meritorious as ever he was," he noted. "This would not constitute us ransomed sinners, but gracious saviours of the world, possessing the whole righteousness and merit of that sacred character."[37]

For many early American Methodists, the universal call in the gospel, born out of a commitment to God's universal love for the world, entailed doctrines that underscored God's benevolent stance toward all of humankind: prevenient grace, universal atonement, and an opposition to the imputation of Christ's righteousness in justification. This was not the end of their revival theology, however. To them, God desires more than pardoned sinners; he wants to raise a holy people, individuals who are eager for good works and filled with divine love.

THE SERIOUS CALL TO HOLINESS: THE ULTIMATE GOAL OF METHODIST REVIVAL THEOLOGY

Most Methodist revivalists in early America were not content with merely preaching the blessings of redemption. To them, repentance, faith, justification, and regeneration were not endpoints but means to something greater, namely, the people of God experiencing the fullness of divine love that flowed out to both God and the world. As we saw earlier, the central vision animating the Wesley

---

[35]Ibid., 172; see also 207.
[36]Bangs, *Errors of Hopkinsianism,* 69.
[37]Shinn, *Plan of Salvation,* 208.

brothers was the biblical ideal of holiness and its practical result, raising up a holy people. This ideal manifested itself in two controversial doctrines that became fundamental to Methodist revival theology: the doctrine of Christian perfection and the affirmation that true Christians can fall away from grace. Practically, both of these doctrines kept the upward call to a holy life ever before the Christian pilgrim. Because Christians are truly freed from sin in the gospel, they are called to grow up into that freedom by seeking, experiencing, and maintaining a zealous love for God and the world that essentially mutes the exertions of their sinfulness. Because Christians can truly fall away from saving grace, they are never to rest on the laurels of previous achievements by entertaining spiritual sloth and neglect, but are ever to press forward in their callings lest sin overtake them, leading them to apostasy. Consequently, Methodists came to view Calvinism as inherently antinomian because its doctrines—most specifically eternal election and the doctrine of perseverance—directly undercut this serious call to holiness. Why engage in the struggles of sanctification when heaven is guaranteed by divine decree? To the Methodist mind, these positions coddled Christians in spiritual lethargy, exposing them to the dangers of damnation. Calvinism "encourages lawless presumption," Shinn observed, "by assuring the elect that they are such eternal favorites of God, that his decree secures their salvation as absolutely as the pillars of heaven are secured."[38] Asbury often noted the connection between Calvinism and antinomianism throughout his travels. At one stop he observed that "the people here appear unengaged: the preaching of unconditional election, and its usual attendant, Antinomianism, seems to have hardened their hearts."[39]

The Methodist doctrine of Christian perfection, though often misunderstood, derives from a rather simple theological logic inherent in the doctrine of sanctification. If, as Scripture declares, Christians have truly been set free from sin by Christ, then why place limits on the degree of sinlessness a believer can experience? Why constantly remind Christians, as Calvinists do, that the active presence of sin will ever disturb their pilgrimage this side of heaven when Scripture appears to present a different picture? Paul declares that Christians are "dead to sin," "freed from sin," and "crucified with him, that the body of sin might be destroyed, that henceforth [they] should not serve sin" (Rom 6:2, 7, 6). John notes that whoever is "born of God doth not commit sin; for his seed remaineth

---

[38]Ibid., 240.
[39]Asbury, *Journal of Rev. Francis Asbury*, 1:428.

in him: and he cannot sin, because he is born of God" (1 Jn 3:9). Jesus himself calls his disciples to be "perfect, even as [their] Father which is in heaven is perfect" (Mt 5:48). Surely these declarations were not merely theoretical ideals that are out of reach for Christians, but real possibilities that Christians can experience now. In fact, Methodists noted that the Old Testament records several examples of this perfection: Noah "was a just man and perfect in his generations," and Job was a man "perfect and upright" (Gen 6:9; Job 1:1).[40]

To the Methodist mind these texts implied that Christians can reach a point in their sanctification, through rigorous mortification and the infilling of God's Spirit, where the impulses of sin are essentially muted or placed into a state of hibernation. Divine love so fills the soul of the "perfected" or "sanctified" Christian that it can temporarily displace an individual's inclination to sin. The "fruits of the Spirit," noted R. Treffry, can be "brought to such maturity, [so] as to exclude every opposing principle, and every contrary temper."[41] Nathan Bangs concurred: the "*Christian* may arrive to such a state of perfection as to keep the gracious law under which the gospel of Christ places him, so as, in this sense to be delivered from sin."[42] Methodist revivalists were the first to point out that this is not the sinless perfection that the saints enjoy in heaven. In heaven, the saints cannot fall away, whereas the sanctified Christian here can fall back into sin and even ultimately fall away from grace. Furthermore, Bangs noted that Christian perfection is consistent with "involuntary transgressions" of the law of love by virtue of the fact that our reasoning powers are still impaired and our bodies still corrupt this side of heaven. Because of this, all Christians, even the perfected, continually need to rely on the atoning merits of Christ and the Spirit's help.[43]

Practically, Methodist revivalists encouraged every Christian to seek the blessing of Christian perfection. In his journal from January 1780, Freeborn Garrettson records his ministry to "Sister Smith," a recent convert who was in the final days of her life due to an illness. During conference, Smith related to Garrettson her conversion story and the great peace and joy that flowed into her soul after a long period of spiritual distress. She still, however, confessed to current trials and her hopes to be rid of them. Garrettson then broached the subject of Christian perfection.

---

[40]For scriptural support Methodists used for the concept of Christian perfection, see Bangs, *Errors of Hopkinsianism*, 182-97.

[41]R. Treffry, "A Sermon on Christian Perfection," *Methodist Magazine* 5 (1822): 85.

[42]Bangs, *Errors of Hopkinsianism*, 183.

[43]Ibid., 156-58.

I asked her if she felt sin in her heart. "Oh yes," said she, "I am troubled with the remains of sin." I begged her to look to the Lord and he would cut short his work. I had much freedom to pray for a total deliverance from sin. Glory be to God for his goodness, He paid us a sweet visit. This night I rested in sweet peace.

   Tuesday [January 11, 1780]—I asked her if she was happy. "Happy? Oh yes," she said, "my soul is happy. I am made a new creature whilst you were at prayer, the Lord cleansed my heart from sin, now I love Him with my whole heart. O God how good thou art, thou art love." I left her praising, of the best of friends. I have no doubt that I shall meet her in glory. Lord grant it.[44]

When asked how one is to seek the blessing of perfection, the answer usually involved a mixture of faith, prayerful expectation, and a regimented use of the means of grace. Garrettson's exhortation to Sister Smith to "look to the Lord" underscored that Methodists viewed seeking perfection to be an extension of faith. One cannot earn it or achieve it, yet one can prepare for it by employing the means of grace. Treffry gives a more extended list of directives: "Be diligent in the practice of self-examination . . . leave no latent evil undiscovered . . . practice self denial and mortification . . . above all be diligent in prayer."[45] He encourages seekers "not only to believe for it, and pray for it, but expect it, and expect it this hour, this moment," yet notes that only God in his own time can instantaneously grant it to someone.[46] Methodists viewed perfection as the ultimate flourishing of the Christian pilgrim this side of glory. They also believed it grounded believers in a state of holiness from which it would be very hard to fall. It was, as Treffry noted, "the only certain preventative of final apostacy [sic]."[47]

   Final apostasy, or genuine Christians falling away from grace, was another doctrine with which Methodists took issue in the Reformed tradition. For centuries Calvinists assured embattled believers that no matter how great sin rages in their hearts, God will never abandon those he has chosen for eternal life. The backslider who has experienced true conversion would eventually return, they maintained, and grace would ultimately triumph.[48] Methodists objected to this, for they again discerned in it the makings of antinomianism. Why tend to the Christian graces

---

[44]Garrettson, *American Methodist Pioneer*, 167. I have updated Garrettson's misdating of Tuesday as January 10.

[45]Treffry, "Sermon on Christian Perfection," 123-24.

[46]Ibid., 125-26.

[47]Ibid., 128.

[48]Referencing 1 Jn 2:19, Calvinists generally understood the apostate who did not return to the faith as one who was never truly converted in the first place.

if there is no possibility of ever entirely losing them? Furthermore, Methodists knew by experience many that had fallen away, and they were not shy to narrate such stories.

One such narrative, titled "The Miserable End of an Apostate," relays the account of a Mr. "R. A." of Maryland, who died around 1819.[49] The minister relating the story noted how, as a young man of twenty, R. A. "found the pearl of great price, and appeared to rejoice in a present salvation" after a period of conviction and seeking. "He walked in all the means of grace for several years," until he married a "gay, handsome young lady" who was "a stranger to religious seriousness." It was this marriage that was the young man's undoing. After years of trying to win his bride over to the faith, and years of her efforts to draw him away from it, he found himself drifting away from the Lord. In time, he "lost his desires for all the means of grace, and entirely forsook the company of the people of God; he gave himself up to the customs and maxims of the world, without having regard even to morality." Years passed, until the anonymous minister who authored the story became an acquaintance of R. A. and subsequently inquired into the state of his soul. "I asked him what he thought would become of him, if he died in his present state? 'Why' said he, 'as sure as God is in heaven, I shall be damned.'" On further inquiry, the minister was surprised to find such fatalistic certitude in R. A. "I as much believe my damnation is sealed, as I believe I am sitting conversing with you," he noted. While many Methodists could date the hour of their conversion, R. A. knew "the very time when the Spirit of God took its flight [from me], and what you may be more surprised at that all I have yet said, is, I am not troubled about it, no, no more than if there was no God to punish sin, nor a hell to punish sinners in."

After two years, R. A. was on his deathbed, where "his conscience roared like thunder against him, and every sense within him appeared to be awakened to torment him." Christian friends visited him to provide comfort and hope but found that he would take no comfort. "You might as well pray for the devil as for me—You would have as much success," he lamented. His last moments are recorded with chilling vividness.

Just before he departed, after he had been rolling for some time from side to side, with horror depicted in every feature of his face, he called out to his wife, to bring

---

[49]The following quotes derive from "The Miserable End of an Apostate," *Methodist Magazine* 3 (1820): 347-51.

him a cup of cold water, "For" said he, "in one hour I shall be where I shall never get another drop."—She brought him the water, he took and drank it with greediness— he reached back the cup with his trembling hand, and stared her in the face; his eyes flashing terror all around him, he cried out, "Becky, Becky, you are the cause of my eternal damnation." He turned over, and with an awful groan left the world, and launched into a boundless eternity.

Though we will never know how many details of this narrative have been embellished for dramatic effect, the very act of publishing such an account reveals the Methodists' plain theological conviction that true believers can fall away from grace. Careless Christians can make drastic mistakes, wander from the Lord, and become so hardened against the gospel that damnation is certain. Such awful stories like this were designed to warn readers to take extreme care of their Christian lives and guard themselves from wandering away from grace like R. A.

Methodists argued for their position on both scriptural and theological grounds. Scripturally, Bangs pointed to texts that indicate the sad end awaiting those people of God who reject his ways. David's charge to Solomon (1 Chron 28:9) is direct and clear—"If thou seek him, he will be found of thee; but if thou forsake him, he will cast thee off for ever"—and reflects the sentiment of other Old Testament texts (Is 1:28; Ezek 33:18). Jesus indicates that the branch that does not abide in the vine will wither, be cast into the fire, and burned (Jn 15:6). Hebrews 6:4-6 notes how it is impossible for those who have fallen away to be renewed again to repentance. The text furthermore notes (Heb 6:4) that these apostates had once been "enlightened, and [had] tasted of the heavenly gift, and were made partakers of the Holy Ghost." Certainly, they argued, these are characteristics that describe genuine believers who subsequently fell away, not false pretenders who never experienced God's grace.[50] Texts like these fortified Methodists with scriptural evidence that Christians should not rest in the joy of their salvation but be ever challenged by the call to holiness lest sin disqualify them from eternal life.

Theologically, the doctrine of falling away from grace derived from their emphasis on free will. The freedom to embrace or resist Christ prior to conversion must continue after conversion for the simple reason that grace does not nullify human free agency. If this is true, then it implies that true converts can, in the

---

[50]Bangs, *Errors of Hopkinsianism*, 233-34.

exercise of their freedom, genuinely reject the grace they enjoy, resist it to the point of hardening, and be damned as a result. Methodists like Peter Cartwright found it ridiculous when some, like those of the Arminian-leaning Cumberland Presbyterian Church, tried to "split . . . the difference between the Predestinarians and the Methodists, rejecting a partial atonement or special election and repro-bation, but retaining the doctrine of the final unconditional perseverance of the saints." The main issue fueling Cartwright's resentment at such a hybrid position centered on the consistency of free agency one enjoys before and after conversion. "What an absurdity!" He continued, "While a man remains a sinner he may come, as a free agent, to Christ, if he will, and if he does not come his damnation will be just, because he refused offered mercy; but as soon as he gets converted his free agency is destroyed."[51] If we are free to come to Christ, Cartwright noted, we must be free to leave him after coming because freedom is central to moral agency, responsibility, and sanctification.

The Methodist understanding of apostasy was in many ways the flip side to their doctrine of Christian perfection. Both doctrines called the Christian pilgrim to take God's call to holiness seriously. Believers cannot sit idly in the world en-joying the hope of final salvation while sin, the world, and the devil actively con-spire against them. The doors of Christian perfection are open, and the reality of damnation still lurks. Suspended between these two options, the central message they preached to Christians was simple: seek holiness and you shall live!

SUMMARY

Methodist revival theology represented the first great surge in the popularity of Arminian soteriology in the English-speaking evangelical world. Its fundamental components included the following:

- an emphasis on the *God of love*, who loves all human beings and has created them with free will so that they can enter lovingly into a genuine redemptive relationship with him through faith in Christ

- an emphasis on the *universal offer of the gospel*, which offers a sincere, free pardon to all who will listen; the limiting doctrines of predestination, inability, and limited atonement form no part of Methodist revival theology

---

[51]Peter Cartwright, *Autobiography of Peter Cartwright: The Backwoods Preacher* (New York: Carlton & Por-ter, 1857), 47.

- an emphasis on the *serious call to holiness* and *Christian perfection* as the ultimate goal of Christian living

Methodist revival theology took root in America at a time when many Americans were laying aside theological traditions inherited from the Old World. It offered a deeply stirring and vigorously energetic version of pietistic Protestantism grounded in Scripture. Its leaders were self-sacrificing, charismatic, and extraordinarily gifted communicators who were not afraid of theological and evangelistic innovation. As such, Methodism appealed to many Americans, which ensured that Methodist revival theology would remain a viable option for American evangelicals for decades to come.

Methodists were not the only popular denomination that benefited from America's distaste for traditional denominations. Baptists as well prized a similar version of autonomy and freedom, sentiments that informed their vision of the local church. In the next chapter we will examine several different kinds of revival theologies circulating among early American Baptists. Though Baptists were all united in the importance of believer's baptism to church membership, they espoused numerous types of revival theologies.

CHAPTER SIX

REVIVAL THEOLOGIES AMONG EARLY AMERICAN BAPTISTS

FROM THE 1780s TO THE 1850s BAPTISTS EMERGED as one of the largest denominational groupings within American evangelicalism.[1] Like the Methodists, their growth was due in part to their zealous participation in evangelism and revivals. Unlike the Methodists, however, Baptists did not espouse a unified revival theology. The reason for this is simple: their identity as Baptists did not arise primarily from their soteriology but rather from their ecclesiology. In other words, ecclesiological issues—the church as a covenanting body of rightly baptized believers (according to believer's baptism), the autonomy of the local congregation, and religious liberty—defined them more fundamentally than matters related to their revival theology. Because of this, we find the full spectrum of revival theologies reflected in early American Baptists. Some were Arminian, some embraced Edwardsean revival theology, while others were traditional Calvinists of varying degrees. Thus this section will not explore *the* revival theology of early American Baptists for the plain reason that only one did not exist. Instead we will sample selections from among the multiple revival theologies advocated

---

[1] Robert Baird notes that there were around 35,000 Baptists in the United States in 1784 and roughly 950,000 in 1855; Robert Baird, *Religion in America* (New York: Harper & Brothers, 1856), 462, 503 (the latter number comprising Regular Baptists, Anti-Mission Baptists, Freewill Baptists, and Seventh-Day Baptists). See also Edwin Scott Gaustad and Philip L. Barlow, *New Historical Atlas of Religion in America* (New York: Oxford University Press, 2001), 79, which notes that Baptists totaled 125,000 in 1800 and just under a million by midcentury.

by different Baptist leaders of the period. In many ways, Baptists mirrored the diversity found among early American evangelicalism at large.[2]

In what follows, we will sample, chronologically, the spectrum of revival theologies among early American Baptists. This topic is complex and largely unexamined. Our first stop will be to examine the Baptists who welcomed the popular revivalism of the period and fanned its flames with zeal. The so-called Separate Baptists, who evangelized the Carolinas and rural South, as well as the Freewill Baptists, who articulated a Baptist version of Wesleyan soteriology throughout New England, will be treated. Second, we will turn our attention to the long-forgotten proponents of Edwardsean revival theology among Baptists, such as Jonathan Maxcy and the first president of the Southern Baptist Convention, William B. Johnson. Last, we will examine the more traditional Calvinist views of Jesse Mercer, editor of the influential *Christian Index*, a Georgia Baptist periodical. The goal here is not so much to show the unique Baptist revival theology but to demonstrate the diversity of revival theologies harbored historically in the Baptist tradition in the early decades of the United States.

REVIVALIST ZEAL AMONG THE SEPARATE AND FREEWILL BAPTISTS

The late eighteenth century saw the rise of two new Baptist movements that fully embraced the revivalist zeal of the First Great Awakening: the Separate Baptists, who spread rapidly throughout the South after the 1750s, and the Freewill Baptists in New England in the 1780s and beyond. Both groups were led by revivalists who were affected by Whitefield's ministry. Both also had origins in the more anti-intellectual, anti-establishment wings of revivalism. Neither group published much until the nineteenth century; they were evangelists, not writers. Subsequently, they were not fundamentally motivated by theology, even though they came from and were influenced by identifiable theological traditions. The Separate Baptists came from Calvinist backgrounds, even though the Calvinism they advocated was somewhat moderated by many of its leaders. By contrast, the Freewill Baptists were avowedly shaped by the evangelical Arminianism of Henry Alline and the Methodists.

---

[2]For recent works on the history and theology of Baptists in America and beyond, see Thomas S. Kidd and Barry Hankins, *Baptists in America: A History* (New York: Oxford University Press, 2015); Anthony L. Chute, Nathan A. Finn, and Michael A. G. Haykin, *The Baptist Story: From English Sect to Global Movement* (Nashville: B&H Academic, 2015); and James Leo Garrett, *Baptist Theology: A Four-Century Study* (Macon, GA: Mercer University Press, 2009).

Separate Baptists. The Separate Baptists of the South, who pervaded much of the Carolinas, Georgia, Virginia, and Kentucky by 1800, trace their origins to the New Light separatism that arose in New England Congregationalism during the 1740s and 1750s.[3] These separatists championed pure-church sentiments to such a degree that they concluded that only true Christians who had undergone a New Light conversion experience could be admitted to church membership and to the ordinance of the Lord's Supper. Given this outlook, it was only time before some of them began to advocate the position that a pure church entailed the belief that only truly converted believers are candidates for baptism. This point engendered the rise of Baptists from separatist Congregationalists. Two leaders of note who went through this transformation were Shubal Stearns (1706–1771) and Daniel Marshall (1706–1784). Both were powerfully influenced by Whitefield's 1745 preaching tour of New England (Stearns was converted at this time), and both became grounded in Congregational separatism in New England before embracing Baptist principles. By the mid-1750s Stearns and Marshall had teamed up in Sandy Creek, central North Carolina (now Randolf County), for planting Baptist churches. Within three years, the duo's powerful preaching and skillful administration had led to the successful planting of three large churches in the region, with a total membership of nine hundred. By 1771, the year of Stearns's death, the Sandy Creek Church had planted a total of 42 churches throughout the region and ordained 125 ministers.[4] They were not alone. Other similar-minded Baptists who promoted the deeply emotional revivals of Stearns and Marshall operated throughout the backcountry of the Carolinas, Georgia, Virginia, and Kentucky. These Baptists were not the same as the confessional Calvinist Baptist groups that had for generations existed on the Atlantic coast. Throughout the later eighteenth century, the revivalistic Baptists of the interior became known as Separate Baptists, as distinguished from the confessionally oriented "Regular" Baptists of the Charleston and Philadelphia Associations.

What was the revival theology of the Separate Baptists? This is difficult to ascertain primarily because the Separate Baptists left behind very few written sources. Historians point out that the Separates were mostly about soul winning,

---

[3]See C. C. Goen, *Revivalism and Separatism in New England, 1740–1800* (New Haven, CT: Yale University Press, 1962), 208-95; William L. Lumpkin, *Baptist Foundations in the South: Tracing Through the Separates the Influence of the Great Awakening, 1754–1787* (Nashville: Broadman, 1961), 1-23.

[4]Lumpkin, *Baptist Foundations in the South*, 59.

not about ironing out the intricacies of predestination or limited atonement.[5] The scant evidence we do have supports this understanding, leading to the conclusion that the Separates hailed from a Calvinist background and embraced some of the features of Calvinism but did not let theological squabbling or the need for acute theological clarity hinder their evangelistic endeavors. The Sandy Creek Church covenant (1757), which might have been written by Stearns, has an explicitly Calvinistic statement regarding election: "[Holding] . . . particular election of grace by the predestination of God in Christ."[6] A story Lemuel Burkitt relayed about an intruding Arminian preacher passing through the Kehukee Baptist Association of North Carolina also reveals Calvinist instincts. After a brief period of considerable success in their region, the Arminian Baptist, a Mr. Frost, took ill in the middle of a sermon. "He was dead in less than three hours," Burkitt noted. "Thus did God avenge his suffering church in these towns, for this fox was spoiling the tender grapes."[7]

Such Calvinist bravado must, however, be understood in the context of a movement that hosted debates which indicated that Calvinism was not embraced by all Separates. In 1775, Virginia Separates debated the extent of the atonement at their general association, where a slight majority affirmed the traditional Calvinist position.[8] Similarly, a union of Separate and Regular Baptists in Kentucky adopted a statement in 1801 that indicated that "the preaching (that) Christ tasted death for every man, shall be no bar to communion."[9] That the extent of the atonement was an issue up for debate indicates that diversity existed among its leaders and that they were not solely confessional Calvinists who uniformly adopted the entire system of traditional Calvinism. Their theology can be summed up in an often-quoted statement by John Leland, who ministered among Virginia Separates around 1790. "I conclude that the *eternal purposes* of God, and the *freedom of the human will*, are both truths; and it is a matter of fact, that the preaching that has been most blessed of God, and most profitable to men, is *the doctrine of sovereign grace in the salvation of souls, mixed with a little of what is*

---

[5]Ibid., 60-62; Goen, *Revivalism and Separatism*, 285; John B. Boles, *The Great Revival, 1787–1805: The Origins of the Southern Evangelical Mind* (Lexington: University Press of Kentucky, 1972), 135-36.

[6]Quoted in Lumpkin, *Baptist Foundations in the South*, 62.

[7]Lemuel Burkitt and Jesse Read, *A Concise History of the Kehukee Baptist Association* (Tarborough, NC: George Howard, 1834), 152.

[8]Lumpkin, *Baptist Foundations in the South*, 103.

[9]Ibid., 146.

called Arminianism."[10] In sum, it is most likely the case that the Separates came from a Calvinist background and that some of their adherents embraced the broad outlines of Calvinism, but Calvinism was not the fundamental core of their identity; revivalism was, and they were very good at it.

Generally, the revivalistic practices of the Separates were deeply emotional. Evangelistic services were often accompanied by persons trembling with fear, weeping, and crying out, "What shall I do to be saved?" Preaching was designed to impress the great solemnities of hell, heaven, and the necessity of the new birth. The results under such sermons were remarkable. At an 1801 revival in the Kehukee Association, it was said that thousands came to Christ and were baptized in an eight-month period.

> The word preached was attended with such a divine power, that at some meetings two or three hundred would be in a flood of tears, and many crying out loudly *what shall we do to be saved.* Another thing observed, *old Christians* were so revived they were all on fire to see their neighbor, their neighbors' children and their own families so much engaged. Their soul seems melted down in love, and their *strength renewed like the eagles.* Many *backsliders* who had been runaway for many years, returned weeping home. The ministers seemed all united in love, and no strife nor contention among them, and all appeared engaged to carry on the work, and did not seem to care whose labors were the most blessed so the work went on; and none of them seemed desirous to take the glory of it to themselves, which ought carefully to be observed.[11]

Several scholars have noted that the practice known as the invitation system— which featured a specific call inviting sinners to repent and place their faith in Jesus Christ—was pioneered among the Separate Baptists of the 1770s and 1780s.[12] Bennett, however, questions the timing entailed in this judgment, because none of the original sources give precise dates as to when the practice arose.[13] It appears that we will never know the exact origins of this practice. We do, however, have an explicit reference to something very similar to the practice described in an 1801

---

[10]John Leland, "Letter of Valediction, on Leaving Virginia, in 1791," in *The Writings of the Late Elder John Leland* (New York: G. W. Wood, 1845), 172.

[11]Burkitt and Read, *History of Kehukee Baptists*, 112-13.

[12]Boles, *Great Revival*, 76; Lumpkin, *Baptist Foundations in the South*, 56; H. Leon McBeth, *The Baptist Heritage* (Nashville: Broadman, 1987), 231.

[13]David Bennett, *The Altar Call: Its Origins and Present Usage* (Lanham, MD: University Press of America, 2000), 35-37.

revival among the Kehukee Baptists of North Carolina. The authors, Lemuel Burkitt and Jesse Read, noted that the ministers often called people who were under conviction to come forward to the front of the church for pastoral prayer. "The ministers usually, at the close of preaching, would tell the congregation, that if there were any persons who felt themselves lost and condemned, under the guilt and burden of their sins, that if they would come near the stage, and kneel down, [the ministers] would pray for them." While at first "shame . . . kept many back," the authors noted that as the revival grew, "numbers apparently under strong conviction would come and fall down before the Lord at the feet of the ministers, and crave an interest in their prayers." It was not uncommon for "twenty to thirty" to come at once, with upwards of several hundred coming at "Union Meetings."[14]

The authors, who appear to be Calvinists of some sort,[15] present the practice in a positive light for several reasons. First, the sight of an individual going forward served as a means of the conviction of family members and friends. Second, the practice had the "good effect" of inculcating the solemn responsibility entailed in committing themself to Christ; "they knew the eyes of the congregation were on them, and if they did fall off afterwards it would be a disgrace to them." Most importantly, the authors noted that many dated the moment of their salvation with the time they went forward for pastoral prayer: "Many confessed that the Lord heard the prayers of his ministers, and they had reason to hope their souls were relieved from the burden of their sins, through the blood of Christ."[16] For these apparent Calvinists, there was no question that this practice was appropriate, fruitful, and consistent with the gospel call.

In summary, the Separate Baptists of the late eighteenth century championed a vigorous revivalism that was passionate, sometimes noisy, broadly Calvinistic, and explicitly Baptist. With the exception of their Baptist principles, they were in many ways reduplicating the revivalism of their radical First Great Awakening predecessors and tailoring its practices to their own specific settings.

Freewill Baptists. Contrary to the Separate Baptists, the Freewill Baptists of the Northeast were a small revivalist denomination founded in conscious opposition to Calvinism. Freewill Baptists, who took root primarily in New England

---

[14]Burkitt and Read, *History of Kehukee Baptists*, 115.
[15]See ibid., 128, for an explicit approval of the doctrine of "particular election, and free, unmerited grace in Christ Jesus," as well as pages 151-52 for the strongly worded anti-Arminian statements against Mr. Frost.
[16]Ibid., 115-16.

in the late eighteenth century, caught the antitraditionalist zeal prevalent in the Revolutionary period, which meant that they sought to build a Baptist denomination with little reference to the traditional Baptist bodies that already existed in North America. In their innovating they essentially embraced much of the revivalist ethos and soteriology pioneered by Methodism and cast it within a Baptist ecclesiological framework.

Their founder and leading light was Benjamin Randall (1749–1808), a sailmaker and tailor from New Castle, New Hampshire.[17] As a young man Randall's religious convictions were not particularly solidified, so when George Whitefield came to preach in Portsmouth in late September 1770, he went as a curious attendee, since it seemed that most of the town went to hear the famed evangelist. Interestingly, the three sermons he heard Whitefield deliver on September 24, 25, and 28 left Randall unaffected. It was only after Whitefield's sudden death two days later (September 30) that Randall was plunged into a deep period of conviction because he had scorned Whitefield while he was alive, and Whitefield now was, Randall believed, in glory, while Randall remained on the road to hell. "O, that voice is now silent in death; I would sacrifice any thing if I could but hear it again."[18] Randall's conviction ran so deep that it brought him to consider whether it would be better for him to be damned lest God's justice be infringed, a point he likely heard from New Divinity sources that were prevalent in his day. He did, however, recoil from the idea.

> But I do not believe the idea; for if the scriptures be true, and I believe they are, God is not willing that any should perish; and he never required that any of his *creatures* should *will* that which *he* himself does not will. I was never willing to be damned, but I felt as if it would be better for me to be damned, that that the glory of God should be eclipsed.[19]

After several weeks Randall was led to meditate on Hebrews 9:26 ("But now once in the end of the world hath he appeared to put away sin by the sacrifice of himself"), after which an unexpected calm flooded his soul and he felt the burden of his sins lifted. The world now appeared odious to him, and God, Jesus, and the

---

[17]For biographical details of Randall, see Scott Bryant, *The Awakening of the Freewill Baptists: Benjamin Randall and the Founding of an American Religious Tradition* (Macon, GA: Mercer University Press, 2011), 65-138. Also see John Buzzell, *The Life of Elder Benjamin Randall Principally Taken from Documents Written by Himself* (Limerick, ME: Hobbs, Woodman, & Co., 1827).

[18]Buzzell, *Life of Elder Benjamin Randall*, 14.

[19]Ibid., 16.

way of salvation now caught his attention with delight. "Ah, it seemed if I had ten thousand souls, I could trust them all with Jesus. I saw in him a universal love, a universal atonement, a universal call to mankind, and was confident that none would ever perish, but those who refused to obey it."[20] Randall's deep sense of the universal love of God at his conversion would eventually transform his theology, but only after a decade of ministerial preparation that began first in a Congregationalist church, which did not appreciate his New Light sympathies, and second in a Particular Baptist church that was Calvinist. There Randall began lay preaching and questioning the truths of Calvinism.[21]

In July 1780, Randall experienced his cornfield vision, which confirmed to him his Arminian theological sentiments. After a period of great theological struggle, Randall went to a "remote place" in a cornfield to meditate on Scripture. There in great "agony" he came to feel God drawing him to cast aside the doctrines of his Particular Baptist tradition. On surrendering to this sense, a "flaming power . . . instantly passed through my soul. . . . It was so amazingly powerful, and [it] began to strip away every thing from me, in such a manner, that I thought I was going to lose all I ever had."[22] Subsequently, Randall saw himself in a vision draped in a white robe, and he was then presented with a Bible and heard a "still small voice, saying look therein."

> I looked in at the beginning of Genesis, and looked out at Revelation. I saw all the scriptures in perfect harmony; and those texts, about which my [Calvinist] opposers were contending, were all opened to my mind; and I saw that they ran in perfect connection with the universal love of God to men—the universal atonement in the work of redemption, by Jesus Christ, who tasted death for every man—the universal appearance of grace to all men, and with the universal call of the gospel; and, glory to God! my soul has never been in any trials about the meaning of those scriptures since.[23]

Such confirming experiences were not uncommon among Methodists and the more experientially leaning New Lights. From this point, Randall was completely committed to the themes of universality in his theological vision: the universal reach of God's love, the gracious universal ability granted to all in the atonement

[20]Ibid., 20.
[21]Bryant, *Awakening of the Freewill Baptists*, 78-85.
[22]Buzzell, *Life of Elder Benjamin Randall*, 88.
[23]Ibid., 89.

to embrace Christ, and the universal responsibility that all live under to comply with the demands of the gospel. Unfortunately, Randall never committed the exegetical details of his vision to paper. Rather, he channeled his energies to spreading the good news of God's universal love in Christ and in the process established a Baptist denomination based squarely on the principles of free will.[24]

The revival theology of the early Freewill Baptists did not emerge from the academy but from Randall's spiritual and theological instincts, which were informed by both his revivalism and his reading of Scripture. These instincts were later clothed with greater theological sophistication derived from sources external to the Freewill Baptist movement, including the work of Methodist theologians as well as the writings of Henry Alline, the Maritimes New Light revivalist whose writings provided the Freewill Baptists with a "ready-made theological system" that was anti-Calvinistic.[25] Randall summarized his core theology in a letter he wrote to the denomination in 1804 when he thought he was dying (he would live another four years). Not surprisingly, the theme of universality is featured prominently. "I am strong in the belief of the universal love of God to all men in the atonement; and in the universal appearance of the light, love and grace of God to all men," he writes.[26] Here the limiting particularities of his Calvinist background are absent; divine favor reaches everyone, not merely the elect. This insight would later be fleshed out by Freewill Baptist theologians: through the atonement, the malevolent effects of the fall were universally counteracted in such a way that guilt is not imputed to a person until that person explicitly sins.[27] Once people have sinned and are condemned sinners, the Holy Spirit strives with all who hear the presentation of the gospel, graciously enabling them to respond positively to the glad tidings in Christ.[28] Hence Randall's next point in his compact statement of faith: "And [I am strong in the belief] that the salvation or damnation of mankind, turns upon their receiving

[24]By 1830 the Freewill Baptists was a modestly sized denomination, with 450 churches, 375 ministers, and roughly 21,000 members. See I. D. Stewart, *The History of the Freewill Baptists* (Dover, NH: William Burr, 1862), 1:450.
[25]For details of Alline's influence among the Freewill Baptists, see G. A. Rawlyk, *Ravished by the Spirit: Religious Revivals, Baptists, and Henry Alline* (Kingston, ON: McGill-Queen's University Press, 1984), 39-69.
[26]Buzzell, *Life of Elder Benjamin Randall*, 251.
[27]Anonymous, *A Letter to the Rev. J. Butler, Containing a Review of his "Friendly Letters to a Lady;" Together with a General Outline of the Doctrine of the Freewill Baptists* (Limerick, ME: W. Burr, 1832), 27; here the author approvingly quotes from a sermon by the Methodist Wilbur Fisk.
[28]Ibid., 55.

or rejecting the [grace of God]."[29] His statement then turns to counter several Calvinist doctrines that he believed were spiritually detrimental. "I know from God," he mentioned, "that the doctrine which teacheth that it is impossible for any of those for whom Christ died to sin themselves to hell, is a doctrine of error, invented to destroy souls; . . . [I] bear my testimony against it; and against that shocking, inconsistent, Calvinistic doctrine, of eternal election and reprobation. I rejoice to see how fast Christ is consuming it by the breath of his mouth, and the brightness of his appearing."[30] From Randall's perspective, Calvinism was crumbling as the gospel spread more and more throughout the world.

Both the Freewill and Separate Baptists illustrate that revivalist experientialism privileges immediate conversions. The highly emotional atmosphere charged with song, powerful preaching, spiritual anxiety, and the joys of new life all promoted the sense and expectation that God's new work in the soul can happen *now* at this meeting. Many folks knew the exact moment they felt the burden of their sins lifted and new life coursing through their breasts. The older practices associated with moderate evangelical revival theology—practicing the means of grace, conferencing with a trained minister who weighed one's spiritual experiences, seeking God for a new heart, and waiting—were falling out of favor among many revivalists later in the eighteenth century, who advocated spiritually charged revivals. This setting also may have aided in the erosion of Calvinism, as Separate Baptists, eager to promote the flames of redeeming love throughout the rural South, relaxed the stringent application of their Calvinist heritage in their ministries and as Freewill Baptists discarded it altogether. Such was not the case, however, with another revivalistic group of Baptists, the Edwardseans, who promoted a vigorous and pious revivalism in tandem with a solid commitment to the Calvinistic doctrines of election and reprobation. To them we now turn our attention.

EDWARDSEAN BAPTISTS OF THE
SECOND GREAT AWAKENING

Edwardsean revival theology was found among Baptists of the Second Great Awakening. Edwards's writings on spiritual theology, revival, and the will were prized among many Baptists of the late eighteenth century on both sides of the Atlantic, who, like the Northampton sage, sought to wed a strong predestinarian

---

[29]Buzzell, *Life of Elder Benjamin Randall*, 251.
[30]Ibid.

theology with a vigorous commitment to revival. Edwards's understanding of the will, particularly his distinction between the fallen will's natural ability and moral inability to choose Christ, found a zealous promoter in Andrew Fuller (1754–1815), who pushed his fellow Particular Baptists in Britain to embrace a revivalist ethos. Fuller's work, with its Edwardsean affirmations, was well-known among American Baptists. Jonathan Maxcy (1768–1820) was an even more proximate source for Edwardsean theology among American Baptists of the Second Great Awakening. Maxcy's legacy resides not so much in his publications (he had only a few) but rather among the many pastors he helped train throughout his tenure as president of three colleges: Rhode Island College (1792–1802; later Brown University), Union College (1802–1804; where Maxcy took over after Jonathan Edwards Jr. died), and finally South Carolina College (1804–1820; later the University of South Carolina; Maxcy was its first president). Together, these three sources—Edwards himself, Fuller, and Maxcy—ensured that Edwardsean theology would be a significant theological option among American Baptists.

One significant piece of the Edwardsean system was embraced broadly by many Baptists in the Second Great Awakening, namely, the affirmation of the will's natural ability to accept Christ in a fallen state. For instance, both Jesse Mercer (1769–1841) and William T. Brantly (1787–1845) embraced Edwards's famous distinction.[31] In these cases, however, we do not find a robust embrace of the entire Edwardsean system. What they reveal is the utility of Edwards's doctrine of the will for many theologically oriented Baptists. Both of these Baptist leaders were committed Calvinists, and they found Edwards's understanding of the will suitable to uniting their evangelistic zeal with a strongly predestinarian theology.

We do find several examples of the full-blown Edwardsean system among American Baptists of the Second Great Awakening. Jonathan Maxcy, mentioned above, did publish an important summary of the atonement in which he demonstrates his allegiance to New Divinity theology.[32] One of his students, William B. Johnson (1782–1862), who would later become the first president of the Southern

---

[31]For Mercer, see Anthony Chute, *A Piety Above a Common Standard: Jesse Mercer and Evangelistic Calvinism* (Macon, GA: Mercer University Press, 2004), 75-76; for Brantly, see Robert Arthur Snyder, "William T. Brantly (1787–1845): A Southern Unionist and the Breakup of the Triennial Convention" (PhD diss., The Southern Baptist Theological Seminary, 2005), 120-36.

[32]Jonathan Maxcy, "A Discourse Designed to Explain the Doctrine of the Atonement," in *Sermons, Essays, and Extracts, by Various Authors: Selected with Special Respect to the Great Doctrine of Atonement* (New York: George Forman, 1811), 179-212. Maxcy originally delivered this sermon in 1796.

Baptist Convention, delivered a sermon titled "Love Characteristic of the Deity" before the Charleston Baptist Association in 1822, which likewise reveals deep Edwardsean commitments. Both authors anchor their work in a universal vision of God's disposition to glorify himself through the communication of his internal fullness to creation. Writes Maxcy, "God, therefore, created [the world] with a view to diffuse and communicate, in different forms, that immense fullness which dwelt in himself. God must love and regard the highest excellency most; but this is nowhere but in himself."[33] Though God seeks himself as the greatest end in all his acts, he seeks himself through the communication of himself to the created order, and thus his regard to himself and to the greatest good of the universe co-incide. Divine love or benevolence is not manifested toward individuals only, but, in language echoing Edwards, Johnson mentions that God's love is "the exercise of infinite benevolence or good will to being, in general, or in other words, a su-preme regard to the highest good of the universe."[34] He goes on to note that God manifests himself to creation as "the great moral Governor of the Universe," whose ultimate plan is the display of his "natural and moral attributes" to moral creatures.[35] Maxcy notes that divine glory is displayed ultimately through the magnification of the divine law throughout the moral order. "The law, whose essence is love," writes Maxcy, "tends in its nature to secure the highest happiness of all rational creatures."[36] Thus love (divine benevolence), law, and the display of God's internal fullness to the entire created order ground Maxcy's and Johnson's theological vision in ways reminiscent of Bellamy's and Hopkins's New Divinity project.

The addition of sin to this equation afforded God both an opportunity and a problem. First, Johnson observes that through the apostasy of the angels "the occasion of a higher display of his glory" is exhibited to the moral world, since through their condemnation divine justice is made known.[37] The full display of God's attributes thus requires the presence of sin in the moral order. The intro-duction of sin into the moral order also allows for the display of divine grace throughout the universe, which would even heighten the grandeur of the divine glory. Johnson here is clearly following the standard Hopkinsian theodicy.

---

[33]Ibid., 193-94.

[34]William B. Johnson, "Love Characteristic of the Deity," in *Southern Baptist Sermons on Sovereignty and Responsibility*, ed. Thomas J. Nettles (Harrisonburg, VA: Gano Books, 1984), 42.

[35]Ibid., 44-45.

[36]Maxcy, "Doctrine of the Atonement," 188.

[37]Johnson, "Love Characteristic of the Deity," 47.

A problem arises, however, in this line of thought: How can God display mercy while at the same time holding to his commitment to his justice? Does not pardoning make the law appear weak and threaten God's status as the supreme moral governor of the universe? Maxcy summarizes this fundamental problem:

> This God is just and merciful. He is disposed to punish and to pardon. How then shall his justice and his mercy be displayed towards the transgressor, without infringing or destroying each other? God threatens punishment to sin. Sin is committed. God, instead of punishing, pardons. Where is his justice? Where is his truth? Where is the regard due to his law, his character and government? If he punish, where is his mercy? These difficulties will be obviated by a right understanding of the atonement which Christ made for sin.[38]

In true Edwardsean fashion, both Maxcy and Johnson are very clear that the solution to this problem does *not* lie in understanding the atonement as the payment of a debt, as in the substitutionary model of the atonement. If it were understood as the payment of a debt, they noted, then God would be obligated to pardon and the sinner be in a position to demand salvation. "If an equivalent price be paid for their redemption, may they not on the ground of justice demand salvation?"[39] How can understanding the atonement as a debt payment coincide with the biblical notions of grace and pardon?

These difficulties led Maxcy and Johnson to opt for the moral government theory of the atonement. Here, as we saw earlier, the atonement is not about purchasing specific sinners from condemnation. "In itself considered," Johnson writes, "the atonement of Christ does not deliver any soul from condemnation."[40] Rather, Christ's atoning work renders it possible for God to uphold the strictness of the divine law while simultaneously demonstrating mercy. Through Christ's suffering and death the law is "satisfied," not in the sense that every infringement has been "paid for," but in the sense that the moral foundations of the universe, inherent in the moral law, stand firm because God's wrath on sin has been publicly displayed in the sufferings of Christ. "The atonement made by Christ presented the law, the nature of sin, and the displeasure of God against it, in such a light, that no injury would accrue to the moral system, no imputations would be against the righteousness of the great Legislator, though he should forgive the sinner, and

---

[38]Maxcy, "Doctrine of the Atonement," 182.
[39]Ibid., 203.
[40]Johnson, "Love Characteristic of the Deity," 56.

instate him in eternal felicity."[41] In the wake of such an awful display of justice, God can magnify his grace by extending a pardon to whomever he wills without damaging the law's threatening power. Through Christ's atonement, God's moral governorship stands firm even though sinners are pardoned.

Two corollaries flow from this model of the atonement. First, both Maxcy and Johnson note its universal extent. If the nature of the atonement is about rendering it possible for God to display both justice and mercy to the moral world, then that work has been done for every member of the human race.[42] The door of pardon has been opened to all, since all can be pardoned and justice stand unmaligned. Second, divine sovereignty remains, for now God can pardon whomever he wills according to his infinitely wise designs. He in no way is obligated to save anyone, even after Christ's atoning work, but freely extends pardoning grace to those he enables to respond to the gospel with repentance and faith. "The number of instances in which atonement will be applied and pardon granted, will depend wholly on the sovereign will and determination of God. One thing is doubtless certain, salvation will be extended as far as is consistent with infinite perfect benevolence, or as far as the glory of God and the highest good of the universe require."[43]

Here we see the attraction the Edwardsean system had for many early American Baptists. While Separate Baptists might have been guilty in letting revivalism trump theology in such a way that relaxed their Calvinism, Edwardsean Baptists believed they had struck a balance between theology and practice, between predestinarianism and revivalism, by adopting the New Divinity system. God is love and possesses a regard of infinite benevolence toward the entire system of being. Fallen human beings still retain a natural ability to choose God in Christ, and God has made a universal provision for their salvation through Christ's atoning work that sustains God's moral government and renders it fit for him to extend pardon to sinners. His ministers can herald the universal benevolence of God, the wonder of Christ's love, the universal provision of salvation found in his atonement, and the necessity of repentance and belief. In the end, however, it is still God who alone graciously grants salvation. Such was the appeal of the Edwardsean system to many Baptists of the time. Other Baptists, however, were not convinced, believing that

---

[41]Maxcy, "Doctrine of the Atonement," 207.
[42]Ibid., 212; Johnson, "Love Characteristic of the Deity," 56.
[43]Maxcy, "Doctrine of the Atonement," 212.

Edwardseanism was a lamentable defection from pure Calvinism. To them, the older Calvinism needed little updating.

TRADITIONAL CALVINISM AND REVIVAL THEOLOGY AMONG EARLY AMERICAN BAPTISTS

As mentioned earlier, Baptists of a more traditional Calvinistic stance had existed for some time in North America. Located in Philadelphia and Charleston, South Carolina, these Baptists adhered to their own versions of the Westminster Confession of Faith (either the 1689 Baptist Confession of Faith or its fraternal twin, the 1742 Philadelphia Confession of Faith) and were proud of their theology, heritage, and ecclesial order. Generally, they received the news of the frontier revivals with some wariness, a coolness that may have had more to do with social status than strictly with theological differences.[44] This does not mean that they were antirevivalists, however. It does mean that they were careful in their approach to revivals, always making sure that the manifestations of the Spirit in revival, as well as the methods employed during one, cohered with sound theology.

Most of the major writings by traditional Calvinist Baptists in America were published in the middle of the nineteenth century or later, long after the grand swell of the Second Great Awakening had receded.[45] Thus it is difficult to get a clear picture of the specifics of the revival theology of traditional Calvinist Baptists during the early decades of the nineteenth century. Much more can be found in the numerous Baptist newspapers published throughout the country. For our purposes we will briefly confine our attention to Jesse Mercer (1769–1841) to catch a glimpse of a traditional Calvinistic Baptist who was deeply involved in evangelism and revival throughout his career. With the exception of several preaching tours throughout the South, all of Mercer's ministry was conducted in his home state of Georgia, where he pastored several churches in Wilkes County. Deeply concerned with education, Mercer provided endowment money to help fund what would eventually be known as Mercer University in Macon, Georgia. In 1833 he became the owner and editor of the weekly Baptist periodical *The*

---

[44]The Separate Baptists were generally more rural and unrefined than the more "civilized" and theologically driven Baptists of the Philadelphia and Charleston associations.

[45]For example, see John L. Dagg, *Manual of Theology* (Philadelphia: American Baptist Publication Society, 1857); Patrick H. Mell, *Predestination and the Saints' Perseverance* (Charleston: Southern Baptist Publication Society, 1851); James Petigru Boyce, *Abstract of Systematic Theology* (Philadelphia: American Baptist Publication Society, 1887).

Christian Index.[46] Theologically, Mercer was an admirer of the British Baptist Andrew Fuller, who managed to steer Particular Baptists away from their anti-revivalistic hyper-Calvinism. Thus Mercer, like Fuller and Edwards before him, affirmed the distinction between the sinner's natural ability and moral inability to choose Christ. In spite of this, Mercer's theology was more closely aligned to traditional Calvinism than to New Divinity Calvinism, a point made clear by his affirmation of the atonement as a debt payment and by its particular application to the elect only.[47]

As editor of the *Christian Index* Mercer at times had to address issues related to the nexus of Calvinism and the preaching of the gospel, often as a response to questions put to him by inquiring readers. We will briefly examine three of these inquiries. One inquirer raised the question of the compatibility between the invitation system and the Calvinist view of sinners as "blind, and deaf, and dead in sins."[48] Similarly, a second inquirer questioned the appropriateness of the term *struggle* when referring to the sinner's anxiety before experiencing saving grace. "The sinner will never be found 'struggling into' that which his whole soul loaths [*sic*] and abhors," Mr. "R." notes.[49] A third wondered how we are to reconcile the apparent contradiction between God's sole activity in the work of saving grace and the sinner's activity in the use of the means of grace.[50] Each of these questions arose out of the conundrums of Calvinism: namely, how are we to understand the human business of salvation (preaching, employing the means of grace, seeking God) in the context of the predestinarian framework, in which God possesses the ultimate decision in the soul's destiny?

In his answers to these questions Mercer demonstrated his grasp of the complexity of the issues as well as his basic conformity to the pattern of revival theology that we saw among the First Great Awakening revivalists. From the pastor's perspective, preachers are to preach the gospel to "dead men" primarily because Scripture commands this. Like the prophet (Ezek 37) who obeyed God's call to preach to the dry bones in the valley, ministers are to preach the gospel to those who have no moral capacity to respond. Though they are "dead" with respect to

---

[46]Chute, *Piety Above a Common Standard*, 50-53.

[47]Jesse Mercer, Letter III of "Mercer's Letters to White on the Atonement," *Columbian Star and Christian Index* 23 (October 1830): 259-60; Jesse Mercer, "Editorial," *Christian Index* (November 5, 1838): 708.

[48]Jesse Mercer, editorial response to an inquiring letter, *Christian Index* (October 5, 1833): 50.

[49]R., Miscellaneous Letter, *Christian Index* (September 5, 1839): 568.

[50]Jesse Mercer, "Editorial," *Christian Index* (November 15, 1838): 706-7.

"evangelical obedience," they are alive "rationally" and are thus reckoned "accountable beings."[51] Deadness in sin does not render sinners unaccountable before God. When treating *how* ministers are to preach, Mercer noted the following order of scriptural priorities:

> The first duty of a gospel minister is to teach men the ruined state they are in by reason of sin, and the provisions of mercy God has made for their recovery in Christ; then to warn them of their danger, then after that to call them to repentance and faith, and then last of all to invite them perishing, helpless and dying to come to Christ and live. The invitations of the gospel are predicated on some circumstance of distress, which the blessings of salvation are suited to remedy.[52]

As seen here, Mercer was open to inviting sinners to faith in Christ, but he notes that the sinners he extends an invitation to are of a certain type: namely, those who are sensible of their perishing condition. He writes that "we know of no command [in Scripture] which requires a minister of Christ, or even justifies him, in inviting *thoughtless sinners* to come to him for salvation. And why should he? They neither know nor feel their need of the blessings he has to bestow."[53] Thus, while the promises and invitations of the gospel are full and free, the "whosoever will" that comes to drink of the water of eternal life will only be the individual who is aware of their helpless state and need of a savior. In sum, Mercer's response to the first inquiry (why preach the gospel if sinners are dead in their sins?) is essentially this: even though those devoid of the Spirit of God are truly dead in their sins, God calls his ministers to preach the good news to them, warning them of their serious condition and extending an offer of invitation to those who are truly sensible of their dire state.

The second and third inquirers raised questions that concern sinners prior to salvation: What are they to *do*, if anything, and is it proper to call the anxiety they face before salvation a *struggling* into the marvelous light of the gospel? Both questions arose from certain Calvinist Baptists who found the notion of any activity on behalf of the sinner as an infringement on God's sovereignty. In his responses Mercer indicates that he is comfortable with encouraging human effort in sinners' pre-Christian struggles precisely because these are the results of God's work in the soul. Their activity does not lie in presuming on God's grace, claiming it for

---

[51]Mercer, *Christian Index* (October 5, 1833): 50.
[52]Ibid.
[53]Ibid.

themselves when they really do not experience it. Rather, they are to "seek, and mourn, and wait before God, to obtain his pardoning mercy, and during that time they have many fears and tremblings, and we may say many *strugglings* lest they should be finally cast off!"[54] In waiting, Mercer notes that the sinner is not "struggling into the Gospel" per se, but rather "he is in strife in himself, to know whether God will, or even can pardon him."[55] In other words, the sinner is not struggling to muster up faith, but wondering when and whether God will grant a new heart. The ball, in this case, is in God's court. This, for Mercer, is the true nature of the sinner's struggle prior to repentance and faith. Pardoning mercy comes only when the mind is illuminated to see a way of faith and forsaking of sin that was not seen before. Once this way out is seen, the soul repents, turns to Christ in faith, and experiences salvation. Thus, though Mercer notes that it is necessary and certain that God's elect will come to faith, it is also certain that God draws them to faith by illuminating their minds and persuading their hearts of the truth of the gospel in such a way that they willingly embrace Christ "with their own free consent or voluntary choice."[56] Their uncoerced volition is simply the fruit of God's powerful activity in their hearts.

Mercer's example represents the continuation of the revival theology we saw taught and practiced during the First Great Awakening. The gospel is preached freely to all, and all are invited. Sinners who come under conviction are to seek the Lord and wait for his pardoning grace to dawn in their hearts, and invitations are specifically offered to those who are sensible of their true state. Mercer's approach is one end of a broad spectrum of revival theologies that existed among Baptists in the early American period.

SUMMARY

Early American Baptists united around their unique views that prized religious liberty, the autonomy of the local congregation, and especially their emphasis on believer's baptism by immersion, a position that set them apart from the majority of evangelical denominations in America. Beyond these views, however, we find a diversity of opinions embraced by American Baptists when it came to revival theology:

---

[54]Jesse Mercer, *Christian Index* (September 5, 1839): 569.
[55]Ibid.
[56]Mercer, "Editorial," *Christian Index* (November 15, 1838): 707.

- *Separate Baptists* most likely advanced a practical revival theology that, while having roots in New England Calvinism, did not appear to be too deeply concerned with reproducing the fullness of that tradition.

- *Freewill Baptists* embraced much of the Arminian revival theology found among Methodism.

- Some Baptist leaders, such as Maxcy and Johnson, reproduced the system of *Edwardsean Calvinism.*

- Other Baptist leaders, such as Jesse Mercer, advocated a revival theology that approximated the more *traditional Calvinist views.*

Baptists were (and are) a vigorously evangelistic people. It is therefore no wonder that they would reflect the diversity of views found among the revival traditions of the period.

Vigorous evangelism was definitely on the mind of Charles Finney, who pioneered evangelistic methods known as "new measures" revivalism. In the 1820s and 1830s, Finney became America's most famous and effective revivalist—as well as the most controversial. In the later 1830s and beyond, he wrote extensively on his methods and on the theology that undergirded them, penning dozens of articles and sermons as well as a massive two-volume textbook on systematic theology. His work, which we will explore in the next chapter, represents one of the last major expressions of revival theology to appear in America.

CHAPTER SEVEN

THE NEW MEASURES REVIVAL THEOLOGY OF CHARLES FINNEY

AMONG THOSE FAMILIAR WITH THE HISTORY OF REVIVALS, few have had a neutral reaction to the life and ministry of Charles Finney (1792–1875). To many, Finney is the great hero of revivals, who freed American evangelism from the confines of Calvinist inability and bequeathed to later generations the simple, practical evangelistic practice of calling people to make a "decision for Christ." To others, especially conservative Calvinists, Finney is known as America's greatest heretic, the man who not only (astonishingly) claimed that "a revival is not a miracle" but who also brazenly resurrected Pelagianism in the American evangelical church. Strong feelings related to Finney have undoubtedly obscured our understanding of his place in the history of Christianity in America. Admirers often employ his writings to support their own evangelistic methods, while detractors dismiss his ideas as theological quackery. Either way, few have taken the time to read his works and interpret him as a writer in his own context.

When we actually peer into his works, however, we find a robust and zealously activist revival theology, one that was forged in the controversy that swelled up around his early revivals. Finney's revival theology was not the one-of-a-kind system that dropped from the sky, but was actually an extension of the Edwardsean tradition. Finney essentially embraced the scaffolding of Edwardsean theology but rejected one of its central components, its affirmation of moral inability. The resulting system drew severe criticism not only from Old School Calvinists but also from both Edwardsean revivalists and Arminian Methodists. While the theological world seemed to be against Finney, the multitudes who heard him welcomed him with open arms, as massive revivals sprung up wherever he preached. This chapter will survey Finney's controversial revival theology: its Edwardsean origins, its volitional emphases, and the specific practices known as "new measures" that he popularized.

FINNEY'S BIOGRAPHY

The outlines of Charles Finney's biography are well-known.[1] Born in Warren, Connecticut, in 1792, Charles was the seventh child of Sylvester and Rebecca (Rice) Finney. When he was a toddler, his family moved to north-central New York state, where he would spend the rest of his youth. The family was never very religious, though they regularly attended local churches. Finney heard a good dose of Presbyterian and Baptist preaching throughout his upbringing, yet these sermons never brought any transformation to his life.

At age twenty Finney was personally ambitious and set his sights on attending Yale. Toward that end he moved to his birth town to attend Warren Academy, where he spent two years in educational preparation (1812–1814). There he regularly attended the local Congregationalist church, where Peter Starr, a well-known Edwardsean minister and revivalist, preached. Deciding not to attend Yale, Finney spent four years (1814–1818) teaching at a school in New Jersey and then moved back to Jefferson County, New York, to be near his family, at which time he began studying to become a lawyer. There, in Adams, New York, his attention turned to God and to the eternal destiny of his soul. Under the preaching of George Gale, the local Princeton-trained Presbyterian, Finney came under a deep sense of the conviction of sin in early October 1821. These impressions increased so much that he could not carry on his duties at the law office, so on Wednesday morning, October 10, he resolved to set apart several hours for extended contemplation.

---

[1]For two excellent biographies, see Keith J. Hardman, *Charles Grandison Finney, 1792–1875: Revivalist and Reformer* (Syracuse, NY: Syracuse University Press, 1987; repr., Grand Rapids: Baker, 1990); Charles E. Hambrick-Stowe, *Charles G. Finney and the Spirit of American Evangelicalism*, Library of Religious Biography (Grand Rapids: Eerdmans, 1996).

For the first time "the whole question of Gospel salvation opened to my mind," he noted in his *Memoirs*.

> I saw that [Christ's atoning] work was a *finished* work; and that instead of having, or needing, any righteousness of my own to recommend me to God, I had to *submit myself* to the *righteousness of God through Christ*. Indeed the offer of Gospel salvation seemed to me to be an offer of *something to be accepted*, and that it was full and complete; and that all that was necessary on my part, was to get my own consent to give up my sins, and give myself to Christ.[2]

Throughout the morning, Finney tried to pray in a nearby forest but found he could not because of the fear of being seen. The thought of this so overwhelmed him with shame that it melted his heart, enabling him to pray. He then remembered the scriptural promise that those who seek God with their whole hearts will find him (Jer 29:12-13), and he began to recall other scriptural promises as well: "I seized hold of them, appropriated them, and fastened upon them with the grasp of a drowning man."[3] After this a serene calm filled his soul as his spiritual anxieties ceased, yet he found that his heart was not converted and concluded that he had grieved the Holy Spirit.

After some afternoon work at the office, Finney retired to a backroom for prayer after his colleagues had left for the day. There "it seemed as if I met the Lord Jesus Christ *face to face*." In his mind's eye he noted that he "saw him as I would see any other man. He said nothing, but looked at me in such a manner as to break me right down at his feet. . . . I fell down at his feet and poured out my soul to him. I wept aloud like a child, and made such confession as I could with my choked utterance."[4] Subsequently, Finney relates that he received "*a mighty baptism of the Holy Ghost*."[5] "Without expecting it . . . the Holy Spirit descended upon me in a manner that seemed *to go through me*, body and soul. I could feel the impression, *like a wave of electricity*, going through and through me. Indeed it seemed to come in *waves*, and *waves of liquid love*."[6]

Finney had been converted in dramatic fashion! It is important to note that many of the elements of his mature theology and revival practices are seen in his

---

[2]Garth M. Rosell and Richard A. G. Dupuis, eds., *The Memoirs of Charles G. Finney: The Complete Restored Text* (Grand Rapids: Academie Books, 1989), 18.
[3]Ibid., 21.
[4]Ibid., 23.
[5]Ibid.
[6]Ibid.

conversion testimony: a deep-seated sense of conviction, an emphasis on the atonement of Christ, the need to "accept" Christ with one's will, and the deeply emotional experiences that often accompany one's conversion.

After his conversion, Finney immediately threw himself into the work of ministry. He studied theology with his pastor, George Gale, for a time and later was ordained to the ministry by a group of New School Presbyterians. For the next three years (1824–1827) he ministered as an itinerant evangelist throughout New York state, first in the state's "North Country" (Jefferson County and the city of Watertown) and later in central and western New York (especially Oneida County).

Powerful revivals sprung up under his multiweek campaigns, which were so extensive that the region came to be known as the "burnt over district."[7] These revivals gave Finney the opportunity to hone his skills as a preacher and revivalist. Before the onslaught of preaching began, Finney would organize Christians from the town into lengthy prayer meetings, because he believed prayer brought all parties in a revival to rely on the Holy Spirit. In addition, he and his associates would spend days visiting dozens of persons in the community in both their homes and workplaces to counsel them about the state of their souls. By the time the evangelistic preaching began, Finney knew his audience, and they knew him. He would preach—often extemporaneously—with a style that was the epitome of directness, precision, and moral suasion, skills that he undoubtedly acquired during his legal training. Visually, he would direct his penetrating gaze to the audience at all times with eyes that many thought pierced directly to their souls. Verbally, he would raise the issues of sin and guilt not in vague generalities but with specific reference to individuals in the audience, a practice that, though shocking, was one that yielded surprising results, as many came to "melt" into conviction and embrace Christ. During the prayer portion of the evangelistic meeting, he would move about the sanctuary, praying specifically for individuals and their salvation. He would also allow Christian laymen and women to pray publicly in these meetings as well. These methods, which we will examine more thoroughly below, became known as Finney's "new measures."

Controversy arose as many came to believe Finney's new measures were uncouth and manipulative. Criticism hailed not just from Old School Presbyterians but also Edwardsean revival leaders, who felt his approach stirred the baser animal

---

[7]Ibid., 78n24.

passions in individuals rather than truly inspiring genuine religious affections. To avoid a public rupture among revival-friendly ministers, a phalanx of Edwardsean leaders and New School Presbyterians gathered in New Lebanon, New York, in July 1827 to work out a solution. For a week Finney and his confreres debated the issues of revival with a group of New Englanders that included Lyman Beecher, the well-known Boston pastor, and Asahel Nettleton, the great Edwardsean revivalist of the period. Surprisingly, opposition to Finney eroded at New Lebanon—Nettleton, who detested Finney's revival work, dropped out of the meetings altogether, and Beecher slowly warmed to Finney's ministry.

Finney basically emerged from the conference as the next great revivalist of the Northeast, which paved the way for campaigns in larger venues: Philadelphia, New York, Rochester, and Boston. His Rochester campaign from September 1830 to June 1831 was arguably his greatest. There he introduced two new measures, those he is best known for: the protracted meeting and the anxious bench. The protracted meeting was basically an urban version of the camp meeting without the campouts. Three sermons a day would be delivered by Finney and his associates over a three- to four-day period that was interspersed with prayer meetings. Similarly, the anxious bench was basically a repackaging of the altar call, which had been pioneered by revivalists in the West. Finney would provide a place toward the front of the sanctuary, such as a bench, pew, or room off to the side, where convicted sinners (the "anxious") were called to leave their seats and move forward for spiritual counsel. The design was to bring sinners to a point of public decision. Finney believed that if one left sinners in the pews, they would flatter themselves and incorrectly conclude that they had been touched by God and were now converted. Yet as soon as one called them to take a public stand of their supposed change of heart, their sincerity would evaporate: "Thus you see that when a person is called upon to give a pledge, if he is found not to be decided, he makes it manifest that he was not sincere."[8]

Neither of these measures were really new, as they were employed in the great revivals of the West. They were new to Presbyterian and Congregationalist revivals in the Northeast, which probably goes far in explaining their controversial nature, since many in the Northeast found the western revivals to be uncouth and not fitting for East Coast sensibilities. What was remarkable about Finney's new

---

[8]Charles Finney, *Lectures on Revivals of Religion* (New York: Leavitt, Lord, 1835), 247.

measures was the way they struck a chord with the educated community elites. Most places he went, businessmen, judges, bankers, and politicians took Finney's message to heart and publicly declared their faith in Christ.[9]

By 1832, years of full-time itinerancy had taken a toll on his health and his family life. Lengthy evangelistic campaigns were difficult for Finney's wife, Lydia, and their growing family.[10] With the encouragement and financial backing of the wealthy Tappan brothers, he made the transition to becoming a full-time pastor in New York City, first at the Chatham Street Chapel (a Free Presbyterian Church) and then at the Broadway Tabernacle (1836–1837). Finney's tenure as a New York City pastor was far from serene—he had to battle long-term illness (cholera), theological controversy, and rising tensions over the issue of slavery in his community. During this time, he became a bestselling author, publishing his immensely popular *Lectures on Revivals of Religion* (1835), which encapsulated his philosophy of conducting revivals, and two volumes of sermons (*Sermons on Important Subjects* [1836] and *Lectures to Professing Christians* [1837]).[11] Presbyterian criticism of his *Lectures on Revivals* was so severe that Finney left Presbyterianism to join the Congregationalists in 1836.

In 1837 Finney was called west to join the faculty of Oberlin College, located just outside Cleveland. For the rest of his life he would call Oberlin home. There Finney taught courses in pastoral and systematic theology, ministered regularly at the First Congregational Church of Oberlin, conducted numerous itinerant revival campaigns, and eventually served as Oberlin's second president (1851–1866). The school became famous for promoting progressive evangelical moral causes, such as temperance, women's rights, the abolition of slavery, Sabbatarianism, and the promotion of a "Reformed" version of Christian perfection known as Oberlin Perfectionism. Finney published his massive multivolume *Lectures on Systematic Theology* (1846–1847) during this time and contributed frequently to Oberlin's theological periodical, *The Oberlin Evangelist*.[12] He conducted two lengthy evangelistic tours through England in 1849–1850 and 1859–1860. Toward the end of his life, friends encouraged Finney to compile his *Memoirs*, which focused heavily

---

[9]For example, see Hambrick-Stowe, *Charles G. Finney*, 65.

[10]Finney married Lydia Root Andrews in 1824, and they had six children. She died in 1847 at the age of forty-three. Finney married two more times during his long life.

[11]Charles Finney, *Sermons on Important Subjects* (New York: John S. Taylor, 1836); Charles Finney, *Lectures to Professing Christians* (New York: John S. Taylor, 1837).

[12]Charles Finney, *Lectures on Systematic Theology*, 2 vols. (Oberlin, OH: James M. Fitch, 1846–1847).

on his revivals. He died in August 1875, just two weeks shy of his eighty-third birthday. He was undoubtedly the best-known evangelist of his generation.

THE EDWARDSEAN SUPERSTRUCTURE OF FINNEY'S REVIVAL THEOLOGY

It goes without saying that Charles Finney was not your average theologian in the classical sense of the term. Deep down he was a pragmatist, a man of action who channeled his energies toward evangelistic ends. He did have an intellectual side—his legal training gave him the ability to define terms with precision and handle subtle distinctions—yet the entire shape of his theology, from the minute details of human ability to the superstructure of God's moral governance over creation, had one thing in view: evangelistic action. Consequently, Finney strongly opposed any theological position that threatened to impede the spread of the gospel.

As we begin analyzing the structure of Finney's theology, it immediately becomes apparent that he was deeply shaped by the Edwardsean theological tradition.[13] After treating the usual Christian theological preliminaries—the existence and attributes of God, the Trinity, and Christology—we find the Edwardsean features emerging once he begins to address God's stance toward the created order.[14] His starting point is simple: God is the moral governor of the universe. What this means is that God's sovereign providence or government over the universe comes in two forms. Over the physical world, God governs by direct control of substances, where he uses necessity and force to obtain his ends. His government over the moral world, the world of responsible moral agents, is different, for "it is a government of motive as opposed to force."[15] God does not govern moral subjects through physical force or compulsion but rather via motives, persuasive argumentation, and "inducements" designed to excite free agents to choose divine ends. "Motives are the grand instrument of moving mind[s]," he noted.[16] Without motive there would be anarchy.[17] Consequently, the Spirit does not transform souls via

---

[13]For the Edwardsean backdrop to Finney's theology, see Allen C. Guelzo, "An Heir or a Rebel? Charles Grandison Finney and the New England Theology," *Journal of the Early Republic* 17 (Spring 1997): 61-94.

[14]The two volumes of Finney's *Lectures on Systematic Theology* actually do not contain these theological preliminaries (i.e., the existence and attributes of God, the Trinity, and Christology). These topics were intended to appear in an entire volume that would have been volume one of a larger three-volume work. However, Finney never completed this volume. The outlines of its contents can be found in an earlier draft of his theology titled *Skeletons of a Course of Theological Lectures*, vol. 1 (Oberlin, OH: James Steele, 1840).

[15]Finney, *Systematic Theology*, 1:17.

[16]Charles Finney, "Traditions of the Elders," in *Sermons on Important Subjects*, 57.

[17]Ibid., 58.

physical contact but by truth presented to the heart as motives, so that sinners can change their hearts.[18] "God converts the soul by motives."[19]

If God's government is moral, then the Spirit's influences are "moral, persuasive, and not physical."[20] This system presupposes that human beings have free moral agency, a point that most Edwardseans would affirm with special qualifications (moral inability) and one which Finney would significantly modify, as we will see below. The system also mandates that God communicate the essence of his character to his creatures to serve as a basis for their moral behavior. The moral law occupies this role both as a means to "declare the perfections of God" and to serve as a "faithful witness of the entire depravity of man."[21] Through the moral law God exhibits benevolence and divine justice. "In short, [God's moral law] is manifestly designed, and calculated to declare the perfection of God, and the total depravity of man. For as it is a faithful portrait of the perfection of God's moral character on the one hand; so it is a faithful witness of the entire depravity of man on the other."[22]

Not only is God a moral governor, but he is a *disinterested*, benevolent moral governor. What this means is that, in his governance of the moral world, God operates out of a regard for the maximal happiness and well-being of the whole universe. Since his actions are done with a supreme regard for the happiness of the entire creation and not merely for himself or for some portion of the whole, God is understood to be "disinterested," that is, interested in the good of all.[23] Since his actions tend to communicate blessedness to creation, he is understood to be benevolent. To Finney, God's benevolence is the master attribute that sums up his character and basically is another term for love. "We are told that God is love; that is, he is benevolent. Benevolence comprises his whole character. All his moral attributes are only so many modifications of benevolence."[24]

Finney maintained that all of God's dealings with creation overflow from his benevolent nature. He gives the moral law to exhibit his benevolence so that human beings might learn that they are to love him supremely and their neighbor as themselves.[25] His "great and disinterested love to sinners" and to "the universe

---

[18]Charles Finney, "Sinners Bound to Change Their Own Hearts," in *Sermons on Important Subjects*, 27.

[19]Ibid., 40a; the text of *Sermons on Important Subjects* has two sets of pp. 29-42. I will indicate the first set of pages with the letter *a* after the page number, the second set of pages with the letter *b*.

[20]Finney, *Systematic Theology*, 1:28.

[21]Finney, "Traditions of the Elders," 61.

[22]Ibid.

[23]This supreme regard does not disregard God's own happiness; they are one and the same.

[24]Charles Finney, "True and False Conversion," in *Lectures to Professing Christians*, 157.

[25]Finney, "Traditions of the Elders," 60.

at large" was the wellspring of sending his Son into the world to be an atoning sacrifice for sin.[26] Justification too finds its foundation in God's benevolent disposition toward the world.[27]

Finney illustrates the benevolent origins of God's work most clearly in his discussion on the nature of election. Election is that doctrine where "certain individuals, making a certain number of mankind, are chosen by God to eternal salvation through the sanctification of the Spirit and belief in the truth."[28] Though "certain individuals" are chosen, this does not mean that God shows partiality to a few in his predestinating work. Rather, his electing work is a byproduct of his universal work to produce the greatest amount of blessedness in the universal moral world. God, in other words, aims at maximizing the well-being in the whole (universal scope), even though this maximization entails that only some will ultimately be saved. "He works upon vast and comprehensive scale," Finney writes. "He has no partialities for individuals, but moves forward in the administration of his government with his eye upon the general good, designing to convert the greatest number and produce the greatest amount of happiness within his kingdom."[29]

God executes his work of election in the following way. In his infinitely comprehensive knowledge of the universal whole, he knew who *could* be converted and consequently brings sufficient moral influence into their lives to influence them unto conversion.

> The elect then must be those whom God foresaw could be converted under the wisest administration of his government. That administering it in a way that would be most beneficial to all worlds, exerting such an amount of moral influence on every individual, as would result upon the whole, in the greatest good to his divine kingdom, he foresaw that certain individuals could with the wisest amount of moral influence be reclaimed and sanctified, and for this reason they were chosen to eternal life.[30]

Thus there are elements of both particularity and universality in Finney's doctrine of election. While only some sinners eventually are converted through the Holy Spirit's inducements on specific individuals, these operations are merely the

---

[26]Finney, *Systematic Theology*, 1:402.
[27]Ibid., 2:163-64.
[28]Ibid., 2:427.
[29]Charles Finney, "Doctrine of Election," in *Sermons on Important Subjects*, 216; for a similar statement, see Finney, *Systematic Theology*, 2:438.
[30]Finney, "Doctrine of Election," 213-14.

byproduct of his universal providence, which wisely charts a course that effects the greatest happiness for the whole. Hence his operations are universal and general in scope: all are benefactors of his work of benevolence, though only some experience full salvation.[31] This, he concludes, is ultimately the best God could have done.

When Finney described the shape and ends of human moral behavior, he naturally employed the categories of disinterested benevolence to frame his discussion. Human ethics takes its cue from God's ways, and thus the ethical ideal is conditioned after disinterested benevolent actions, in which individuals sacrificially seek the well-being of others and of God. "The highest well being of God and of the universe of sentient existence is the end on which ultimate preference, choice, intention, ought to terminate. In other words the well being of God and of the universe is the absolute and ultimate good and therefore it should be chosen by every moral agent."[32] Similar to Bellamy's understanding of the law, Finney maintained that "the whole law is properly expressed in one word, Love," and that "this love is benevolence or good willing; [which] consists in choosing the highest good of God and of universal being as an ultimate end, or for its own intrinsic value; in a spirit or state of entire consecration to this as the ultimate end of existence."[33]

The opposite course, selfishness, is when human beings seek their "own happiness above other interests of greater value; such as the glory of God and the good of the universe."[34] Pursuing a course that is limited in scope to the private sphere of one's own well-being is the essence of humanity's "natural state . . . before conversion."[35] True "gospel benevolence," by contrast, "seeks the good of others for its own sake . . . [and] rejoices in the happiness of others, and desires their happiness for its own sake."[36] Thus, even though the Christian pursues selfless ends at great personal cost, that person is actually finding great joy because the pursuit of others' happiness is the pursuit of their own.

> Your happiness will be in proportion to your disinterestedness. . . . If you aim at doing
> good for its own sake, then you will be happy in proportion as you do good. But if
> you aim directly at your own happiness, and if you do good simply as a means of

---

[31]Finney notes that God does not save all human beings, because this would not result in the greatest amount of happiness to the universal whole. See Finney, "Doctrine of Election," 213.

[32]Finney, *Systematic Theology*, 1:43.

[33]Ibid., 1:210.

[34]Finney, "True and False Conversion," 157.

[35]Ibid.

[36]Ibid.

securing your own happiness, you will fail. You will be like the child pursuing his own shadow; he can never overtake it, because it always keeps just so far before him.[37]

These concepts are straight out of the Edwardsean playbook. It is thus no surprise to see Finney advocating theological positions similar to the rest of the Edwardsean system. He affirmed the principle of personal merit and blameworthiness: sins, guilt, virtue, and righteousness cannot be transferred or imputed between persons; they must be personally related to that person's own willing. "Voluntariness is indispensable to moral character," he noted.[38] Sinners thus are condemned for their own personal sins, not because Adam's guilt has been imputed to them.[39] Similarly, when God justifies sinners, he does so not because Christ's righteousness has been imputed to them. "Gospel Justification is not the imputed righteousness of Jesus Christ. Under the gospel, sinners are not justified by having the obedience of Jesus Christ set down to their account, as if he had obeyed the law for them, or in their stead." Such an idea, he noted, is "absurd and impossible" precisely because it counters the principle of personal merit.[40] Justification is merely the act of God extending a pardon to sinners who acknowledge their guilt, repent, and place their faith in Christ; no imputation of an alien righteousness is required.

Relatedly, Finney's view of the atonement followed the standard logic of the Edwardsean moral government theory. The atonement is not to be understood as a payment of debt, a penal substitute, or a commercial transaction, whereby the righteousness of Christ is imputed to sinners.[41] Rather, the atonement allows God to display his integrity as a just moral governor who supports the universal law while at the same time extending a pardon to sinners who trust in Jesus. The theory is substitutionary not because Christ pays for the actual sins of sinners, but because the public display of his suffering honors the moral law. Thus his atoning work serves as a substitute for their eternal judgment. God remains holy in relaxing the strictness of the law and extending pardon, because in the public sufferings of Christ the law's demands have been satisfied. "The Atonement is an exhibition of God suffering as a substitute for his rebellious subjects."[42]

---

[37]Ibid., 167-68.
[38]Charles Finney, "How to Change Your Heart," in *Sermons on Important Subjects*, 32b.
[39]We will explore this further below.
[40]Charles Finney, "Justification by Faith," in *Lectures to Professing Christians*, 215.
[41]Finney, *Systematic Theology*, 1:398-99.
[42]Ibid., 1:409.

None of these positions were really new. As we have seen, versions of them had been circulating widely among Congregationalists and New School Presbyterians for decades. However, Finney's unique streamlining of Edwardsean themes, centered exclusively on personal voluntariness, generated much controversy. The next two sections will analyze the unique features of Finney's revival theology. Most of his practical innovations arose from his theological anthropology. Thus we will first explore these theoretical doctrines before turning our attention to how Finney practically applied this theology in his evangelistic endeavors.

THEORETICAL: FINNEY'S THEOLOGICAL ANTHROPOLOGY

The center of Finney's revival theology lies in his doctrine of the will. In his extensive experience with sinners, he had come across dozens of excuses as to why they claimed they were not ready to repent and believe. Many complained that they professed an inability to believe; others noted that they were "waiting on the Lord's time" for a new heart; still others confessed that they had not experienced the terror of the law in their hearts. When he turned to the theologies circulating among revivalists, he noted that ministers were providing sinners with both theological and practical justification for their excuses:

- Sinners possess a *spiritual inability* to comply with the terms of the gospel.

- Sinners must *use the means of grace* and *wait* for proper *conviction of sin* before they are ready to believe.

- *Regeneration is a passive renewal of the soul* by the Holy Spirit; therefore one must "wait God's time."

- *Conversion is a lengthy affair* and cannot occur within a short timespan.

Finney believed that the cumulative effect of these views dampened hope, encouraged spiritual procrastination, and left people without any course of action in the midst of their religious anxieties.

To address this situation Finney did not have to look far; indeed, the answer lay right in the middle of the Edwardsean theological tradition: *the will has a natural ability to repent immediately and submit to the claims of the gospel.* If this is the case, he argued, then evangelists must do all they can to remove any hindrances that keep people from exercising that ability. He deeply believed the foundations of evangelistic method must be reevaluated in light of this insight, so he set his sights on cleaning out the clutter that impeded evangelistic efficacy.

The starting point of this campaign centered on the topic of human volition, most notably the freedom of the will to obey God. Freedom, Finney noted, is embedded in the mind as a fundamental principle of reason, a "first truth" or "intuition" of reason that does not require proof or defense because it is virtually self-evident.[43] "But the fact is, that in all cases, and in every case the assumption has lain deep in the mind as a first truth of reason that men are free in the sense of being naturally able to obey God: and this assumption is a necessary condition of the affirmation that moral character belongs to man."[44] Scripturally, Finney grounded his understanding of the liberty of the will in the basic notion that "moral obligation," or those moral "oughts" found in the commands of Scripture, necessarily implies a power or ability to obey. "It is a dictate of reason, of conscience, of common sense, and of our natural sense of justice, that if God require of us the performance of any duty or act, he is bound in justice to give us power to obey; i.e. he must give us the faculties and strength to perform the act."[45] Without this fundamental concept of common moral sense, God's moral government could not stand, and neither could one make sense of every biblical command which implies "the liberty of the human will, and the natural ability of men to obey God."[46]

This was a significant move by an Edwardsean. As we have seen in earlier chapters, Edwardseans such as Hopkins, Bellamy, and Griffin employed the natural ability/moral inability distinction to adhere to both divine sovereignty and human responsibility. Though Finney was reared in the Edwardsean tradition, he came to reject this distinction. Essentially, he argued that moral inability and natural inability are basically the same thing: if you have the former, then you have the latter. Given Finney's starting point—that it is a first truth of reason that the will is free—it is no surprise that he possessed a negative assessment of this Edwardsean distinction: moral ability, defined as Edwards defined it, "is no ability at all, and nothing but an empty name, a metaphysico-theological FICTION."[47]

Finney's own view, by contrast, is reminiscent of New Haven theology: in order for an act to be morally praiseworthy (or blameworthy), every volition must be free to choose *or not choose* the action that is to be performed. "True freedom or liberty of will must consist in the power or ability to will in every instance either

---

[43]Ibid., 2:17-19, 44, 57.
[44]Ibid., 2:19.
[45]Finney, "Sinners Bound to Change Their Own Hearts," 25; see also 17.
[46]Finney, *Systematic Theology*, 2:17.
[47]Ibid., 2:14.

in accordance with, or in opposition to moral obligation."[48] Hence we see a fundamental distinction between the mainstream Edwardsean Calvinists and the
extreme Edwardseanism of Finney's system. Mainstream Edwardseans, while
they spoke of freedom and responsibility in their own unique way (natural ability,
willing according to human nature), ultimately retained the emphasis of God's
sovereign choice in the work of regeneration. Finney, by contrast, laid the accent
on the sinner's will. While he spoke of God's election and of the necessity of the
Spirit's "inducements" on sinners' wills in the conversion process, he ultimately
argued that individuals retain the freedom to choose or not to choose salvation
offered in Christ. In short, his rejection of the Edwardsean distinction between
natural ability and moral inability coupled with his understanding of the freedom
of the will dramatically transformed his revival theology.

By focusing on the freedom of the will, Finney was led to rethink his theological anthropology, specifically the doctrines of total depravity and original sin.
His fundamental strategy with regard to this doctrine is easy to identify: if the will
is truly free, not bound to sin by necessity, then the doctrines of total depravity
and original sin must be understood in a way that does not undermine human
liberty. Specifically, these doctrines must be given their due, but they must not be
portrayed in a way that leads to the conclusion that the will is in total bondage to
sin or that sinners possess an ultimate inability from doing anything about their
situation. That would effectively undermine human liberty, moral obligation, and
ultimately, he contended, God's moral government. How does he explain this?

He begins with an analysis of the tripartite makeup of the soul. Finney maintained that the human psyche consists of three parts: the *intellect*, which reasons
and discerns truth from error; the "*sensibility*," which emotes and seeks pleasure
in that which is good (or that which is perceived to be good); and the *will*, which
makes choices.[49] Finney argued that the first two faculties are "purely passive"
states of mind, that is, they do not possess moral character in their exercise because they are designed to be reactors to circumstances rather than moral actors.
For instance, the intellect is designed to behold truth and reject error. Knowing
that two plus two does not equal six is not a moral act; it is merely the intellectual consciousness of truth. Likewise, feelings of joy over a victory or sadness
at the death of a loved one are not moral actions but rather involuntary reactions

---

[48]Ibid., 2:16.
[49]Ibid., 2:53, 65-67.

that arise in the circumstances of life. "The emotions are purely involuntary states of mind," Finney wrote on the sensibility. "They naturally and necessarily exist in the mind under certain circumstances calculated to excite them."[50] Together, knowing and emoting are involuntary activities of the soul. We do not predicate "moral character" to them, that is, we do not call them either good or evil because they are passive, involuntary inner states that are hardwired into our psyches.[51]

The will, by contrast, is the only locus of moral activity among the three faculties of the soul. By it individuals make choices that can be denominated either virtuous or vicious. In other words, the actions of the will alone possess moral character.

This seems to be a rather simple insight, but for Finney it became an extremely important point when factored into a discussion of human depravity. If it is true that the will alone is the locus of moral accountability, if "voluntariness is indispensable to moral character,"[52] then discussions of human depravity and original sin must be restricted to the orbit of actual human volitions. Human beings, in other words, are accountable for actions they have actually committed; they are not held accountable for aspects of their existence that lie beyond volitional control, like some "sinful human nature" that "lies behind" the will causing a person to sin. For generations, theologians and evangelists had employed some version of the idea that a sinful, corrupted human nature, inherited from Adam, binds human willing in such a way that sin is the necessary result. Finney believed this was rubbish. There is no invisible nature, physical constitution, or created substance of sinfulness external to the will that causes our wills to sin. We sin because we voluntarily commit sin.

> O the darkness, and confusion, and utter nonsense of that view of depravity which exhibits it, as something, lying back [behind the will], and the cause of all actual transgression. Something created in the sinner, and born with him. Some physical pollution, transmitted from Adam, through the agency of God or the devil, which is in itself sinful, and deserving the wrath of God, previous to the exercise of voluntary agency on the part of the sinner. This is absurd and impossible.[53]

---

[50]Finney, *Lectures on Revivals*, 34.
[51]Finney, *Systematic Theology*, 2:65.
[52]Finney, "How to Change Your Heart," 32b.
[53]Charles Finney, "Total Depravity," in *Sermons on Important Subjects*, 136-37.

His rejection of the traditional view centered on the fact that only wills commit acts of moral character. Natures or substances, by contrast, do not will things; consequently, we are not to predicate "sinfulness" or "virtuousness" to them. "What ground is there for the assertion that Adam's nature became in itself sinful by the fall? This is a groundless, not to say ridiculous assumption and a flat absurdity. Sin as [an] attribute of nature! A sinful substance! Sin a substance! Is it a solid, a fluid, a material or a spiritual substance?"[54]

Finney's positive statements about the nature of human depravity center on human choices characterized by selfishness and an active hatred of God. Depravity is a "depravity of free will," he noted, "not of the faculty itself, but of its free action. It consists in a violation of moral law. . . . It is a choice at variance with moral law, moral right. It is synonymous with sin or sinfulness."[55] Its essence consists in selfishness, where individuals seek their own private happiness to the exclusion of the universal good. A selfish volition occurs when the will gratifies the impulses of sensibility (or feelings) rather than obeying the law of reason discerned by the mind. This is sin in a nutshell.[56] These selfish acts essentially amount to a hatred of God, since they run counter to God's universal, disinterested benevolence. The individual might not be aware of this hatred, but once the facets of the gospel are laid out before the mind—repenting of sin, trusting in Christ, following in universal obedience to God, and becoming a selfless servant of God's purposes—then the individual's own selfish preferences come into full view, preferences that amount to a hatred of God.

In his preaching Finney frequently noted the vast degree to which sinners display their hatred for God. "Sinners hate God supremely. That is, they hate him more than they do any thing, and every thing; any body; and every body else in the universe."[57] In language reminiscent of Hopkins, Finney noted how completely devoid sinners are of obedience. "If you are an impenitent sinner, you have never, in a single instance, obeyed your Maker";[58] "when God has fanned your heaving lungs, you have breathed out your poisonous breath in rebellion against the eternal God. . . . Ought not God then to hate you with all his heart?"[59] The

---

[54]Finney, *Systematic Theology*, 1:474.
[55]Ibid., 1:448.
[56]Ibid., 1:478.
[57]Finney, "Total Depravity," 131.
[58]Finney, "How to Change Your Heart," 47.
[59]Ibid.; see also Finney, *Systematic Theology*, 1:453.

reason for this pessimistic portrait is simple: it is impossible for individuals to love their own private interests and God's universal interests at the same time. Because sinners will not let go of their own private interests, every volition they make is sinful and at enmity with God. "It will therefore, always be natural for a sinner to sin, until he changes the supreme preference of his mind, and prefers the glory of God and the interests of his kingdom to his own separate and opposing interests."[60]

How does selfishness come to characterize the totality of human choices? Finney answered this first with respect to how it arises in human beings individually and second with respect to how individual selfishness is related to Adam's sin. Individually, Finney accounted for moral depravity in the following way. As we have seen, he maintained that the inner nature of a human being is composed of three faculties: the mind, the sensibility, and the will. At birth Finney observed that the sensibility is fully developed, whereas reason has only begun its development. This creates an imbalance in the human constitution that does not itself constitute sin but can definitely contribute to it. Because of this imbalance, the "sensibility acts as a powerful impulse to the will from the moment of birth, and secures the consent and activity of the will to procure its gratification, before the reason is at all developed."[61] As the child develops, the will becomes so habituated to gratifying the sensibility that once an awareness of moral obligation is discerned by the mind, the child willfully rejects what is rationally discerned to be the moral way and remains committed to seeking his or her own self-gratification. Here is the first moral act of the person, that individual's own personal fall. Prior to this moment Finney maintains that the infant had no moral character.[62] After this moment, the will becomes increasingly committed to favoring the appetites of the sensibility (that is, the "flesh") rather than the dictates of reason. "Selfishness confirms and strengthens and perpetuates itself by a natural process. It grows with the sinner's growth and strengthens with his strength, and will do so forever unless overcome by the Holy Spirit through the truth."[63]

Interestingly, when Finney commented on how Adam and Eve's sin is related to ours, he focused on the similarity between the way their sin arose and the way

---

[60]Charles Finney, "Why Sinners Hate God," in *Sermons on Important Subjects*, 155.
[61]Finney, *Systematic Theology*, 1:481.
[62]Finney, "Why Sinners Hate God," 156. Finney does not speculate as to when infants commit their first moral action, but given that he speaks of the subject with regard to infants, he believes that it is early in life. See ibid., 156-58.
[63]Finney, *Systematic Theology*, 1:485.

ours arises. In Adam and Eve moral depravity was induced when the "unperverted susceptibilities of their nature" were "excited," leading them to succumb to temptation.[64] Note his language here: our first parents' natures, though created "unperverted" or without sin, contained "susceptibilities" that resulted in temptation and ultimately sin. These "susceptibilities" surfaced due to the "impulses of the sensibility" in a process that is very similar to what he described when the will, at the tempting of Satan, yields to the impulses of sense rather than "abiding by the law of God as revealed to the intelligence."[65] In sum, both Adam and his posterity come into the world without sin, yet certain "susceptibilities" inherent in the tripartite makeup of the soul are present, capable of being thrown out of balance through the wiles of Satan and the unchecked appetites of the sensibility. While Finney acknowledges that Adam's original transgression did indeed affect the entire human race as it "exposed his posterity to aggravated temptation," he ultimately maintained that every individual experiences his or her own fall.[66]

The importance of this point should not be underestimated. By accentuating the parallels between Adam's sin and that of his offspring, Finney is essentially doing away with the doctrine of original sin as it has been traditionally articulated.[67] Sinners are not under judgment because they have passively inherited a defective human nature from Adam, from which they sin of necessity. Nor are they hell-bound because, as descendants of Adam, God holds them responsible for Adam's transgression through the covenant of works and immediate imputation. No. For Finney, they are liable to judgment because early in life, at the first moment of moral accountability, all individuals have willfully, actively, and freely chosen to reject God's benevolent ways and seek their own selfish ends.

This conclusion is the direct result of the centrality of the will in Finney's theology. The will is free; we thus sin freely and are not necessarily bound to it. His view had the benefit of enhancing his evangelistic preaching, since it allowed him to place the blame for sinners' damnation squarely in their own hands. No longer does anybody have the excuse of inability to hide behind; nor can anyone reassign blame to some powerful nature causing their sin. They alone are the culprits; they

---

[64]Ibid., 1:484.

[65]Ibid., 1:479.

[66]Ibid., 1:485.

[67]As a matter of fact, Finney's *Systematic Theology* does not have a separate chapter or section on the subject of original sin. Rather, he treats the issue under the heading of "moral depravity." See Finney, *Systematic Theology*, 1:447-89.

have earned their wages. In a sermon on Romans 6:23 ("the wages of sin is death") Finney solemnly declares their end: "You will get your *wages*, just what you have earned, your due; nothing more, nothing less; and as the smoke of your torment, like a thick cloud, ascends forever and ever, you will see written upon its curling folds, in great staring letters of light, this awful word, wages, *wages*, WAGES."[68]

This view also, however, raises questions about the necessity of the Holy Spirit in revival. If sin is not necessary, then can it be overcome by merely redirecting the course of the will? Is there any room for supernatural agency in the process of salvation? Finney wants to answer yes to both of these questions: we have a power of choice to change the eternal destinies at the same time that the Holy Spirit is the necessary supernatural agent in conversion. In the next section, where we treat the practical side of Finney's revival theology, we will see how he addressed the confluence of divine and human agencies in revival.

PRACTICAL: NEW MEASURES AND THE WAY OF SALVATION

Finney's practical revival theology emerged from the details of his theological anthropology. If the will is genuinely free and if moral depravity is the result of one's own choices, then sinners possess both a natural and moral ability to repent and believe in Christ unto salvation. Though the influences of the flesh, Satan, and the world predominate, it is not the case that sinners are left without any power to change their situation. If depravity is the result of one's own choices, then the essence of conversion consists not in prayerfully waiting around for some miraculous change to take place to one's nature, but in the willful determination to stop sinning now and embrace the gospel message. Finney's evangelistic message was succinct, direct, and to the point. He does not leave anyone guessing what needs to be done to be saved. The practical problem he ran into had to do with the reality of sin: sinners habitually seek their own private interests rather than God's universal benevolent interests. Given the fact that sinners can immediately comply with the gospel, how are they to be brought from death to life in Christ? This was the central question of Finney's revival theology, one he spent his life trying to answer.

Finney's basic answer to this question ran as follows: *God has ordained the various agents of revival to bring the truth of the gospel to bear on the minds of sinners in order to "induce" them to accept the gospel immediately.*[69] Finney maintained that

---

[68]Cited by Charles P. Bush, *Reminiscences of Rev. Charles G. Finney* (Oberlin, OH: E. J. Goodrich, 1876), 12.
[69]Finney used the word *induce* to mean "strongly persuade." He employed the term to avoid the concept of

there are multiple agents in revival, actors who actually do something in the great work of human salvation. He usually identified three: the Holy Spirit, who emblazons the truth of the gospel on the sinner's mind; the preacher, who employs various measures designed to direct the sinner's attention to the verities of the gospel; and the sinner, who makes the choice to comply with the gospel via repenting and believing in Christ. Finney did not bother a great deal in delineating the exact boundaries between these various agents when asked how he specifically prioritized them. He saw each of them in Scripture and was thus satisfied with giving an imprecise both/and kind of answer to the question.

The following exploration of Finney's practical theology will be divided up according to the different agents of revival he identified. First we will examine Finney's understanding of the Holy Spirit's agency in the salvation process, noting the necessity of his work and the vast need for prayer as a means to invite God's blessing on a revival. Next we will address the preacher's role in revival, including how the means of grace are to be understood as well as how new measures are to be employed. And third, we will explore Finney's view of sinners' role in salvation, how it is that they are bound to change their hearts.

The Holy Spirit: Necessary agent of revival. Finney is often characterized as a mechanizer of revival, one who has so thoroughly overthought the human side of the revival process that there seems to be no place for the Holy Spirit in a genuine revival of religion. This caricature is inaccurate, however. When we peer into his writings we find him repeatedly noting the utter necessity of the Holy Spirit's supernatural efficacy in the conversion process and the vast importance of remaining utterly dependent on him for grace. "[The] truth by itself will never produce the effect [of salvation], without the Spirit of God," he noted.[70] The Spirit is necessary for the obedience of repentance: "Unless God interpose the influence of his Spirit, not a man on earth will ever obey the commands of God."[71] If sinners grieve the Holy Spirit during conviction, "it is very probable that they will be lost for ever."[72]

How does Finney hold together the necessity of the Spirit's agency in conversion with human agency? As noted earlier, Finney was a practical evangelist

---

causality in speaking about the relationship between the Spirit's agency and an individual's volition in the conversion process. Thus the Holy Spirit induces sinners to accept Christ; he does not cause them to do so.
[70]Finney, *Lectures on Revivals*, 45.
[71]Ibid., 9.
[72]Ibid., 192.

and did not iron out all the subtle details involved in this question. He rather chose to offer a common-sense answer to the question by employing a simple illustration of Niagara Falls, which demonstrates the multiple agencies at work in the conversion process.

> Suppose yourself to be standing on the bank of the Falls of Niagara. As you stand upon the verge of the precipice, you behold a man lost in deep reverie, approaching its verge unconscious of his danger. He approaches nearer and nearer, until he actually lifts his foot to take the final step that shall plunge him in destruction. At this moment you lift your warning voice above the roar of the foaming waters, and cry out, *Stop*. The voice pierces his ear, and breaks the charm that binds him; he turns instantly upon his heel, all pale and aghast he retires, quivering, from the verge of death.[73]

When we ask the question, "Who saved this man's life?" numerous answers come to mind. We can say the one who cried "Stop!" saved him; we can say that the word *stop* itself saved him; we can say that that man, who heard the message and stopped taking that last step, saved himself; and we can say that God, who providentially arranged each aspect of the event, saved him. There is a sense in which each of these answers to the question is true. Finney maintained that this illustration well illustrates the multiple agencies in a revival. The man who cried "Stop!" is likened to the preacher of the gospel; the word *stop* is likened to the message of life; the man who stops is the one who responds positively to the message heard; and God is the one who providentially arranged the entire affair.

Though Finney believed this illustration nicely pictured the confluence of agencies involved in revival, he does note a "defect" in it. The conversion of the sinner is not merely the product of God's providential ordering of events. Rather, the Spirit of God is much more actively at work in the minds of sinners convincing them of the gospel; "for here not only does the providence of God so order it, that the preacher cries, Stop, but the Spirit of God forces the truth home upon him with such tremendous power as to induce him to turn."[74] This, for Finney, was the essence of the Holy Spirit's work in conversion and the reason he is the necessary agent in a revival. His central work is to present the truth to sinners' minds forcefully and offer motives designed to effect change in the will. The Spirit, in other words, acts as a persuasive prosecuting attorney who "gathers

---

[73]Finney, "Sinners Bound to Change Their Own Hearts," 20-21; see whole sections in ibid., 20-23, as well as Finney, *Lectures on Revivals*, 181-83.
[74]Finney, "Sinners Bound to Change their Own Hearts," 21.

a world of motive, and pours them in such a focal blaze upon [the] soul," inducing them to embrace the truth.[75] Because human obstinacy, selfishness, and sin so characterize the will, natural means—such as the prayers of friends, the warnings of ministers, the rebukes of providence—are often rendered useless to dissuade the individual from doing evil "because no human persuasion, no motive that man or angel can get home upon the mind, will cause him to turn; therefore the Spirit of God must interpose to shake his preference, and turn him back from hell."[76] Finney is careful to point out that the Holy Spirit does not work "physically" in the soul through a work of re-creation. Nor does his work consist in forcing human beings to make choices against their wills. His work, his supernatural work, consists in emblazoning on the minds of obstinate sinners the realities of the gospel and presenting powerful motives to their minds that only he can present given his intimate knowledge of people. "Thus the strivings of the Spirit of God with men, is not a physical scuffling, but a debate; a strife not of body with body, but of mind with mind; and that in the action and reaction of vehement argumentation."[77] This convicting ministry, tailored directly to the individual's own situation, is the essence of the Holy Spirit's supernatural work in the conversion process. Without this element, no degree of natural means will avail.

Preachers and the detailed application of the new measures. Having made this point, it is not the case that no natural means are required in the conversion process. As we saw in his Niagara illustration, there is a confluence of supernatural and natural means in Finney's revival theology. The preacher's activity along with the sinner's are the natural agents in his system of conversion. While the Spirit's agency is utterly necessary to conversion, Finney was led to believe that there will be no revival without someone preaching the gospel and sinners repenting and believing in Christ. These activities Finney believed were natural activities: preaching is merely the natural communication of gospel information by a messenger; repentance and belief are merely the redirection of belief and action made by the individual's will. Combined with the Holy Spirit's convicting work, the preacher's efforts and the sinner's turning to God culminate in a miraculous affair in which sinners experience salvation to the glory of God.

[75]Ibid., 26.
[76]Ibid., 27.
[77]Ibid., 28.

According to Finney, what are the preacher's duties during a revival? This is a vast subject in Finney's writings. In our overview we must content ourselves with looking at three major aspects of the answer. The first aspect relates to what the preacher expects during the sinner's conversion process, an expectation that is fraught with a noticeable tension. Ultimately, the preacher's goal is to lead sinners to immediate repentance. Sinners have the ability to repent of sins now, and preachers must tailor all their evangelizing efforts toward this end, allowing the sinner no shelter short of repentance and belief. This is calculated to inculcate a degree of religious anxiety in the sinner, a spiritual restlessness that can only find rest once they have submitted to the gospel. "The requirement of the gospel is, repent now, and believe that your soul may live. It gives not the sinner a moment's time to wait; it presses upon him with all the weight of Jehovah's authority, instantly to ground his weapons, and submit to God."[78] Elsewhere Finney writes that "sinners ought to be made to feel that they have something to do, and that is to repent; that it is something which no other being can do for them, neither God nor man, and something which they can do, and do now."[79]

Yet in spite of this message of immediacy, Finney maintained that the route to compliance with the gospel entails a period of intense conviction of sin prior to coming to faith. There are "always, in a genuine revival, deep convictions of sin, and often cases of abandoning all hope," he notes.[80] The preaching of the law with its message of universal obedience and disinterested benevolence is employed to impress on the heart its sinfulness and guilt. The goal is not merely to inculcate a mild religious unease, but to fan a blaze of great spiritual anxiety in the heart of the nonbeliever. Finney did not believe this was cruel. Rather, it was a means to their salvation, since conviction pointed anxious sinners to repentance and faith. Often, the greater the conviction, the more immediate the repentance. Thus Finney advised ministers to turn up the intensity of the sense of conviction. "If possible, melt [the sinner] down on the spot. When once you have got a sinner's attention, very often his conviction and conversion is the work of a few moments. You can sometimes do more in five minutes, than in years or a whole life while he is careless or indifferent."[81] In sum, ministers are to expect both preparatory convictions and immediate repentance during the conversion process.

---

[78]Finney, "Traditions of the Elders," 74.
[79]Finney, *Lectures on Revivals*, 191.
[80]Ibid., 14.
[81]Ibid., 50.

The second thing ministers are to do during revivals is employ the means of grace with a great deal of specificity. Finney regarded the means of grace as necessary to revivals and to a sinner's conversion. "Where sinners continue to neglect the means of grace," he notes, "their case is hopeless."[82] The means of grace are designed to testify to the truths of God and the gospel. Thus ministers are to direct sinners to employ all the means necessary in seeking salvation. In addition, ministers can the employ the means of grace as well: they can pray, exhort, visit, counsel, and do other things that serve as means by which the gospel spreads. When I indicate that Finney encouraged ministers to use the means with specificity, I mean that Finney encouraged a highly detailed, over-the-top application of specific means of grace in his advice to ministers. We can see this with regard to how he encouraged ministers in the duties of prayer and visitation.

Prayer was the means of grace that Finney perhaps advocated the most. He maintained that prayer is the "essential link in the chain of causes that lead to a revival" because it "is intended to move God to pour out his Spirit."[83] Finney, of course, does not intend that prayer actually changes God; it rather "produces such a change in us as renders it consistent for God to do as it would not be consistent for him to do otherwise."[84] What is particularly striking is how much detail he gives to ministers as they lead prayer. He did not merely encourage ministers and Christians to pray for revival. Rather, he encouraged them to host prayer meetings at different parts of a town sometimes for weeks before the commencement of evangelistic preaching. These meetings were designed to unite Christians in a spirit of prayer, deepen a yearning for God's work and a hatred for sin, and further convict sinners present.[85] He gave specific directions for how prayer meetings are to be conducted. While prayer meetings are to be allowed to take their own course, ministers can give directions that ensure that they do not stray off course: they can call on specific Christians (especially those who are very spiritual) to pray, they can encourage short prayers, they can impress sinners to repent immediately, and they can discourage too much singing and the introduction of controversial theological subjects.[86] These directions were not designed to interfere with the Spirit's supernatural work; they

---

[82] Finney, "How to Change Your Heart," 53.
[83] Finney, *Lectures on Revivals*, 45, 129.
[84] Ibid., 45; see also 115.
[85] Ibid., 114-16.
[86] Ibid., 116-26.

merely were offered to keep a prayer meeting focused on the successful spread of the gospel.

Finney also advocated the intense "travailing" prayer among Christians on behalf of revival. This

> spirit of prayer is a state of continual desire and anxiety of mind for the salvation of sinners. . . . A Christian who has this spirit of prayer feels anxious for souls. It is the subject of his thoughts all the time, and makes him look and act as if he had a load on his mind. He thinks of it by day, and dreams of it by night. . . . [Such persons] have had an actual travail of soul for sinners, till they were as helpless as children.[87]

In short, Finney did not just advocate prayer as a means of grace for both ministers and laypersons; he also advocated an intense and fervent version of it.

Another means of grace he commended to ministers of the gospel was visiting members of the community for spiritual counsel and interviews. Before the commencement of revival preaching Finney and his colaborers routinely visited dozens of members of the community, often non-Christians, for spiritual counsel, prayer, and one-on-one ministry. From these visits he learned the spiritual and moral geography of the community and used this information in preaching and public prayer meetings. "Preachers ought to know the religious opinions of every single sinner in his congregation," he charged.[88] Without such knowledge,

> how otherwise can he preach to them? How can he know how to bring forth things new and old, and adapt truth to their case? How can he hunt them out unless he knows where they hide themselves? He may ring changes on a few fundamental doctrines, Repentance and Faith, and Faith and Repentance, till the day of judgment, and never make any impression on many minds. Every sinner has some hiding place, some intrenchment where he lingers. He is in possession of some darling LIE with which he is quieting himself. Let the minister find it out and get it away, either in the pulpit or in private, or the man will go to hell in his sins, and his blood will be found in the minister's skirts.[89]

By knowing his audience intimately, the minister can tailor the gospel to specific situations. In his public prayers and in his preaching Finney would sometimes bring up specific sins of specific persons in the community by name. He

---

[87]Ibid., 26-27.
[88]Ibid., 185.
[89]Ibid.

maintained that this was not manipulative but rather the application of the gospel to actual situations, specifically targeted to real people. "Preaching should be direct. The gospel should be preached to men, and not about them. The minister must address his hearers."[90] This direct approach served to facilitate spiritual urgency, conviction, and the conversion process much better than communicating the gospel in mere generalities.

Third, Finney argued that ministers of the gospel had the duty of using "new measures" during revivals. Finney was famous for his new measures revival techniques. New measures were basically a specific subset of the means of grace designed to fix the attention of sinners on the truths of the gospel.[91] They were "new" in the sense that they generally had not been used before with much popularity. Finney believed that Scripture does not provide a standard set of means designed to promote revivals of religion, "but has left it to ministers to adopt such as are wisely calculated to secure the end."[92] In the past God had blessed numerous measures that were considered new at the time but later became routinized and no longer fixed individuals' attention on the gospel. In the history of worship, the use of psalm books, hymn lining, choirs, organs, and instrumental music were originally greeted with scorn and contempt merely because of their newness.[93] Later these measures were accepted. Similarly, in the history of revivals, many new measures that were originally scorned had now become accepted: lay preaching and exhorting as well as extemporaneous and outdoor preaching (think Whitefield) were all measures that were originally opposed but had since become accepted practices. Finney maintained that in his own generation the three new measures that worked the best were the anxious meeting, the protracted meeting, and the anxious bench.[94] "By [the anxious bench] I mean the appointment of some particular seat in the place of meeting, where the anxious may come and be addressed particularly, and be made subjects of prayer, and sometimes conversed with individually."[95] The bench is merely the outworking of his hyperdetailed application of the means of grace. Sinners are to be addressed individually: they have been personally visited by the minister, the

---

[90]Ibid.
[91]Finney, "How to Change Your Heart," 56.
[92]Finney, *Lectures on Revivals*, 168.
[93]Ibid., 233-49.
[94]Ibid., 242.
[95]Ibid., 246-47.

gospel has been preached to them with specificity, the Holy Spirit strives with them particularly, and now during the evangelistic service a place is made available for them to come, where their own situations can be reviewed and where they can receive direct spiritual counsel and prayer.

In sum, Finney maintained that ministers are extremely important to revivals of religion. Like farmers who sow seed, they are to do all they can to ensure that the harvest will be plentiful. Though only the Holy Spirit can bring the "rain" of conviction on sinners, ministers of the gospel must preach the gospel, direct sinners to immediate repentance, and employ all the means of grace possible to point sinners to Christ. At the end of the day, however, their efforts are useless if sinners themselves refuse to comply with the claims of the gospel.

Sinners bound to change their own hearts. Having treated the work that the Holy Spirit and preachers do in revivals, we now turn our attention to Finney's understanding of the sinner's duty in conversion. Finney's entire system was devoted to removing all the unnecessary obstacles that impeded the sinner's route to salvation. To his mind, numerous theological errors, mostly hailing from Old School Calvinism, had erected multiple roadblocks that prevented immediate repentance.

> They have been perplexed and confounded by abstract doctrines, metaphysical subtleties, absurd exhibition of the sovereignty of God, inability, physical regeneration, and constitutional depravity, until the agonized mind, discouraged and mad from contradiction from the pulpit and absurdity in conversation, dismissed the subject as altogether incomprehensible, and postponed the performance of duty as impossible.[96]

According to Finney, the entire system of Old School Presbyterianism accomplished nothing positive. All it did was engender spiritual passivity and defeatism that crippled the sinner's active striving to seek the narrow gate of salvation. The reality of the situation, Finney maintained, is that God has already done all that he can for human salvation. He has sent his Son to procure atonement for sins and sends his Spirit and ministers to strive with sinners, who by nature have volitional ability to comply with the terms of the gospel. All that is needed is that nonbelievers change their moral character and get a new heart, something only they can do: "God commands you to do it, expects you to do it, and if it ever is done, you must do it."[97]

---

[96]Finney, "Sinners Bound to Change Their Own Hearts," 41a.
[97]Ibid., 23.

How does a sinner get a new heart? Sinners must change the governing preference of their minds and consent to the gospel. In so doing they exercise their
natural ability to change their hearts and convert to Christ. Practically, however,
when Finney counseled with sinners he avoided theological sophistication and
stuck close to scriptural language: sinners are to repent from sin and believe in his
word.[98] He used other simple phrases that captured the same idea: sinners are to
"give their hearts to God," "submit to God," "forsake their sins," or "choose this day
whom they will serve."[99] The latitude of vocabulary found in Scripture demonstrated to Finney that one standard set of terms does not fit every situation, since
God works variously with each individual as each one's situation is different.[100] Yet
fundamentally, at the core of each of these directions is the call that sinners change
their wills with regard to sin and submit to God.

This centrality of the will in Finney's thought is further seen in how he responded to questions that arose in the course of individual counsel. "What if God
won't pardon me?" This question, Finney maintained, is the wrong question to
ask, since it presupposes an unwillingness in God for the salvation of the world.
God has already demonstrated his willingness in sending his Son, in sending the
minister to preach the gospel, and in granting the individual the ability to choose
or reject his message of eternal life. The ball is really in the court of the sinner,
since the only requirement necessary is their own consent. "The question is not,
whether he will pardon you, but whether you will obey him. . . . The question for
you to settle, is, whether you will obey him, and leave the question of your salvation for him to settle. . . . One thing is requisite, that is a willing mind. Your
consent is all that is needed. Be willing to do your duty, and the work is done."[101]

What about feelings? Are not feelings of terror prior to faith and feelings of
divine love afterward essential to salvation? These questions surfaced no doubt
because many revivals were deeply emotional affairs and because some had degenerated into religious frenzies altogether. Finney's approach to religious emotion
during revivals was one of moderation and caution. On the one hand religious
excitement is necessary in revivals: the Holy Spirit convicts, preaching often stirs
religious anxiety, and new converts experience joy in their salvation. Yet, as we saw

---

[98]Finney, "How to Change Your Heart," 48; *Lectures on Revivals*, 337-39.
[99]Finney, *Lectures on Revivals*, 337-44.
[100]Ibid., 337.
[101]Finney, "How to Change Your Heart," 50.

earlier, Finney believed that the sensibility (feelings) is designed to react to events that the mind perceives; it is not designed to lead the soul. If the sensibility is over-excited during a revival, then the mind and will cannot operate rationally. Finney noted that the "strain of preaching" that appeals "to the sympathies and the feelings [rather] than to the intelligence" can "never result in good."[102] His measures at promoting revival, by contrast, were designed to secure the attention of the mind on the truths of the gospel so that the will can act accordingly, both rationally and sensibly. "All the measures used to awaken interest, and our whole policy in regu-lating this awakened interest should be such as will not disturb the operations of the intelligence or divert its attention from the truth to which the heart is bound to submit."[103] Thus, while feelings are important, they are not the primary object of concern in a sinner's conversion. By contrast, attention needs to be focused on one's moral obligation, what one is to do in light of one's knowledge of the truth, not how one is to feel: "Remember, the present object is, not directly to call into existence certain emotions, but, by leading your mind to a full understanding of your obligations, to induce you to yield to principle, and to choose what is right."[104]

From an objective point of view, Finney argued that the act of repenting and believing *is* the act of regeneration. This contrasted starkly with the traditional Calvinist position, in which regeneration was understood to be God's work of grace in the sinner, whereas the individual's work of repentance and belief was categorized under the heading of conversion. To ensure God's sovereign initiative in the salvation process, regeneration was understood to be antecedent to (or logically prior to) the human act of converting. Furthermore, God's regenerating work was often understood as being miraculous, in which the Holy Spirit reno-vates the soul, begetting a new creature. The sinner, by contrast, is passive in re-generation but active in conversion.

Finney found the Calvinist approach to be woefully inadequate for a number of reasons. Biblically, Finney found evidence that regeneration is not solely the work of divine agency. "Regeneration is ascribed to man in the gospel," he notes, drawing attention to Paul's note in 1 Corinthians 4:15, where the apostle indicates that "I have begotten you through the gospel."[105] If this is correct, then regeneration

---

[102]Charles Finney, *Reflections on Revival by Charles G. Finney*, compiled by Donald W. Dayton (Minneapolis: Bethany Fellowship, 1979), 43.
[103]Ibid.
[104]Finney, "How to Change Your Heart," 38b.
[105]Finney, *Systematic Theology*, 1:492.

involves human agency. Theologically, Finney did not believe that salvation involved the re-creative work of the Holy Spirit in the human soul, a process he called physical regeneration. As we saw earlier, the Spirit's primary work in salvation is of a persuasive nature, not a re-creative one. "But men are to be converted, not by physical force, or by a change wrought in their nature or constitution by creative power, but by the truth made effectual by the Holy Spirit."[106] Practically, the Old Calvinist position encouraged sinners to adopt the waiting system, which Finney believed brought sinners no closer to God.

To resolve these problems Finney rejected the distinction between conversion and regeneration. True to his position that we see a confluence of divine and human agency in all the aspects of salvation, Finney basically equated the acts of regeneration and conversion: "Both terms [regeneration and conversion] imply the simultaneous exercise of both human and divine agency."[107] Because the term *regeneration* is also closely associated with the biblical concept of a "new heart,"[108] Finney made the three terms synonymous. To get a new heart is not something sinners are to wait for God to accomplish in them, nor is it the result of God's creative renovation of their souls. It is merely changing the moral orientation of their lives: "A new heart is the choice of Jehovah as the supreme ruler."[109] Thus sinners do not only have the ability to change their hearts, but also they are under the moral obligation to get a new heart, convert, and regenerate themselves. As the title of one of his popular sermons says, "Sinners [are] bound to change their own hearts."

This confluence of agencies in Finney's theology goes a long way to explain one of his most famous—or infamous—quotes in his writings, in which he declares that a revival of religion is "not a miracle."

> [A revival of religion] is not a miracle according to another definition of the term miracle—something above the powers of nature. There is nothing in religion beyond the ordinary powers of nature. It consists entirely in the right exercise of the powers of nature. It is just that, and nothing else. When mankind become religious, they are not enabled to put forth exertions which they were unable before to put forth. They only exert the powers they had before in a different way, and use them for the glory of God.[110]

---

[106]Finney, *Lectures on Revivals*, 308.
[107]Finney, *Systematic Theology*, 1:493.
[108]Ibid., 1:492.
[109]Finney, "Sinners Bound to Change Their Own Hearts," 10.
[110]Finney, *Lectures on Revival*, 12.

Finney's point in this paragraph is not to say that there is no supernatural agency occurring in a revival. We have already seen Finney's emphasis on the necessity of the Spirit's work in convicting and persuading sinners of their duty. Rather, what he is saying here is that from the human perspective the great affair of salvation does not lie beyond one's own volitional powers in some mysterious transubstantiation of the heart that only God can effect. Salvation is merely directing one's will away from selfish ends toward holy ones. There is nothing "miraculous" or "above the powers of nature" in this.

SUMMARY

Finney's revival theology was essentially an intensely practical version of New School revival theology that was indebted to Taylorism. Its central features included the following:

- an understanding of free will that rejected the traditional Edwardsean notion of inability; biblical commands to repent and believe implying the moral ability of a sinner to comply

- the extensive elaboration of the means of grace tailored to specific individuals and audiences (these practices—such as public prayers for specific individuals, protracted meetings, and the anxious bench—came to be known as "new measures")

- the assertion that there are three agencies that work simultaneously in the conversion process:

  » the Spirit's work of bringing the truth to focus in sinners' minds and providing motives to the sinner to induce them to submit to God

  » the minister's work of preaching, counseling, and employing new measures

  » the convert's work of making themself a new heart by changing the supreme preference of the soul

While Finney highlighted the freedom of the will, his theology was not technically Arminian in the sense we saw among the Methodists (though, admittedly, there are similarities in the application of both revival theologies). His theology was a progressive, some might say extreme, version of the Edwardsean theological tradition. It was also the last new and extensive system of revival theology advanced by American theologians.

Finney's new measures revival theology appeared at a time when many American Christians were beginning to ask serious questions about the direction and accuracy of modern revivalism. In the final chapter we will explore two very different ways American Protestants responded to the modern revivals of the Second Great Awakening.

CHAPTER EIGHT

TWO RESPONSES TO MODERN REVIVAL THEOLOGY

PRINCETON SEMINARY *and*
the RESTORATION MOVEMENT

NOT EVERY CHURCHGOER WELCOMED THE PHENOMENA of revivals
in early nineteenth-century America. Alternative visions of the Christian faith
were available that did not lay such a great emphasis on individual conversion
experiences or corporate revivals. Christian groups, both orthodox and progressive, claimed that God and Christ could be known through the avenues of the
church's sacraments, through reason, or through ethical living. Many came to eye
revivals altogether with an air of suspicion, believing that their leaders approximated the spiritual version of snake-oil salesmen who peddled false versions of
Christianity to the uneducated masses. This attitude has often been called antirevivalism because of its committed opposition to the entire affair of revivals.[1]

Antirevivalism, however, did not suit many American Christians who saw
themselves as heirs of the broader evangelical heritage but who were also not that
enthusiastic about modern revivals. Those who found themselves in this category
felt compelled to respond to modern revival theologies in one of two ways. First,
there was the high Calvinist response offered by Princeton Seminary theologians
Archibald Alexander and Charles Hodge. Both of these Presbyterian loyalists
were deeply troubled by the profusion of theological errors they discerned in

---

[1]For antirevivalism, see the set of writings in James D. Bratt, *Antirevivalism in Antebellum America: A Collection of Religious Voices* (Piscataway, NJ: Rutgers University Press, 2006).

modern revival theologies.[2] In its place they offered an Old School Presbyterian and high Calvinist vision of the Christian faith, which cautiously commended the older revivals of the First Great Awakening as an ideal but also emphasized the importance of committed Christian parenting as one of the best means for propagating the gospel. Second, there was what I will call the biblicist response to modern revival theology offered by Alexander Campbell of the Restoration Movement. Campbell believed that all revival theologies were erected on the faulty foundation of complicated theological systems that yielded numerous errors, including lengthy conversions and an excessive preoccupation with religious experiences. The antidote, he claimed, lay in a plain reading of Scripture, which portrays conversion in a simple, nonemotional manner that underscores faith, repentance, and baptism as its three main features.

This chapter will briefly examine these two very different responses to modern revival theology. Both groups offered a robust critique of modern revivalism and commended an alternative vision that Christians should embrace in its place. Our comments will be brief, though entire studies could be devoted to exploring each group. The goal here is merely to demonstrate that other options were available to American Christians who cherished Scripture and faith in Christ but who were not fully onboard with modern revivals.

PRINCETON SEMINARY: THE HIGH CALVINIST RESPONSE OF ARCHIBALD ALEXANDER AND CHARLES HODGE

Charles Hodge (1797–1878) is well-known for saying that no new idea ever originated in Princeton Seminary. To him, Princeton theology had basically advanced the same theology that Calvin, the Swiss reformers, and the great Puritan divines had taught for centuries. This is not the place to assess the validity of this claim, but there can be no doubt that the Presbyterians who taught at "Old Princeton" throughout the nineteenth century were conservative stalwarts who repeatedly drew inspiration from the older Reformed writers, such as John Calvin, John Owen, and Francis Turretin. Because of this strong historical orientation, it is no surprise to see the Princeton theologians interpreting the revivals of the Second Great Awakening through the historical lens of the classical Reformed tradition.

---

[2]The "modern revival theologies" the Old School Presbyterians were against comprise not only Finney's views but also the revival theologies of New School Presbyterians, which drew much from Taylorism, as well as the views of many of the Edwardsean theologians.

Princeton Seminary was founded in 1812 to be a Presbyterian graduate institution for training ministers. Known for its Calvinistic conservatism, its robust defense of Scripture, and its comprehensive theological apologetic, it rose to become the preeminent seminary in the United States by midcentury, attracting students from around the world. Its two most important theologians of the period we are examining (1820–1850) were Archibald Alexander and Charles Hodge. Born in 1772, Alexander was dramatically converted as a teenager, pastored numerous churches, where he led revivals, and served as president of Hampden-Sydney College before becoming Princeton's first professor of theology in 1812. He remained there until his death in 1851. He was known as a giant of both heart and mind who led students into the depths of the spiritual life while also calling them to master the intricacies of Reformed scholasticism.[3] Alexander, who had significant experience as a pastor-revivalist, was generally more open to revivals than Hodge was, which illustrates that differences of opinion on the subject did exist at Princeton Seminary during the first half of the nineteenth century.

While Alexander helped establish the seminary, the work of his star student, Charles Hodge, would extend Princeton's theological influence far and wide. Raised by his devout Presbyterian mother in Philadelphia, the young Hodge was converted as an undergraduate at the College of New Jersey before attending nearby Princeton Seminary, where he studied under Alexander. By 1830 Hodge had mastered the biblical languages, the history of Reformed theology, and the current theological scene in Germany, having spent two years of study there (1826–1828). For the next forty years he taught over two thousand divinity students and edited Princeton's widely influential theological journal. Outside his extensive work with the journal, his most important writings include his commentary on Romans (1836), his brief manual of the Christian life, *The Way of Life* (1842), and his three-volume *Systematic Theology* (1872–1873).[4]

Both Alexander and Hodge had much to say about the state of revivals in America in the 1830s and 1840s, the full critique of which is beyond the scope of this study. Our examination will focus on their criticism of the doctrines of original sin and regeneration as found in New School Presbyterianism and

---

[3] For biographical details on Alexander, see W. Andrew Hoffecker, *Piety and the Princeton Theologians* (Phillipsburg, NJ: P&R, 1981), 1-43.

[4] For details of Hodge's life and ministry, see Paul C. Gutjahr, *Charles Hodge: Guardian of American Orthodoxy* (New York: Oxford University Press, 2011); and W. Andrew Hoffecker, *Charles Hodge: The Pride of Princeton* (Phillipsburg, NJ: P&R, 2011).

Finney's new measures. To both men, the new revival theologies had strayed from the Reformed standard. Errors here could only preponderate throughout the theological system, threatening the orthodoxy of what was preached and, ultimately, the presentation of the gospel.

The Princeton critique of modern revivals. Hodge's critique of modern revival theology centered on a key concept that he believed many New School Presbyterians had rejected: the concept of a "principle of nature" in their theological anthropology. Traditionally Christian theologians had acknowledged the existence of a "principle of nature" in the psychological makeup of a human being, a principle that lies behind the will, conditions one's volitions, and possesses moral character. This principle has been known under numerous names in Christian tradition: "disposition," "inclination," "temper," "sinful/holy nature," "habit," or "heart." Hodge notes that principles of nature "cannot be resolved either into essential attributes of the soul, fixed preferences, or subordinate acts."[5] Thus there are three essential components to the human soul: its existence, its nature, and its acts. Moral character is attributed not just to the soul's acts (or volition) but to its nature as well, which lies behind an individual's volition. To possess a "sinful nature" is to be morally sinful even though one has not yet actively sinned. Conversely, when God regenerates a sinner, he transforms the person's nature, enabling the individual to desire holy things, which translates into the actions of repentance and faith in Christ. This, essentially, is the process of God granting the convert a new heart.

As we saw earlier, Finney and some New School Presbyterians had rejected the existence of a principle of nature operating in the soul. This primarily was due to the way they equated sin with explicit acts of the will. A will sins; a sinful nature does not, Finney maintained. The soul thus merely consists of its substance and its acts. Hodge believed people who reject this concept basically commit themselves to several significant errors.

First, he noted how many New School theologians constantly misread Old School theological positions. Specifically, because these New Schoolers rejected the concept of a principle of nature operating in the soul, they constantly charged Old Schoolers with affirming the doctrine of "physical regeneration," or the idea that God creates something brand-new in the substance of the soul on conversion.

---

[5]Charles Hodge, "Regeneration," in *Essays and Reviews* (New York: Robert Carter & Brothers, 1857), 24.

Hodge countered that this assessment is basically incorrect: Old School theologians do not affirm the doctrine of physical regeneration. He notes their erroneous logic:

> The principle assumed is, that there is nothing in the soul but its substance, with its essential attributes, and its acts. Therefore, if regeneration be not a change in its acts, it must be a change in its substance. If sin be not an act, then it is a substance, "an entity," "a disease of the texture of the soul." This, we take it, is the ground of the [accusation] that Calvinists believe in physical depravity and physical regeneration.[6]

Hodge's basic response to this is that it simply is not true: "[We] profess to believe regeneration to be a moral and not a physical change; and that it takes place without any violence being done to the soul or any of its laws."[7] Furthermore, he affirmed that the mainstream Reformed tradition agrees with him on this point. John Owen, for instance, states that

> the power which the Holy Spirit puts forth in our regeneration, is such in its actings or exercise, as our minds, will, and affections are suited to be wrought upon, and to be affected by, according to their natures and natural operations. He doth neither act in them any otherwise than they themselves are meet to be moved and to move, to be acted and to act, according to their own nature, power, and ability.[8]

In short, according to Hodge, the main writers of the Reformed tradition have always held that the Spirit does not recreate the essence of the soul in the work of regeneration. Rather, his work lies essentially in giving the individual a new, holy principle of nature (a "new heart"), from which the individual desires God, repents, and believes in Christ.

Second, and more significantly, Hodge argued that the position that there is "nothing in the soul but its substance and acts" led modern revivalists to embrace significant theological errors mainly related to the doctrines of original sin and regeneration. If there is no sinful nature, as some New School revivalists maintained, then Hodge noted that the following conclusions naturally flow:

- Children are born morally neutral or without moral character, since they do not make any volitional choices.

---

[6]Ibid., 16-17.

[7]Ibid., 11.

[8]Ibid., 8. Hodge quotes from John Owen, *Pneumatologia, or A Discourse Concerning the Holy Spirit*, ed. William H. Goold (London, 1674; repr., London: Johnstone and Hunter, 1852), 318.

- Adam himself was morally neutral at his creation, possessing no principle of holiness that inclined him to God.[9]

- Human beings by nature possess the capacity to change the course of their willing, since no power, principle, or nature inclines them otherwise. This, Hodge maintained, essentially places regeneration in the hands of the sinner.[10]

- The Holy Spirit's operations in salvation lie predominantly in persuading the sinner to embrace the claims of the gospel.[11]

As we saw in the previous chapter, Finney, who was the most prominent of the New School theologians, adopted each of these principles.

The problem Alexander and Hodge found with this set of views is that it eerily reminded them of the old Pelagian heresy. The error of Pelagianism lay in its over-emphasis on nature in the salvation process, which virtually eliminates any supernatural agency. In his survey on the "Early History of Pelagianism," Alexander notes the striking similarities between the new revival theology and the fifth-century Pelagians by quoting the latter at length. "When it is declared that all have sinned in Adam," wrote Pelagius, "it should not be understood of any original sin contracted by their birth, but of imitation." Relatedly, Pelagius asked, "How can a man be considered guilty by God of that sin which he knows not to be his own? For if it is necessary, it is not his own; but if it is his own, it is voluntary; and if voluntary it can be avoided."[12] Hodge noted the significant effects these points have on evangelistic preaching and revival: "The obvious tendency and un-avoidable effect of this philosophy has been to lower all the scriptural doctrines concerning sin, holiness, regeneration, and the divine life."[13] In sum, Alexander and Hodge believed that in rejecting the concept of a "principle of nature" operating in the soul, the modern revivalists basically opened their theologies up to the charge of Pelagianism.

In spite of this, Hodge did acknowledge orthodox views in the preaching of the modern revivalists. For instance, they affirmed the certainty of moral depravity and the necessity of the Spirit's agency in conversion. But overall he remained

---

[9]Charles Hodge, "The New Divinity Tried," in *Biblical Repertory and Theological Review* 4 (1832): 288.
[10]Charles Hodge, "Finney's Lectures on Theology," in *Essays and Reviews*, 251-53; Hodge, "New Divinity Tried," 300.
[11]Hodge, "Regeneration," 42; Charles Hodge, "Bushnell on Christian Nurture," in *Essays and Reviews*, 323.
[12]Archibald Alexander, "The Early History of Pelagianism," in *Biblical Repertory and Theological Review* 2 (1830): 102.
[13]Hodge, "Bushnell on Christian Nurture," 322-23.

pessimistic about the eventual direction of this hybrid system because he believed the Pelagian themes would ultimately prevail.

> How far the assumption of the fundamental principles of a system has a tendency to lead to its thorough adoption, every man must judge for himself. For ourselves we fear the worst. Because, we think consistency requires an advance, and because history informs us, that when men have taken the first step [in the direction of heresy], they or their followers soon take the second.[14]

The safer course was to stick to the revival theology that emerged from the Reformed tradition, where a strong view of sin informs one's soteriology. This includes the affirmation of the immediate imputation of Adam's sin as well as the affirmation that principles of nature really do exist and operate as a foundation for human willing. First, because Adam is the representative head of the human race, God saw fit, subsequent to Adam's fall, to impute his guilt as a covenant transgressor to all his descendants. Thus as soon as they come into the world they are regarded as transgressors liable to eternal judgment. Second, human beings inherit a corrupt, sinful nature from Adam that inclines their wills to sinning from the beginning of their lives. This bondage to sin is consistent with their status as responsible human agents despite being sinners unable to effect a change in their natures. Third, the only hope for a fallen human being is for God to regenerate the individual by supernaturally transforming "the heart" or the habitual nature of the soul. Such a work does not alter the ontological stuff of the soul. Rather, a new, holy nature is wrought in sinners, which serves as the foundation for regeneration and enables individuals to repent and believe in the gospel unto salvation. Hodge and Alexander believed that only by honoring these Reformed positions could one avoid sliding into heresy.

The alternative vision: Cautious advocacy of First Great Awakening revivalism coupled with Christian nurture. The alternative vision of revival that Alexander and Hodge put forth is really not new but agrees roughly with that presented by the moderate evangelicals in the First Great Awakening. Revival preaching should be shaped by the central doctrines of Reformed theology: sinners are by nature "dead" in their sins, unable to change their hearts;[15] though

---

[14]Charles Hodge, "Of an Article in the June number of the Christian Spectator, entitled, 'Inquiries Respecting the Doctrine of Imputation,'" *Biblical Repertory and Theological Review* 2 (1830): 429.

[15]Archibald Alexander, "The Inability of Sinners," in *Princeton Versus the New Divinity* (Carlisle, PA: Banner of Truth, 2001), 131-32.

dead, anxious sinners are to employ the means of grace to gain a sensible awareness of their guilty condition before God;[16] sinners are to anticipate being convicted of sin and waiting on God expectantly until he sovereignly transforms their affections, which enables them to repent and believe.[17]

Alexander and Hodge did diverge on their positive regard to revivals. Alexander's experience as pastor and revivalist rendered him more favorable to the phenomenon than Hodge, whose views were colored more by the defective theologies advanced by modern revivalists. Though sometimes considered an antirevivalist, Hodge's stern statements were usually made with regard to the revivalism of the New School or Finney's new measures. When considering revivals such as those led by Edwards, Whitefield, and the Tennents of the First Great Awakening, he was generally more positive: "We avow our full belief," he noted,

> that the Spirit of God does at times accompany the means of grace with extraordinary power, so that many unrenewed men are brought to the saving knowledge of the truth and a high degree of spiritual life is induced among the people of God. We believe also that such seasons have been among the most signal blessings of God to his church, from the day of Pentecost to our own times.[18]

Part of Hodge's lack of enthusiasm for revivalism lay in his believing revivals divert attention away from the ordinary means that God employs to grow his church. In a review essay on Horace Bushnell's *Discourses on Christian Nurture* (1847), Hodge explored one topic he believed had been overlooked because of the church's preoccupation with revival, namely, the issue of Christian nurture of children by godly parents. While Christian salvation is experienced individually in the sense that no one can repent and believe in Christ on another's behalf, this fact must not obscure the communal nature of the family, an entity that God significantly employs to aid the conversion process. Bushnell's point, which Hodge so appreciated, is that the corporate structure of the family can be a powerful tool in the conversion of children. There "is such a divinely constituted relation between the piety of parents and that of their children," Hodge pointed out, "as to lay a scriptural foundation for a confident expectation, in the use of appointed

---

[16]Archibald Alexander, *Thoughts on Religious Experience* (Philadelphia: Presbyterian Board, 1841), 31.

[17]Charles Hodge, *The Way of Life*, ed. Mark A. Noll, Sources of American Spirituality (New York: Paulist, 1987), 104-19, 151-80.

[18]Hodge, "Bushnell on Christian Nurture," 320. He lists Edwards, Whitefield, the Tennents, and Samuel Davies as examples of solid revival preaching.

means, that the children of believers will become truly the children of God."[19] Through "parental nurture, [and] Christian training," parents can create a "religious culture" in their homes that daily exhibits the gospel to their children as they mature. "The truth concerning God and Christ, the way of salvation and of duty, is inculcated from the beginning, and as fast as it can be comprehended. The child is sedulously guarded as far as possible from all corrupting influence, and subject to those which tend to lead him to God."[20] Though children possess native depravity, they can be encouraged that they stand in a unique relation to God because of their godly families and because of their baptisms:

> [The child] is constantly taught that he stands in a peculiar relation to God, as being included in his covenant and baptized in his name; that he has in virtue of that relation a right to claim God as his Father, Christ as his Saviour, and the Holy Ghost as his sanctifier; and assured that God will recognize that claim and receive him as his child, if he is faithful to his baptismal vows. The child thus trained grows up in the fear of God. . . . When he comes to maturity, the nature of the covenant of grace is fully explained to him, he intelligently and deliberately assents to it, publically confesses himself to be a worshipper and follower of Christ, and acts consistently with his engagements.[21]

Such an approach does not consider the salvation of the child as automatic or taken for granted. Nor is this a natural process that undercuts the Spirit's supernatural work. The process, he notes, is essentially a covenantal one, since it "refers to the connection to the promise of God and his blessing on faithful parental training."[22] The experience of salvation in such a context is thus long and drawn out, taking years to complete. While regeneration is instantaneous, it is experienced in the Christian nurture model as part of a protracted process of religious upbringing such that the adult convert who exhibits genuine fruits of the Spirit might not know exactly when the moment of conversion occurred. Hodge preferred this method of propagating the Christian faith because he believed it was analogous to the way the spiritual life progresses in the individual believer—through discipline, growth, and studied attention to the great truths of the faith. This, he noted, lay in stark contrast to the modern revival method, which he

---

[19]Hodge, "Bushnell on Christian Nurture," 305.
[20]Ibid., 310.
[21]Ibid.
[22]Ibid., 325.

believed abandoned the normal means of growth for intense, spectacular periods of religious excitement fraught with "violent paroxysms of exertion."[23]

In their response to modern revivals, both Alexander and Hodge called Christians back to the Reformed theological tradition because they believed it to be a stable shelter that protected Christians from the vicissitudes of religious enthusiasm and the slippery slope of heresy. As we turn our attention to the Restoration Movement, however, we find a very different response to modern revivals, one that resolutely rejected past theological traditions, opting instead for a plain biblical critique of modern revival theology and an easily understandable, commonsense approach to conversion.

THE RESTORATION MOVEMENT: ALEXANDER CAMPBELL'S "BIBLICIST" RESPONSE TO MODERN REVIVALS

The early decades of the nineteenth century witnessed an explosion of new Christian movements in America. Emboldened by a wave of antitraditionalism, many Christian leaders saw the absence of a state-sanctioned church as a golden opportunity to restore the church to its original, primitive ways, based on a plain reading of Scripture. They thought that if the Scriptures alone were allowed to set the agenda—rather than creeds or complicated theological systems—then a restored and unified New Testament church would emerge. The result was the birth of the Restoration Movement.

The origins and history of Restorationism in America are very complex, containing numerous leaders and multiple trajectories. We will confine our attention to the writings of Alexander Campbell (1788–1866), not only because he is viewed as one of the three main leaders of the "Disciples" or "Churches of Christ,"[24] but also because his doctrine of salvation came to characterize much of the Restoration Movement at large.[25]

Campbell was an Irish-born Scot who was educated at the University of Glasgow. In 1809 he immigrated to America, where he joined his father, Thomas,

---

[23]Ibid., 320.

[24]The other two early Restoration leaders are Barton Stone (1772–1844) and Walter Scott (1796–1861).

[25]Thus, while the roots of Restorationism had associations with extravagant revivals (i.e., Barton Stone was the leader of the great Cane Ridge Camp Meeting while he was still a Presbyterian), the ultimate soteriological trajectory of the movement gravitated in the direction of Campbell; see Robert C. Kurka, "The Role of the Holy Spirit in Conversion: Why Restorationists Appear to Be Out of the Evangelical Mainstream," in *Evangelicalism and the Stone-Campbell Movement*, ed. William R. Baker (Downers Grove, IL: InterVarsity Press, 2002), 142.

who was ministering in southwest Pennsylvania. There Campbell associated with Baptists and came to champion Restorationist ideals through his religious periodicals.[26] Though sharing similar positions with Baptists on ecclesiology—the autonomy of the local church and the practice of believer's baptism—Campbell introduced teachings that many Baptists considered innovative: a weekly celebration of the Lord's Supper, a rejection of the use of instruments in worship, a vigorous anti-Calvinist polemic, and the language that baptism by immersion is "for the remission of sins." By the early 1830s, Campbell's "Disciples" movement had left the Baptists and formed a loose alliance with Barton Stone's "Christian" movement that coalesced into the denomination known under the names "Churches of Christ" or "Disciples of Christ."

Campbell's unique response to modern revivals was fueled by his vision of Christian unity and world evangelization. To his mind these two ideals were intimately connected: *"Nothing is [as] essential to the conversion of the world but the union of and co-operation of Christians."*[27] Consequently, he became staunchly opposed to anything that brought schism or denominational division to Christians and repeatedly identified two issues that constantly divide. The first is human theological systems. Campbell believed that many of the terms, concepts, and "isms" that Christians have concocted over the centuries have no grounding in Scripture but derive instead from an elite, educated class of human theologians. Their collective utterances are not only overly speculative but are completely ineffective in drawing people to salvation. "The Arianism, Athanasianism, Arminianism, Calvinism, Trinitarianism, Uritarianisms [sic], Sabellianisms," he notes, "are mere philosophies, and whether true or false, at their respective meridians, never saved man, woman, or child from the guilt of sin."[28] Human theological traditions, in short, divide the church and keep people from understanding the Scriptures. Second, Campbell believed that the church's reliance on creeds and confessions has also needlessly generated division among Christians. The only use for creeds is to "to build and keep up a party; to cause professors to revile, slander, and hate one another; to hold formalists, hypocrites, and prevaricators

---

[26] *The Christian Baptist* in the 1820s and *The Millennial Harbinger* in the 1830s and afterward.

[27] Alexander Campbell, *The Christian System, in reference to the Union of Christians, and a Restoration of Primitive Christianity, as pleaded in the Current Reformation* (London: Simpkin, Marshall, & Co., 1843), 112.

[28] Alexander Campbell, *The Writings of Alexander Campbell, Selections from the Millennial Harbinger*, ed. W. A. Morris (Austin, TX: Eugene Von Boeckmann, 1896), 227.

together; and to exclude weak Christians and honest disciples from popular establishments."[29] In short, *"No human creed in Protestant christendom can be found that has not made a division for every generation of its existence."*[30]

The way forward, Campbell asserted, lies in what we might call a merely "biblicist" return to the Scriptures. What this means is that Christians are to allow the simple Scriptures to speak plainly for themselves. God does not speak to his people as the theologians do in their "metaphysical and speculative dialect, peculiar to their abstract theses and their reasonings thereupon." He speaks through the apostles "in the common idiom of the common people, in their common intercourse with one another."[31] Campbell's biblicist hermeneutic led him on a lifelong crusade against modern revivals because he believed these had all emerged from defective theologies. Fundamentally, he believed that the revival theologies in circulation were overly subjective and introspective. Christians must turn away from the subjectivism of modern conversions—fraught with conviction, terrors, mystical raptures, the endless testing of the heart—and return to what he called the simple "Christian system," that is, the plain verities of the salvation process as exhibited in the New Testament: faith, repentance, baptism, and regeneration.

Campbell's critique of modern revivals. In his "Sermon on the Law," an early work (1816) preached to the Regular Baptist Association in Cross Creek, Virginia, Campbell not only strove to outline the proper relationship between the law and the gospel but also laid the foundation for a significant critique of popular revival theology. To Campbell, law and gospel are two "contradistinguished" principles throughout Scripture. Though the law displays the inherent holiness of God, it is ultimately rendered powerless in both salvation and sanctification because of the undermining effects of human sin. Consequently, the law is a ministration of both condemnation and death in the human race. Campbell extended this verdict over the entire law of Moses—moral, ceremonial, and judicial—because he argued that this threefold division was entirely "unknown in the Apostolic age, and of course never used by the Apostles."[32] Since the entire law has been transcended by the gospel, Christians are to bind themselves to Christ's teachings as the disciples did, not to any part of the Mosaic law. "The law or Ten Commandments is

[29]Alexander Campbell, "Creeds," in *Writings*, 523.
[30]Campbell, *Christian System*, 114.
[31]Alexander Campbell, "Regeneration in Fact and in Theory," in *Writings*, 125.
[32]Alexander Campbell, "Sermon on the Law," in *Writings*, 32.

not a rule of life to Christians any further than it is enjoined by Christ; . . . it is only what Christ says [that] we must observe."[33]

The implications of Campbell's approach for preaching the gospel are huge. "We conclude from the above premises that there is no necessity for preaching the law in order to prepare men for salvation."[34] This was a significant change in evangelistic preaching. As we have seen, most of the revival theologies we have surveyed have emphasized the centrality of legal preaching. Such preaching was designed to inculcate conviction of sin, which began the process of seeking salvation. Campbell argued that this method, based on a faulty understanding of the relationship between the law and the gospel, committed modern revivalists to an erroneous theology of conversion. He noted three consequences that unfold from the practice.

First, legal preaching turns the conversion process into an extremely lengthy affair. "Modern conversions" are "very systematic, and lingering," events that drive folks "to despair by the thunders of Mount Sinai." Persons are held in "anxious suspense," wondering whether the "wounds of conviction are deep enough" or "whether their desires are sufficiently keen." Waiting for the proper religious experiences, it is "not rare to find some in a way of being converted for years; and, indeed, it is generally a work of many months." Campbell notes the sharp contrast between these examples and those ancient conversions found in the New Testament, where "we read of many converted in a day, who yesterday were as ignorant of law and gospel as the modern Hindoos [sic] or Birmans [sic]."[35]

Second, the popular method of legal preaching centered too much on the subjective aspects entailed in the conversion process. By calling listeners to cultivate a heart of conviction and then to seek a new heart, the minister is bound to direct the attention of seekers away from the gospel and toward their own inner states. Revivalists erroneously expected persons to pass through "some terrible process of terror and despair through which a person must pass, as through the pious Bunyan's slough of *Despond*, before he can believe the gospel. It is all equivalent to this, that a man must become a desponding, trembling infidel, before he can become a believer."[36] Other Restorationists agreed. Walter Scott, the well-known

---

[33]Campbell, "Sermon on the Law," 47. This essentially was the position advocated by antinomianism.
[34]Ibid., 50.
[35]Ibid., 57.
[36]Alexander Campbell, "Address to the Readers of the Christian Baptist, No. IV," in *The Christian Baptist*, ed. Alexander Campbell (Buffalo, VA: A. Campbell, 1827; repr., Nashville: Gospel Advocate Company, 1955), 1:148.

evangelist of the Stone-Campbellites, sharply criticized the "modern error" of substituting "feeling for faith" in his lengthy evangelistic manual *The Gospel Restored* (1836).[37] In his evangelistic labors, Scott had come across many who feared that they could not truly believe the gospel because they had not been adequately prepared emotionally. "I do not feel as I ought to feel, in order to obey the gospel" was the common objection. Scott reckoned they learned this "mode of speech" from modern revivals, in which persons were told to tend to their Christian experiences, "which [consist] generally, of a history of those intervals and moments of mental misery and happiness, for which the lives of the faithless and secular professors of modern times are distinguished, being occasionally exalted to the heights of enthusiasm, and again sunken to the depths of despair."[38] Such a method is not found in the New Testament, he argued, where the gospel is presented as good news first and foremost, not something that can only be experienced after spiritual despondency has set in. Scott thought this evangelistic method needed to be scrapped and replaced with the simple preaching of faith in Christ. The "doctrine of spiritual operations, and the absurd and uncertain custom of waiting for frames and feelings, must all be thrown out from before faith or belief, and this principle [of faith must] be brought into the very front, and be made stand forth in bold relief in the grand master-piece of the gospel."[39]

Third, legal preaching, lengthy conversions, and the overly subjective nature of modern conversions generated a faulty reading of Scripture that destroyed the simple order of salvation in the Bible. As we will see in the next section, both Campbell and Scott strongly emphasized the natural order that Scripture gives to the conversion process. Subsequently, they lamented the erroneous arrangements given by other groups. Scott noted that the common order found among Presbyterians and Congregationalists—"infant baptism, the special operations of the Holy Spirit, the forgiveness of sins, faith, repentance, and the resurrection"—is a "pernicious arrangement" that should be "rejected with disdain as a most unscriptural gospel." "This error," he continued, "reflects upon the perfection of the holy scriptures, and causes men to neglect them, and to look up to God through the medium of their frames and feelings rather than through the medium of these holy oracles."[40]

---

[37]Walter Scott, *The Gospel Restored, A Discourse of the True Gospel of Jesus Christ* (Cincinnati: O. H. Donogh, 1836).

[38]Ibid., 245.

[39]Ibid.

[40]Ibid., 99.

Campbell believed that the underlying theological error to these practices derived from placing regeneration and repentance before faith in the order of salvation, a position held by Calvinists. This is wrong, Campbell argued. First, repentance cannot precede faith because biblical repentance already implies the presence of true faith; "how could any one repent of sin against God, if he did not believe that he had sinned against God? And how could the mercy of God afford any encouragement to repentance unless that mercy is reported to us as believed?"[41] Faith, then, is the foundation of biblical repentance. Second, regeneration cannot precede faith because that would lead us to admit the ridiculous possibility that some persons are regenerated before they have exercised true faith. Campbell tells of a man he knew who declared that *"he was [for] three years a 'godly unbeliever' . . .* acceptable to God *'without faith.'"* Such an absurd conclusion, propagated by "Bellamy, Hopkins, and Fuller," can only surface among theologians who have become unfamiliar with simple teachings of Scripture. "Such is the effect of metaphysical theology."[42]

The alternative vision: The plain conversion theology of Campbell's "Christian system." Campbell's answer to revival theology was a practical soteriology that he believed was easily comprehensible to everyone. His approach broadly followed two characteristics: a common-sense theology of conversion that underscored the simplicity of faith in the gospel and a holistic soteriology that strove to strike the scriptural balance between internal belief (faith in Christ) and external obedience (repentance and baptism). From this foundation, a natural order to the conversion process emerges, one that must be maintained if one is to be saved. In a nutshell, this order ran as follows. First, on hearing the gospel, the individual comes to believe in the veracity of the apostolic testimony concerning Christ (i.e., faith) and trusts him for salvation. Second, faith naturally leads the new believer to turn away from sin in the act of repentance. Third, Campbell argued that the individual then undergoes baptism for the remission of sins. This visible testimony of the Spirit's work in the life of the believer engenders assurance and is simultaneous with the believer's justification, sanctification, and adoption. Last, the believer experiences regeneration, defined as being transferred completely from a state of condemnation into salvation. In sum, not only did Campbell believe this order to be biblical, but he contended that it is a natural, understandable process that the common churchgoer can easily comprehend.

---

[41]Alexander Campbell, "Repentance unto Life," in *Writings*, 71.
[42]Campbell, "Address to the Readers of the Christian Baptist, No. IV," 1:148-49.

Throughout his writings, Campbell displayed his plain biblicism by sticking close to the order of salvation portrayed in the New Testament. "Order is heaven's first law," he maintained. "There is an order of antecedents and consequents in all the economy of the universe. There is an order in causation, and an order in consequence in all the words of God."[43] Applied to the salvation process, Campbell was particularly at pains to stress the causal sequence he found in the New Testament. While he noted many things that accompany an individual's salvation (justification, conversion, sanctification, and adoption), three items emerge as the center of gravity to his reflections: faith, repentance, and baptism. "But now the Lord be praised and glorified forever!" he notes in a section on the universality of God's grace,

> It is most cordially and most importunately *granted*—tendered to all the nations of the earth, with the assurance that Jesus has not only become the propitiation for the sins of the Jews, but also for the sins of the whole world; so that faith, repentance, and baptism, are, by the commandment of the everlasting God, now announced to all the world for the remission of sins.[44]

Elsewhere, he notes how "Faith, Repentance, Baptism, [and] Regeneration" are all comprehended under the term *grace* and that "each and every one, [is] necessary to our reconciliation, pardon, justification, sanctification, adoption and ultimate glorification."[45] Similarly, Walter Scott was well-known for his simple evangelistic summary of the gospel, which featured the same concepts: faith, repentance, baptism, remission of sins, receiving of the Holy Spirit, and the resurrection.[46] Thus, while revivalists from other traditions prominently featured the doctrines of original sin, justification by faith, regeneration as the new birth, and the abilities (or inabilities) of the will in embracing Christ through faith, Campbell and his coreligionists centered the focus of their message on this basic trio (faith, repentance, and baptism) and then treated other topics (justification, regeneration) in light of them. Consequently, our approach to Campbell's conversion theology will center on these pillars of their message.

For Campbell, faith is the grand entryway into the Christian religion. His views on the topic demonstrate his desire to define faith in a basic, matter-of-fact

---

[43]Alexander Campbell, "Metanoeoo—Metanoia: Repent—Repentance. Reform—Reformation," in *Writings*, 86.

[44]Campbell, "Repentance unto Life," 73.

[45]Alexander Campbell, "Grace, Faith, Repentance, Baptism, Regeneration," in *Writings*, 116.

[46]These six points formed the framework for *The Gospel Restored*.

way that avoids theological speculation and subjectivity. Faith "has nothing to do with opinions, theories, or speculative reasonings of any sort whatever," he notes.[47] Neither is it to be confused with the emotional and volitional sides of our being; "it is not choosing, nor refusing; it is not loving, hating, fearing, desiring nor hoping."[48] Faith relates to the simple facts of the gospel, which the mind comes to believe is true based on the credible testimony of the apostles found in Scripture. The "capital principle" of Christianity is "faith in Jesus as the true Messiah and obedience to him as our lawgiver and king."[49] Walter Scott concurred: "The gospel, it will be seen by the reader, is comprehended ultimately in one external fact, that Jesus is the Son of God; and one internal principle, namely, faith. . . . The Christian Religion is, therefore, a system of great simplicity as well as originality, and on that account is admirably adapted to the capacity of those for whom it is intended."[50]

How does one come to faith? Campbell and Scott broke down the components of this process in numerous ways, yet the composite picture looks something like this. Objectively, God has revealed his gospel: the Word became flesh, dwelt among us, and has become the sacrifice for the sins of the world. This true testimony was recorded by faithful witnesses throughout the New Testament, which subsequently has been spoken and preached through the generations. Subjectively, we hear the message of the gospel ("faith cometh by hearing") and then are left to deliberate whether these new facts are true or not. Our recognition of their truthfulness constitutes true belief, and we place our trust in Christ. There is nothing mysterious, mystical, or metaphysical in the entire affair. The process is very similar to learning about other, nonreligious things. In *The Gospel Restored*, Walter Scott noted how the exercise of faith in Christ and that of growing in knowledge are virtually identical processes.[51] In Lockean categories, he describes how God has given human beings "the power of acquiring ideas by sensation, and of reflecting upon them when acquired," a process that leads us to grow in knowledge. When we learn through testimony (like through a parent or teacher), we affirm the "experience" (that is, the report of what was seen or heard) of another to be true. Faith follows this same process, "for faith differs from

---

[47]Alexander Campbell, "Faith and Faith," in *Writings*, 61.
[48]Campbell, *Christian System*, 122.
[49]Ibid., vii.
[50]Scott, *Gospel Restored*, 241-42.
[51]Ibid., 258-60.

knowledge only as other people's experience differs from our own." When we hear the testimony of the apostles' experience of Christ in Scripture and affirm it, we "avail ourselves" of their experience. Believing in Christ is therefore a process that is no different from learning, for in both believing and learning one affirms the testimony about an event that one did not directly experience. Since everyone has a power to learn through education, everyone has a power to believe. Thus Scott found the doctrine of spiritual inability to be ridiculous: "That doctrine, consequently, which says a man cannot believe the gospel, virtually denies that we can avail ourselves of the experience of others; and consequently it makes the gospel, which is reported to us as true upon the experience of others . . . a matter ulterior to human nature."[52]

Though faith and repentance are "inseparably connected" in the experience of salvation, Campbell was insistent that repentance is the product of belief.[53] Faith is to repentance as "cause is to effect" or as "means is to the end."[54] "Gospel repentance is the offspring of gospel light and gospel motive, and therefore it is the effect, and not the cause, of belief of the testimony of God."[55] In his mind, Scripture portrays the call to repentance as a proclamation of mercy that must first be believed for it to be genuinely performed. He repeatedly pointed to Hebrews 11:6 in this regard, noting how it is impossible to do anything spiritual without faith: one must first "believe that [God] is, and that he is a rewarder of them that diligently seek him" (definition of faith) before one can do anything of spiritual value in the economy of salvation (repentance). "A man's repenting of a sin against God without a prior assurance of faith or knowledge that there is a God, assumes a position no less untenable in the court of sound reason than he who assumes that there was a creature before a creator, or a son before his father."[56] This position dramatically reorganized the standard evangelical pathway to faith. No longer did one need to wait for a work of conviction that commences a lengthy period of spiritual angst accompanied by moral reformation (legal repentance), employing the means of grace, seeking a new heart, and waiting for the new birth. To Campbell, this turned the glad tidings of gospel preaching into a morose affair. "Be sorrowful and believe the gospel, never entered into the heart [of the New

---

[52]Ibid., 259.
[53]Campbell, "Repentance unto Life," 67.
[54]Ibid., 71.
[55]Campbell, *Christian System*, 57.
[56]Campbell, "Metanoeoo—Metanoia," 87-88.

Testament writers]. . . . It belongs to the furor of the Calvinistic or Arminian campmeeting."[57] One only needs the simple message of the gospel: believe in the apostolic testimony (something every rational human being is capable of doing) and, subsequent to that, repent of all known sin.[58]

Scripturally, Campbell argued that the process of salvation is not yet complete at the point of faith and repentance. Penitent believers must undergo an external rite, mandated by the apostles, which visibly demonstrates the internal change of heart to the church and world: the rite of immersionist baptism. Early Restorationists argued that Christian baptism introduces its subjects to the blessings of the death and resurrection of Jesus Christ.[59] As Christ died, was buried, and rose again to new life, so too does the penitent believer identify with Christ in his death, burial, and resurrection by being immersed in the waters of baptism. To Campbell, Christian baptism brings to completion the cycle begun with faith and repentance. It is the "final and sealing act of [our] compliance" with the gospel.[60]

These views substantially overlap with Baptist positions—both affirmed believer's baptism and baptism by immersion. Campbell differed with the Baptists, however, in his insistence that baptism is "for the remission of sins" and that baptism is closely associated with regeneration in the New Testament. These assertions made other evangelicals uncomfortable because they appeared to devalue the doctrine of justification by faith alone and teach a doctrine of baptismal regeneration.

Though he did answer these charges, his first strategy when addressing the connection between baptism, justification, and regeneration was to point out the coherence of the Christian system presented in Scripture. In his work *The Christian System*, Campbell gives careful attention to the terms Scripture uses for salvation: faith in Christ, repentance, baptism, confession, conversion, and regeneration.[61] He notes that these terms are the "most important terms and phrases of the Christian system"[62] and thus should frame our theology of salvation. Terms such

---

[57]Ibid., 81.

[58]Campbell's conversion theology is sometimes called rationalistic since it downplays the intense emotionalism of revival conversions and portrays faith and repentance merely as a change of belief. This anti-emotional conversion theology was pioneered by the Sandemanians, a small Scottish denomination founded by John Glas and Robert Sandeman that had churches in New England. For more information, see John Howard Smith, *The Perfect Rule of the Christian Religion: A History of Sandemanianism in the Eighteenth Century* (Albany: State University Press of New York, 2008).

[59]Campbell, *Christian System*, 61.

[60]Alexander Campbell, "Immersion for Remission of Sins, Advocated by Elder Meredith," in *Writings*, 92.

[61]Campbell, *Christian System*, 55-65.

[62]Ibid., 65.

as *justification, adoption,* and *sanctification* are "other predicates" of the Christian system that round out the biblical portrait of salvation, but they should not receive priority in a biblical-theological framework.[63] Thus when Campbell and Scott prominently featured baptism in their theology of salvation, they did so because they believed Scripture inextricably united faith, repentance, and baptism—and what God has joined, let no one separate. "[The apostles] taught the system as a whole; they have required a compliance with the whole; to him who complies with the whole, they have promised the blessing of salvation; but to him who complies only in part, they have made no such promise."[64] He complained that the broader evangelical community shattered the unity of the Christian system by associating remission solely with faith "before compliance with an external rite."[65] Such rear-ranging of the biblical system might serve the purposes of revivalists in their camp meetings, but it "is without a warrant in the records of the divine compact."[66]

When Campbell addressed the connection of baptism with justification, he pointed to how the New Testament closely associates baptism with salvation. Peter tells would-be converts to repent and be baptized "for the remission of sins" (Acts 2:38), and Jesus himself declared prior to his ascension that "he that believeth and is baptized shall be saved" (Mk 16:16). Campbell interpreted these texts to mean that penitent believers' sins are washed away, remitted, and forgiven *when they are baptized.* He contended that this in no way is to be considered works-righteousness. "Baptism is . . . no work of the law, no moral duty, no moral righteousness," he indi-cated. Rather, it is an integral component of the Christian system, the external in-dicator of an internal change of heart. "[Baptism is] a simple putting on of Christ and placing our selves, wholly in His hand and under His guidance."[67]

Campbell maintained that baptism is also the moment of regeneration. To him, the essence of regeneration does not lie in the Spirit's work in the soul of a convert; it simply refers to an individual being brought into a "new state" of being in which they enjoy a new relationship with God, humanity, and Christ.[68] Re-generation occurs when the "consummating act" of the entire salvific process is

---

[63]Ibid., 65-66. See also *Writings,* 247, for his wonder at why there is so much emphasis placed on justification by faith alone when we find Scripture noting at least six other causes of justification.

[64]Campbell, "Immersion for Remission of Sins," 92.

[65]Ibid.

[66]Ibid., 93.

[67]Alexander Campbell, "Justification," in *Writings,* 251-52.

[68]Campbell, "Address to the Readers of the Christian Baptist, No. IV," 147; Campbell, *Christian System,* 279, 283.

completed, "because the process is always supposed incomplete until that act is performed."[69] This consummating act is believer's baptism. Noting the parallels between John 3:5 (where Jesus comments to Nicodemus that one can only enter the kingdom of God by being "born of water and of the Spirit") and Titus 3:5 (where Paul comments that individuals are saved by the "washing of regeneration, and renewing of the Holy Ghost"), Campbell vigorously argued that baptism is *the moment* when the salvation process is finalized. Through it, penitent believers have been brought into a new state in which God is their Father, Christ is their Savior, and all Christ's blessings (forgiveness, justification, adoption) are theirs. The person is now born again, or regenerated. "Being *born of water* in the Saviour's style, and *the bath of regeneration* in the apostles' style, in the judgment of all writers and critics of eminence, refer to one and the same act—viz.: Christian baptism."[70]

SUMMARY

Not everyone welcomed the revival theologies that supported many of the revivals of the Second Great Awakening. This chapter examined the critiques that two different groups leveled against modern revival theology—the high Calvinists of Princeton and several early Restorationists. It also noted the alternative vision of Christian conversion that each group offered as a remedy to the errors they discerned in modern revival theology.

Early Princeton theologians advanced a high Calvinist critique of modern revivals that sharply criticized the theologies of New School Presbyterianism and Finney's new measures. Specifically, Archibald Alexander and Charles Hodge believed that these theologies

- did not articulate the nature of sin correctly;

- were too optimistic about the will's ability to contribute to regeneration; and

- led to positions that came dangerously close to Pelagianism.

Conversely, they called Christians back to an older vision of Reformed theology:

- First, they called Christians to adopt the traditional Reformed positions on numerous issues, including the immediate imputation of Adam's sin, the

---

[69]Campbell, *Christian System*, 279.
[70]Ibid., 280.

inability of sinners, the reality of sinful or holy "natures" that inform the will, and the doctrine that regeneration is a work of the Holy Spirit antecedent to human conversion.

- Second, they called Christians to adopt the older vision of revival found among the moderate evangelicals of the First Great Awakening.

- And, third, they called faithful Christian parents everywhere not to forget the solemn responsibility they have to create a rich religious environment in their homes so that their children might repeatedly see the gospel on display in their lives and hopefully embrace the Christian faith for themselves.

Early Restorationist leaders such as Alexander Campbell and Walter Scott believed that the common approaches to evangelism in the revivals of the early nineteenth century did more to hinder the spread of the gospel than spread it. Their criticism centered on several interconnecting errors that they discerned among the modern revivalists.

- First, they believed the revivalists' emphasis on "law preaching" drew the soul away from faith in Christ. The gospel, they countered, and the simple response of faith should be the center of the preacher's evangelistic endeavors, not the law.

- Second, their observations of the many emotionally animated revivals led them to conclude that "modern conversions" were both too lengthy and overly subjective. True conversions are quick affairs that should not lead the soul's attention into the murky depths of the inner self but to the objective realities of Christ and the salvation he offers.

- Last, Campbell realized that underlying these errors was a defective theology that confused the simple, biblical order of salvation portrayed in the Scriptures.

By contrast, Campbell advanced what we have called a biblicist response to revival theology, one that highlighted a common-sense reading of Scripture that avoided the conundrums associated with human-made theological systems.

- He maintained that the Bible presents a practical soteriology that is easily comprehended by laypeople who read the Bible with their common sense.

- He noted that the Bible presents a simple, biblical order of salvation that strikes a balance between internal belief (faith) and external obedience (repentance and baptism).

- He, along with Walter Scott, stressed that faith is the notional affirmation of the simple facts of the Christian gospel.

- He underscored that the biblical order of salvation is strictly fourfold in its manifestation: it begins with *faith*, which then leads to *repentance*, followed by the rite of *baptism*, and ending finally in *regeneration*.

These plain biblical verities, Campbell maintained, anchor the convert's interior faith to tangible external realities, which corrects the excessive introspection he associated with the conversions found in modern revivals.

CONCLUSION

You see the importance of understanding the philosophy of conversion, and why
it is, that so many sermons are lost, and worse than lost upon the souls of men.

CHARLES FINNEY, "HOW TO CHANGE YOUR HEART"

CHARLES FINNEY SAW THE IMPORTANCE of a philosophy of conversion
to the spread of the gospel. Even though one might find serious flaws in his teaching,
we cannot but appreciate the fact that he had a well-thought-out system con-
necting theology, preaching, and the application of the gospel to individuals' spiritual lives. Evangelicals have always been an experience-oriented people who revel
in "knowing God personally." They have been at their best when they anchor these
spiritual impulses deeply in biblical theology. Throughout this book we have seen
how the major evangelical traditions of the First and Second Great Awakenings
united doctrine with a robust spiritual life and heralded the message of salvation
in Christ to a dying world. Revivalists seemed to move easily between the worlds
of theology, evangelistic method, and spiritual shepherding as they counseled
sinners through the stages of conversion to Christ. As they did so, they developed
the numerous revival theologies we have explored in the preceding chapters.

To recap, our study began with an analysis of the revival theology that characterized the beginnings of evangelicalism, the "moderate evangelical" views of the
First Great Awakening's major leaders. We argued that this was the baseline revival
theology American evangelicals were familiar with in the middle of the eighteenth
century. From there we moved forward historically over a century, noting how
new issues and debates introduced alternative views that led to the rise of other
revival theologies. In sum, we analyzed the following positions in detail:

- *Moderate evangelical revival theology* was Puritan Calvinism with a strong dose of pietism. It emphasized preaching the law to draw sinners into conviction and advocated would-be converts to use the means of grace and wait expectantly for God to give them new hearts. Conversions were emotionally intense and often lengthy events.

- *Free grace revival theology* was taught by Andrew Croswell and other radical evangelicals of the First Great Awakening. It rejected the moderates' emphasis on spiritual activism (means of grace), lengthy preparations, and spiritual doubt. Instead, this position argued that faith is particular (it approaches Christ as *my* Savior who loves *me*) and passively receives salvation. In addition, God has granted the blessings of salvation to the world by "right." Conversions are emotionally intense (verging on "enthusiasm"), certain (doubting is impossible), and quick.

- *Edwardsean Calvinist revival theology* was inspired by Jonathan Edwards and developed by the New Divinity (eighteenth century) and New England theologians of the Second Great Awakening (nineteenth century). Building on Edwards's insights, the Edwardseans taught that, though sinners possess a moral disinclination to believe, they do have a natural ability to embrace the gospel, and because of this they should repent immediately. Their views, which transformed the doctrines of original sin, atonement, and justification, expected conversions to be lengthy events that culminated in the convert's embrace of the disinterested spirituality held by Edwards.

- *Methodist Arminian revival theology* was promoted by early American Methodists throughout the Second Great Awakening. It rejected the evangelistically limiting doctrines of the Calvinists (election, spiritual inability), emphasizing instead an Arminian vision of God who loves the world, who offers the gift of salvation universally to everyone, and who does not interfere with human free will. Methodists called sinners not only to experience quick and emotionally powerful conversions but also to experience the higher blessings of Christian perfection.

These four views were the major different systems of revival theology emerging between the First and Second Great Awakenings. Along the way, we made several other observations that represent numerous iterations or responses to the above systems.

- *Early American Baptists* did not produce a single system of revival theology; rather, their revivalists selected from among the views already existing in the broader evangelical world. Because of this they mirrored the diversity reflected among American evangelicalism at large.

- *Taylorism, or New Haven theology,* represented a progressive version of the Edwardsean system that strongly privileged the sinner's theoretical ability to repent and suggested that the means of grace might actually suspend the sinner's principle of selfishness prior to regeneration. Taylor's theology found adherents among many New School Presbyterians.

- *Charles Finney's revival theology* built a highly practical system erected largely on the foundation of Taylorism. His extensive elaboration of the means of grace, known as the "new measures," was tailored to bring the gospel to bear on the minds of specific audiences and individuals. His revival theology emphasized the agencies of the Holy Spirit, the minister, and the convert, though he was not careful to delineate the boundaries between these agents of salvation.

- *Princeton theologians* Alexander and Hodge leveled a sharp critique of modern revivals by noting that the new views polluted the purity of classic Reformed theology. They cautiously advocated revivals like those found in the First Great Awakening, yet also called Christian parents to revive interest in family religion as an important means to advancing the gospel in the world.

- *Restoration movement leaders* Campbell and Scott argued that the revival theologies of their day were too complex, confusing, and metaphysical. The Bible presents a plain and easy-to-understand vision of salvation that includes the basic actions of belief, repentance, and baptism and avoids the emotionalism and introspection associated with revivals altogether.

FOUR FACTORS OF REVIVAL THEOLOGY

The history of revival theology in early America was propelled by several factors. Indeed, we can pinpoint four factors that generated doctrinal development in revival theology between the awakenings. The first factor relates to the tension between the bondage and freedom of the will. In a world where sin reigns, how are we to articulate the spiritual capacities of the unregenerate? We have seen numerous answers given to this question. Moderate evangelical Calvinists argued that sin keeps sinners in bondage, rendering them unable by nature to initiate the salvation process. In spite of this fact, they argued that sinners are still responsible agents held accountable to their actions. Edwardsean Calvinists similarly argued that sinners possess a moral disinclination to choose God as their ultimate good, but they noted that the unregenerate do possess a natural ability to repent and believe if they so choose. Arminian Methodists argued that the universal effects of Christ's atoning work have supernaturally granted human beings the genuine freedom to repent and believe the gospel. Finney partially agreed yet noted that human freedom was not a supernatural gift but part of humankind's natural ability to comply with the gospel. Others, like Campbell, found the question impractical and metaphysical, noting how scriptural examples of evangelism and conversion bypass these theoretical questions altogether.

A second factor pertains to the tension between particularism and universalism in their revival theologies. All of the revivalists we have treated in this volume are particularists in the sense that none of them believed in universal salvation. Lines must be drawn somewhere. At the same time, they appealed to everyone indiscriminately to seek salvation in Christ; the benefits of salvation, in other words, are theoretically available to all. On what basis are we to make a universal appeal, given the particular restrictions inherent in one's theology? Different revival theologies gave different answers to this question. The theology of the moderate evangelicals was perhaps the most particular given their affirmation of election and limited atonement. Yet they grounded the universal call of the gospel in the fact that anyone can employ the means of grace to their life and seek salvation. Those who seek may find; those who do not seek will definitely find themselves facing God's eternal judgment. Croswell and other free grace revivalists taught that God has universally granted the gospel to humanity. Since Christ and the blessings of salvation belong to everyone "by right or grant," one only needs to claim them as such through personal acceptance and belief. Edwardsean Calvinists affirmed a universal atonement (the moral government theory) in which human beings universally retain a natural ability to comply with the gospel if they so will. Methodists, Finney, and Campbell all affirmed some version of the freedom of the will as the theoretical basis for indiscriminately calling all to repent. To these writers, the vestiges of Calvinist inability have receded into the background; one can be saved if one submits to the claims of the gospel. In each of these revival theologies, the basis for the universal offer of the gospel manifested itself differently.

Third, questions related to the standard length of the conversion process were also a factor in the development of revival theology. While each of the views presented here affirmed that regeneration is an immediate work of God, they were at odds regarding how converts generally experience this transformation in real time. As inheritors of the Puritan tradition, moderate evangelicals generally expected the conversion process to take a period of days or weeks to accomplish. A legal work of preparation needed to run its course in the heart. Also, the one seeking salvation needed to engage God's means of grace with the hopeful expectation that God might, at some point, illuminate the mind and enable the soul to believe savingly. Edwardsean revivalists advocated a similar process, but they prominently featured the doctrine of immediate repentance in their preaching, and some of them (i.e., Hopkins) portrayed the means of grace in a negative light. Croswell and later Finney both affirmed the necessity of conviction prior to faith, but generally they expected that conversions would be rather quick events. And Campbell and Scott, in their response to revival theologies in general, represented the conversion process as reaching its culminating conclusion in the moment of baptism, an event that takes just seconds to accomplish.

A fourth factor that led to a development in American revival theology had to do with the contrast between traditional theological systems and a plain, common-sense reading of Scripture. To what degree do systematic theological constructs—such as the doctrines of sin, spiritual inability, election, and the extent of the atonement—bear on the practicalities of preaching and conversion, especially when scriptural narratives of preaching and conversion do not appear to feature these doctrines prominently? As we have seen, the earlier revival theologies—the moderate evangelicals and the New Divinity theologians—were decidedly Calvinist in orientation. As such, they incorporated the full set of soteriological categories into their preaching and spiritual counseling. Thus the doctrines of original sin, spiritual inability, divine election, regeneration antecedent to faith, and the atonement factored significantly in shaping how they preached to and counseled sinners. This changed after the 1790s with the rise of the popular denominations and the rejection of Old World traditions. Many revivalists came to question the complicated systems of salvation promoted by the older views. The Bible, they countered, presents a simpler picture of salvation: Jesus receives sinners of all types, not specially prepared sinners; the apostles' call to repentance seems to imply an ability to respond; converts submit to Christ immediately, not after a lengthy period of preparation. These observations emerged from a plain, common-sense reading of Scripture, which many revivalists of the Second Great Awakening noted as they constructed their revival theologies.

TRAJECTORIES OF REVIVAL THEOLOGY

These four factors that developed American revival theology also serve as a guide summarizing the major trajectories in the history of revival theology from 1740 to 1840. First, between the First and Second Great Awakenings we see a trajectory away from theories that accentuate the bondage of the will toward theories that highlight the will's freedom. As we have seen, this is not merely a trajectory from Calvinism to Arminianism. Rather, it is the recognition that, after the First Great Awakening, more theological options existed than just the traditional Calvinism of the moderate evangelicals and that these other options underscored volitional freedom in different ways, whether theoretical (Edwardsean Calvinism) or actual (Methodist Arminianism and Finney).

Second, we see a trajectory away from revival theologies that emphasize themes of particularity toward ones that emphasize themes of universality. Moderate evangelical Calvinists did preach the gospel to everyone indiscriminately; they were not hyper-Calvinists who resisted extending the offer of salvation. But to the eyes of others moderate evangelical revival theology appeared to harbor too many theoretical concepts that "particularized" or limited gospel preaching: election, limited atonement, spiritual inability. Many later came to believe that these concepts were not consistent with the wideness in God's mercy portrayed in Scripture. Hence we see an expansion of universal themes in other revival theologies between the awakenings. The New Divinity emphasized the universal implications of the atonement and also argued that every human being theoretically can come to Christ if they so choose (natural ability). Methodists agreed somewhat but noted that human beings universally have an actual freedom to repent and believe. Finney, as we have seen, extended these themes further. In sum, the further we move away from the First Great Awakening, the more we see revivalists emphasizing themes that stress the universal reach of the gospel message.

Third, we see a trajectory away from lengthy conversions to quick conversions. Conversions in the First Great Awakening were lengthy events usually preceded by a long runway of preparation that included thorough conviction, the application of the means of grace, and prayerful waiting for God to give a new heart.

This conversion theology, forged by English Puritans, was well suited to the ordinary rhythms of church ministry in which individuals converted under the preaching and shepherding of a local minister who they saw week after week. With the appearance of extraordinary revivals and passionate preaching by itinerant ministers, who were only in an area for a short time, the gravity shifted to conversions taking place during the revival event. This, coupled with new theological emphases, such as immediate repentance and the increasing popularity of the freedom of the will, ensured that quicker conversions would become more of the norm among American evangelicals.

Last, we see a trajectory away from revival theology that is deeply informed by systematic theological constructs toward more of a practical, common-sense approach to revival theology. The revivals and conversions of the First Great Awakening were held in a context that was deeply saturated by American Puritan tradition, which prized the intricacies of the Reformed faith. Jumping ahead a century, we find many American evangelicals entertaining a different mood, one that was willing to discard sophisticated theological systems of the past and embrace a more practical view of God and his relationship with the world. We saw this sentiment appearing in several of the revival theologies surveyed in the Second Great Awakening: Methodists rejecting the predestinarian conundrums of Calvinism for a more easily graspable vision of the interplay between God's love and human liberty; Finney bypassing the mysteries of spiritual inability in order to call sinners to immediate repentance; and Campbell abandoning the emotionalism of modern revivals altogether for a practical conversion theology that emphasized the simple order of belief, repentance, and baptism. While there were those who still advanced the older views, we increasingly find revivalists and theologians embracing a simpler conversion theology that cohered with good common sense.

AFTER THE SECOND GREAT AWAKENING

After the Second Great Awakening there were no major developments in the history of American revival theology similar to the changes that took place between 1740 and 1840. While revivals were still a part of America's religious landscape after the Civil War, newer, comprehensive systems of revival theology did not emerge that furthered the discussions noted above. Why is this? The reasons are complex, and a full answer is beyond the scope of this study. But we can note a few brief observations.

First, in the latter third of the nineteenth century many American evangelicals increasingly came to abandon the life of the mind. While they definitely were not anti-intellectual by any means, American evangelicals did disengage from the academy.[1] This, of course, was not completely their fault, as Western intellectual life was growing increasingly secular and hostile to traditional Christian faith and as intellectual elites increasingly marginalized Christian voices. But evangelical disengagement from the academy was a real event in the latter part of the nineteenth century. Thus the robust theologies of revival, which grew out of thoughtful, trained theologians in the churches and seminaries from 1740 to 1840, did not, by 1900, continue in this new era of academic disengagement.

Second, the two most visible intellectual traditions that existed among American evangelicals in the middle of the nineteenth century—the Edwardsean Congregationalists and the Princeton Presbyterians—did not pass on the torch of interest in revival theology to later generations. The Princeton theology, as we have seen, was a rich theological heritage that proudly defended Reformed Presbyterianism from secular criticism, most notably defending the inerrancy of Scripture and responding to naturalistic Darwinism. But because they were Old School Presbyterians, they were known more for criticism of modern revivalism rather than for cautious advocacy of moderate evangelical revival theology. By contrast, the Edwardsean theological heritage, which was very pro-revival, essentially dropped off the radar by 1900. This stunning disappearance was basically the result of decades of infighting among different Edwardsean subgroups in the 1830s to 1850s, only to be followed by the wholesale takeover of most Edwardsean seminaries by liberalism toward the century's end.

The result is that, since the Civil War, American evangelicals have not continued advancing discussions related to the nature of revival theology, which is defined as the combination of soteriology, evangelistic preaching methods, and conversion expectations. Even though evangelicals have reengaged the academy in recent generations, few theologians or revivalists have cultivated a robust, systematic revival theology in the way Edwards, Hopkins, Taylor, or even Finney did.[2] Today, revivals are practiced and conducted; yet rarely are they the topic of mature theological consideration.

---

[1] See Mark A. Noll, *The Scandal of the Evangelical Mind* (Grand Rapids: Eerdmans, 1994).
[2] Though see Richard F. Lovelace, *Dynamics of Spiritual Life: An Evangelical Theology of Renewal* (Downers Grove, IL: InterVarsity Press, 1979).

Is there a need for revival theology today? Most evangelicals would indeed welcome a great move of God's Holy Spirit in our churches. As the march of secularization continues, revivalists and ministers will have plenty of material to fill their sermons with cultural critique. Spiritual and cultural decline is indeed the great theme revivalists use to get sinners' attention when they begin preaching the gospel. Yet more may be needed than merely an arsenal of criticisms and a basic understanding of the gospel. A robust revival theology, one that intimately unites head and heart, Scripture, proclamation, and life, would certainly help galvanize preaching, capture the religious imagination of the lost, and aid in imparting a theological vision that draws sinners to life and raises up God-glorifying disciples.

As a young Jonathan Edwards was completing the last stage of his formal theological training—a two-year tutorship at Yale College—his attentions had for some time been turning away from scientific and philosophical pursuits toward the more sublime subject of God and his ways with humankind. On February 12, 1725, he penned these words in his journal: "The very thing I now want, to give me a clearer and more immediate view of the perfections and glory of God, *is as clear a knowledge of the manner of God's exerting himself, with respect to spirits and mind*, as I have, of his operations concerning matter and bodies."[3] How does God "exert himself" in people's minds and spirits? Edwards wanted to know this deeply, thoroughly, exhaustively. Consequently, he embarked on a lifelong study of this topic, producing penetrating treatises and searching sermons as well as counseling saints and sinners with spiritual sensitivity and wisdom. We would do well to go and do likewise.

---

[3]Jonathan Edwards, "Personal Narrative," in *Letters and Personal Writings*, ed. George S. Claghorn, WJE 16 (New Haven, CT: Yale University Press, 1998), 787, emphasis added.

BIBLIOGRAPHY

PRIMARY SOURCES

Alexander, Archibald. "The Early History of Pelagianism." *Biblical Repertory and Theological Review* 2 (1830): 77-113.

———. "The Inability of Sinners." In *Princeton Versus the New Divinity*, 114-40. Carlisle, PA: Banner of Truth, 2001.

———. *Thoughts on Religious Experience*. Philadelphia: Presbyterian Board, 1841.

Asbury, Francis. *Journal of Rev. Francis Asbury: Bishop of the Methodist Episcopal Church*. 3 vols. Vol. 1, New York: Eaton & Mains, 1852. Vols. 2 and 3, Lane & Scott, 1852.

Bangs, Nathan. *The Errors of Hopkinsianism Detected and Refuted*. New York: John C. Totten, 1815.

Barnes, Albert. *The Way of Salvation*. 7th ed. New York: Leavitt, Lord, 1836.

Bellamy, Joseph. *A Blow at the Root of the Refined Antinomianism of the Present Age*. In *The Works of Joseph Bellamy, D.D.*, 1:491-525. Boston: Doctrinal Tract and Book Society, 1853.

———. *Remarks on the Revd. Mr. Croswell's Letter to the Reverend Mr. Cumming*. Boston: S. Kneeland, 1763.

———. *Theron, Paulinus, and Aspasio; Or, Letters and Dialogues upon the Nature of Love to God, Faith in Christ, Assurance of a Title to Eternal Life*. In *The Works of Joseph Bellamy, D.D.*, 2:161-267. Boston: Doctrinal Tract and Book Society, 1853.

———. *True Religion Delineated; Or, Experimental Religion, as Distinguished from Formality on the One Hand, and Enthusiasm on the Other, Set in a Scriptural and Rational Light*. In *The Works of Joseph Bellamy, D.D.*, 1:3-361. Boston: Doctrinal Tract and Book Society, 1853.

Blair, Samuel. *The Doctrine of Predestination Truly and Fairly Stated*. Philadelphia: B. Franklin, 1742.

———. *The Gospel Method of Salvation*. New York: William Bradford, 1737.

———. *A Persuasive to Repentance: A Sermon Preached at Philadelphia, Anno 1739*. Philadelphia: W. Bradford, 1743.

———. *A Short and Faithful Narrative, of the Late Remarkable Revival of Religion in the Congregation of New-Londonderry, and Other Parts of Pennsylvania.* Philadelphia: William Bradford, 1744.

Boyce, James Petigru. *Abstract of Systematic Theology.* Philadelphia: American Baptist Publication Society, 1887.

Buell, Samuel. *A Faithfull Narrative of the Remarkable Revival of Religion in the Congregation of East Hampton on Long-Island.* Aberdeen: 1773.

Campbell, Alexander. "Address to the Readers of the Christian Baptist, No. IV." In *The Christian Baptist,* edited by Alexander Campbell, 1:144-50. Buffalo, VA: A. Campbell, 1827. Reprint, Nashville: Gospel Advocate Company, 1955.

———. *The Christian System, in reference to the Union of Christians, and a Restoration of Primitive Christianity, as pleaded in the Current Reformation.* London: Simpkin, Marshall, 1843.

———. *The Writings of Alexander Campbell, Selections from the Millennial Harbinger.* Edited by W. A. Morris. Austin, TX: Eugene Von Boeckmann, 1896.

Cartwright, Peter. *Autobiography of Peter Cartwright: The Backwoods Preacher.* New York: Carlton & Porter, 1857.

Colman, Benjamin. *A Letter From the Reverend Dr. Colman of Boston, To the Reverend Mr. Williams of Lebanon, Upon Reading the Confession and Retractations of the Reverend Mr. James Davenport.* Boston: G. Rogers and D. Fowle, 1744.

———. *The Wither'd Hand Stretched Forth at the Command of Christ, and Restored.* 2nd ed. Boston: J. Draper, 1740.

Cooper, William. *The Doctrine of Predestination Unto Life, Explained and Vindicated.* Boston: J. Draper, 1740.

Croswell, Andrew. *An Answer to the Rev. Mr. Garden's Three First Letters to the Rev. Mr. Whitefield.* Boston: S. Kneeland and T. Green, 1741.

———. *Free Justification Through Christ's Redemption.* Boston: T. & J. Fleet and Green & Russell, 1765.

———. *Heaven Shut Against All Arminians and Antinomians.* Boston: Rogers and Fowle, 1747.

———. *The Heavenly Doctrine of Man's Justification Only by the Obedience of Jesus Christ.* Boston: Green and Russell, 1758.

———. *A Letter to the Reverend Alexander Cumming.* Boston: D. and J. Kneeland, 1762.

———. *Mr. Croswell's Reply to a Book Lately Publish'd, Entitled, A Display of God's Special Grace.* Boston: Rogers and Fowle, 1742.

———. *A Second Defence of the Old Protestant Doctrine of Justifying Faith.* Boston: Rogers and Fowle, 1747.

————. *What Is Christ to Me, If He Is Not Mine?* Boston: Rogers and Fowle, 1745.

Dagg, John L. *Manual of Theology.* Philadelphia: American Baptist Publication Society, 1857.

Davies, Samuel. *Sermons on Important Subjects.* 3 vols. New York: Robert Carter, 1845.

Dickinson, Jonathan. *A Display of God's Special Grace.* In *Sermons and Tracts, Separately Published at Boston, Philadelphia, etc.,* 379-446. Edinburgh: M. Gray, 1793.

————. *Familiar Letters to a Gentleman, upon A Variety of Seasonable and Important Subjects in Religion.* 3rd ed. Edinburgh: R. Fleming, 1757.

————. "The Nature and Necessity of Regeneration, Considered in a Sermon from John iii.3." In *Sermons and Tracts, Separately Published at Boston, Philadelphia, etc.,* 323-78. Edinburgh: M. Gray, 1793.

————. *The True Scripture Doctrine Concerning Some Important Points of Christian Faith.* In *Sermons and Tracts, Separately Published at Boston, Philadelphia, etc.,* 105-296. Edinburgh: M. Gray, 1793.

————. "The Witness of the Spirit, A Sermon Preached at Newark in New-Jersey, May 7, 1740." In *Sermons and Tracts, Separately Published at Boston, Philadelphia, etc.,* 297-322. Edinburgh: M. Gray, 1793.

Dwight, Timothy. *Theology Explained and Defended in a Series of Sermons.* 4 vols. New Haven, CT: S. Converse, 1823.

Edwards, Jonathan. *An Account of the Life of the Reverend Mr. David Brainerd.* In *The Life of David Brainerd,* edited by Norman Pettit. WJE 7. New Haven, CT: Yale University Press, 1984.

————. *Dissertation I. Concerning the End for Which God Created the World.* In *Ethical Writings,* edited by Paul Ramsey, 405-526. WJE 8. New Haven, CT: Yale University Press, 1989.

————. "Efficacious Grace." In *Writings on the Trinity, Grace, and Faith,* edited by Sang Hyun Lee, 198-290. WJE 21. New Haven, CT: Yale University Press, 2002.

————. *A Faithful Narrative of the Surprising Work of God in the Conversions of Hundreds of Souls in Northampton.* In *The Great Awakening,* edited by C. C. Goen, 144-211. WJE 4. New Haven, CT: Yale University Press, 1972.

————. *Freedom of the Will.* In *Freedom of the Will,* edited by Paul Ramsey. WJE 1. New Haven, CT: Yale University Press, 1957.

————. *The Great Christian Doctrine of Original Sin Defended.* In *Original Sin,* edited by Clyde A. Holbrook. WJE 3. New Haven, CT: Yale University Press, 1970.

————. "The Mind." In *Scientific and Philosophical Writings,* edited by Wallace E. Anderson, 332-93. WJE 6. New Haven, CT: Yale University Press, 1980.

————. *The "Miscellanies," (Entry Nos. 501-832).* Edited by Ava Chamberlain. WJE 18. New Haven, CT: Yale University Press, 2000.

———. *The "Miscellanies," (Entry Nos. a-z, aa-zz, 1-500)*. Edited by Thomas A. Schafer. WJE 13. New Haven, CT: Yale University Press, 1994.

———. "Personal Narrative." In *Letters and Personal Writings*, edited by George S. Claghorn, 790-804. WJE 16. New Haven, CT: Yale University Press, 1998.

———. *Religious Affections*. In *Religious Affections*, edited by John E. Smith. WJE 2. New Haven, CT: Yale University Press, 1959.

———. *Sermons and Discourses, 1730–1733*. Edited by Mark Valeri. WJE 17. New Haven, CT: Yale University Press, 1999.

———. *Sermons and Discourses, 1734–1738*. Edited by M. X. Lesser. WJE 19. New Haven, CT: Yale University Press, 2001.

Edwards, Jonathan, Jr. "Remarks on the Improvements Made in Theology by His Father, President Edwards." In *The Works of Jonathan Edwards, D.D.*, edited by Tryon Edwards, 1:481-92. Andover, MA: Allen, Morrill & Wardwell, 1842.

———. "Three Sermons on the Necessity of Atonement, and the Consistency Between That and Free Grace in Forgiveness." In *The Atonement: Discourses and Treatises*, edited by Edwards Amasa Park, 1-42. Boston: Congregational Board of Publication, 1859.

Emmons, Nathanael. *The Works of Nathanael Emmons, D.D.* Edited by Jacob Ide. 6 vols. Boston: Crocker & Brewster, 1842.

Finney, Charles G. *Lectures on Revivals of Religion*. New York: Leavitt, Lord, 1835.

———. *Lectures on Systematic Theology*. 2 vols. Oberlin, OH: James M. Fitch, 1846–1847.

———. *Lectures to Professing Christians*. New York: John S. Taylor, 1837.

———. *The Memoirs of Charles G. Finney: The Complete Restored Text*. Edited by Garth M. Rosell and Richard A. G. Dupuis. Grand Rapids: Academie Books, 1989.

———. *Reflections on Revival by Charles G. Finney*. Compiled by Donald W. Dayton. Minneapolis: Bethany Fellowship, 1979.

———. *Sermons on Important Subjects*. New York: John S. Taylor, 1836.

———. *Skeletons of a Course of Theological Lectures*. Oberlin, OH: James Steele, 1840.

Fisher, Edward. *The Marrow of Modern Divinity: In Two Parts*. Edited by Thomas Boston. London: Thomas Tegg and Son, 1837.

Garrettson, Freeborn. *American Methodist Pioneer: The Life and Journals of the Rev. Freeborn Garrettson, 1752–1827*. Edited by Robert Drew Simpson. Rutland, VT: Academy Books, 1984.

Griffin, Edward Dorr. *The Doctrine of Divine Efficiency, Defended against Certain Modern Speculations*. New York: Jonathan Leavitt, 1833.

———. *A Series of Lectures, Delivered in Park Street Church, Boston, on Sabbath Evening*. Boston: Nathaniel Willis, 1813.

————. *Sermons by the Late Rev. Edward D. Griffin, D.D.* Edited by William B. Sprague. 2 vols. New York: John S. Taylor, 1839.

————. *Sermons, Not Before Published, on Various Practical Subjects.* New York: M. W. Dodd, 1844.

H. E. "Observations on Being Made Sinners by Adam, and Righteous by Christ." *The Connecticut Evangelical Magazine* (March 1805): 341-46.

Heaton, Hannah. *The World of Hannah Heaton: The Diary of an Eighteenth-Century New England Farm Woman.* Edited by Barbara E. Lacey. DeKalb: Northern Illinois University Press, 2003.

Hervey, James. *Theron and Aspasio, Or, A Series of Dialogues and Letters, upon the Most Important and Interesting Subjects.* London: John and James Rivington, 1755.

Hodge, Charles. "Bushnell on Christian Nurture." In *Essays and Reviews*, 303-40. New York: Robert Carter & Brothers, 1857.

————. "Finney's Lectures on Theology." In *Essays and Reviews*, 245-84. New York: Robert Carter & Brothers, 1857.

————. "The New Divinity Tried." *Biblical Repertory and Theological Review* 4 (1832): 278-304.

————. "Of an Article in the June number of the Christian Spectator, entitled, 'Inquiries Respecting the Doctrine of Imputation.'" *Biblical Repertory and Theological Review* 2 (1830): 425-72.

————. "Regeneration." In *Essays and Reviews*, 1-48. New York: Robert Carter & Brothers, 1857.

————. *The Way of Life.* Edited by Mark A. Noll. Sources of American Spirituality. New York: Paulist Press, 1987.

Hopkins, Samuel. *An Inquiry Concerning the Promises of the Gospel.* In *The Works of Samuel Hopkins, D.D.*, 3:185-275. Boston: Doctrinal Tract and Book Society, 1852.

————. *An Inquiry into the Nature of True Holiness.* In *The Works of Samuel Hopkins, D.D.*, 3:9-141. Boston: Doctrinal Tract and Book Society, 1852.

————. *Sketches of the Life of the Late Rev. Samuel Hopkins, D. D., Pastor of the First Congregational Church in Newport.* Hartford, CT: Hudson and Goodwin, 1805.

————. *System of Doctrines.* In *The Works of Samuel Hopkins, D.D.*, vol. 1 and 2:3-221. Boston: Doctrinal Tract and Book Society, 1852.

————. *The True State and Character of the Unregenerate.* In *The Works of Samuel Hopkins, D.D.*, 3:279-497. Boston: Doctrinal Tract and Book Society, 1852.

Johnson, William B. "Love Characteristic of the Deity." In *Southern Baptist Sermons on Sovereignty and Responsibility*, edited by Thomas J. Nettles, 39-64. Harrisonburg, VA: Gano Books, 1984.

Knowles, James D. *Memoir of Mrs. Ann H. Judson, Late Missionary to Burmah.* 3rd ed. Boston: Lincoln & Edmands, 1829.

Lee, Jesse. *Memoir of the Rev. Jesse Lee.* Edited by Minton Thrift. New York: Meyers & Smith, 1823.

Leland, John. "Letter of Valediction, on Leaving Virginia, in 1791." In *The Writings of the Late Elder John Leland,* 171-78. New York: G. W. Wood, 1845.

A Letter to the Rev. J. Butler, Containing a Review of his "Friendly Letters to a Lady;" Together with a General Outline of the Doctrine of the Freewill Baptists. Limerick, ME: W. Burr, 1832.

Maxcy, Jonathan. "A Discourse Designed to Explain the Doctrine of the Atonement." In *Sermons, Essays, and Extracts, by Various Authors: Selected with Special Respect to the Great Doctrine of Atonement,* 179-212. New York: George Forman, 1811.

McGready, James. *The Posthumous Works of the Reverend and Pious James M'Gready.* 2 vols. Louisville: W. W. Worsley, 1831.

Mell, Patrick H. *Predestination and the Saints' Perseverance.* Charleston, SC: Southern Baptist Publication Society, 1851.

Mercer, Jesse. Letter III of "Mercer's Letters to White on the Atonement." *Columbian Star and Christian Index* 3 (1830): 259-60.

Methodist Episcopal Church. *The Arminian Magazine: Consisting of Extracts and Original Treatises on General Redemption.* 2 vols. Philadelphia: Prichard and Hall, 1789.

———. *The Doctrines and Discipline of the Methodist Episcopal Church.* New York: B. Waugh and T. Mason, 1832.

———. *Minutes of Several Conversations Between the Rev. Thomas Coke, LL. D., the Rev. Francis Asbury and Others.* Philadelphia: Charles Cist, 1785.

"The Miserable End of an Apostate." *Methodist Magazine* 3 (1820): 347-51.

Owen, John. *Pneumatologia, or A Discourse Concerning the Holy Spirit.* Edited by William H. Goold. London: Johnstone and Hunter, 1852.

Park, Edwards Amasa. "The Rise of the Edwardean Theory of the Atonement: An Introductory Essay." In *The Atonement: Discourses and Treatises,* edited by Edwards Amasa Park, vii-lxxx. Boston: Congregational Board of Publication, 1859.

Pemberton, Ebenezer. *Practical Discourses on Various Texts.* Boston: T. Fleet, 1741.

Prince, Thomas. *The Christian History, Containing Accounts of the Revival and Propagation of Religion in Great-Britain and America, For the Year 1743.* Boston: S. Kneeland and T. Green, 1744.

Ralston, Thomas Neely. *Elements of Divinity.* Louisville: Morton & Griswold, 1847.

Scott, Walter. *The Gospel Restored, A Discourse of the True Gospel of Jesus Christ.* Cincinnati: O. H. Donogh, 1836.

Sewall, Joseph. *The Holy Spirit Convincing the World of Sin, of Righteousness, and of Judgment.* Boston: J. Draper, 1741.

Shinn, Asa. *An Essay on the Plan of Salvation.* Baltimore: Neal, Wills and Cole, 1813.

Smalley, John. "Justification Through Christ, an Act of Free Grace." In *The Atonement: Discourses and Treatises*, edited by Edwards Amasa Park, 43-64. Boston: Congregational Board of Publication, 1859.

————. *Sermons, on a Number of Connected Subjects.* Hartford, CT: Lincoln and Gleason, 1803.

Spring, Gardiner. *Memoir of Samuel John Mills.* Boston: Perkins & Marvin, 1829.

Stone, Barton W. *The Biography of Eld. Barton Warren Stone.* Cincinnati: J. A. & U. P. James, 1847.

Strong, Nathan. *Sermons, on Various Subjects, Doctrinal, Experimental and Practical.* Hartford, CT: Hudson and Goodwin, 1798.

Taylor, John. *The Scripture Doctrine of Original Sin.* 3rd ed. London: J. Waugh, 1750.

Taylor, Nathaniel W. *Concio ad Clerum: A Sermon Delivered in the Chapel of Yale College, September 10, 1828.* New Haven, CT: A. H. Maltby and Homan Hallock, 1842.

————. *Essays on the Means of Regeneration.* New Haven, CT: Baldwin and Treadway, 1829.

————. "The Sinner's Duty to Make Himself a New Heart." In *Practical Sermons*, 397-412. New York: Clark, Austin, and Smith, 1858.

Tennent, Gilbert, Samuel Blair, John Blair, William Tennent Jr., John Tennent, Robert Smith, and Samuel Finley. *Sermons and Essays by the Tennents and Their Contemporaries.* Philadelphia: Presbyterian Board of Publication, 1855.

Treffry, R. "A Sermon on Christian Perfection." *Methodist Magazine* 5 (1822): 81-90.

Tyler, Bennet. *Letters on the Origin and Progress of the New Haven Theology.* New York: Robert Carter and Ezra Collier, 1837.

————. *Nettleton and His Labours: Being the Memoir of Dr. Nettleton.* Edinburgh: T&T Clark, 1854.

Webb, John. *Christ's Suit to the Sinner, While He Stands and Knocks at the Door.* Boston: S. Kneeland and T. Green, 1741.

West, Stephen. *Scripture Doctrine of Atonement: Proposed to Careful Examination.* 2nd ed. Stockbridge, MA: Herald Office, 1809.

Whitefield, George. *George Whitefield's Journals.* London: Banner of Truth Trust, 1965.

————. *The Sermons of George Whitefield.* Edited by Lee Gatiss. 2 vols. The Reformed Evangelical Anglican Library 1.1. Stoke-on-Trent, UK: Tentmaker Publications, 2010.

Williams, Solomon. *A Vindication of the Gospel-Doctrine of Justifying Faith.* Boston: Rogers and Fowle, 1746.

SECONDARY SOURCES

Ahlstrom, Sydney A. *A Religious History of the American People*. 2nd ed. New Haven, CT: Yale University Press, 2004.

Baird, Robert. *Religion in America*. New York: Harper & Brothers, 1856.

Bebbington, David W. *Evangelicalism in Modern Britain: A History from the 1730s to the 1980s*. London: Unwin Hyman, 1989. Reprint, New York: Routledge, 2005.

Bennett, David. *The Altar Call: Its Origins and Present Usage*. Lanham, MD: University Press of America, 2000.

Boles, John B. *The Great Revival, 1787–1805: The Origins of the Southern Evangelical Mind*. Lexington: University Press of Kentucky, 1972.

Bozeman, Theodore Dwight. *The Precisianist Strain: Disciplinary Religion and Antinomian Backlash in Puritanism to 1638*. Chapel Hill: University of North Carolina Press, 2004.

Bratt, James D. *Antirevivalism in Antebellum America: A Collection of Religious Voices*. Piscataway, NJ: Rutgers University Press, 2006.

Breitenbach, William. "The Consistent Calvinism of the New Divinity Movement." *The William and Mary Quarterly* 41, no. 2 (1984): 241-64.

———. "Unregenerate Doings: Selflessness and Selfishness in New Divinity Theology." *American Quarterly* 34 (1982): 479-502.

Bryant, Scott. *The Awakening of the Freewill Baptists: Benjamin Randall and the Founding of an American Religious Tradition*. Macon, GA: Mercer University Press, 2011.

Burkitt, Lemuel, and Jesse Read. *A Concise History of the Kehukee Baptist Association*. Tarborough, NC: George Howard, 1834.

Bush, Charles P. *Reminiscences of Rev. Charles G. Finney*. Oberlin, OH: E. J. Goodrich, 1876.

Buzzell, John. *The Life of Elder Benjamin Randall Principally Taken from Documents Written by Himself*. Limerick, ME: Hobbs, Woodman, 1827.

Carwardine, Richard. *Transatlantic Revivalism: Popular Evangelicalism in Britain and America, 1790–1865*. Westport, CT: Greenwood Press, 1978.

Chute, Anthony. *A Piety Above a Common Standard: Jesse Mercer and Evangelistic Calvinism*. Macon, GA: Mercer University Press, 2004.

Chute, Anthony L., Nathan A. Finn, and Michael A. G. Haykin. *The Baptist Story: From English Sect to Global Movement*. Nashville: B&H Academic, 2015.

Coalter, Milton J. *Gilbert Tennent, Son of Thunder: A Case Study of Continental Pietism's Impact on the First Great Awakening in the Middle Colonies*. Contributions to the Study of Religion 18. New York: Greenwood Press, 1986.

Conforti, Joseph A. *Samuel Hopkins and the New Divinity Movement: Calvinism, the*

Congregational Ministry, and Reform in New England Between the Great Awakenings. Grand Rapids: Christian University Press, 1981.

Crawford, Michael J., ed. "The Spiritual Travels of Nathan Cole." *William and Mary Quarterly* 33, no. 1 (1976): 89-126.

Crisp, Oliver D. "Non-penal Substitution." *International Journal of Systematic Theology* 9 (2007): 415-433.

Crisp, Oliver D., and Douglas A. Sweeney, eds. *After Jonathan Edwards: The Courses of the New England Theology.* New York: Oxford University Press, 2012.

Fisher, George Park. "The Augustinian and the Federal Theories of Original Sin Compared." In *Discussions in History and Theology,* 355-409. New York: Scribner, 1880.

Garrett, James Leo. *Baptist Theology: A Four-Century Study.* Macon, GA: Mercer University Press, 2009.

Gatiss, Lee. "Introduction." In *The Sermons of George Whitefield,* edited by Lee Gatiss, 1:13-44. The Reformed Evangelical Anglican Library 1.1. Stoke-on-Trent, UK: Tentmaker Publications, 2010.

Gaustad, Edwin Scott, and Philip L. Barlow. *New Historical Atlas of Religion in America.* New York: Oxford University Press, 2001.

Goen, C. C. *Revivalism and Separatism in New England, 1740–1800.* New Haven, CT: Yale University Press, 1962.

Guelzo, Allen C. *Edwards on the Will: A Century of American Theological Debate.* Middleton, CT: Wesleyan University Press, 1989.

———. "Freedom of the Will." In *The Princeton Companion to Jonathan Edwards,* edited by Sang Hyun Lee, 115-29. Princeton, NJ: Princeton University Press, 2005.

———. "An Heir or a Rebel? Charles Grandison Finney and the New England Theology." *Journal of the Early Republic* 17 (1997): 61-94.

Gutjahr, Paul C. *Charles Hodge: Guardian of American Orthodoxy.* New York: Oxford University Press, 2011.

Hambrick-Stowe, Charles E. *Charles G. Finney and the Spirit of American Evangelicalism.* Library of Religious Biography. Grand Rapids: Eerdmans, 1996.

Hankins, Barry. *The Second Great Awakening and the Transcendentalists.* Westport, CT: Greenwood Press, 2004.

Hardman, Keith J. *Charles Grandison Finney, 1792–1875: Revivalist and Reformer.* Syracuse, NY: Syracuse University Press, 1987. Reprint, Grand Rapids: Baker, 1990.

Harper, George W. *A People So Favored of God: Boston's Congregational Churches and Their Pastors, 1710–1760.* Lanham, MD: University Press of America, 2004.

Hempton, David. *Methodism: Empire of the Spirit.* New Haven, CT: Yale University Press, 2005.

Hindmarsh, D. Bruce. *The Evangelical Conversion Narrative: Spiritual Autobiography in Early Modern England*. New York: Oxford University Press, 2008.

Hoffecker, W. Andrew. *Charles Hodge: The Pride of Princeton*. Phillipsburg, NJ: P&R, 2011.

———. *Piety and the Princeton Theologians*. Phillipsburg, NJ: P&R, 1981.

Holifield, E. Brooks. *Theology in America: Christian Thought from the Age of the Puritans to the Civil War*. New Haven, CT: Yale University Press, 2003.

Howe, Daniel Walker. *What Hath God Wrought: The Transformation of America, 1815–1848*. New York: Oxford University Press, 2009.

Jauhiainen, Peter. "Samuel Hopkins and Hopkinsianism." In *After Jonathan Edwards: The Courses of the New England Theology*, edited by Oliver D. Crisp and Douglas A. Sweeney, 107-17. New York: Oxford University Press, 2012.

Jones, Mark. *Antinomianism: Reformed Theology's Unwelcome Guest?* Phillipsburg, NJ: P&R, 2013.

Kidd, Thomas S. *George Whitefield: America's Spiritual Founding Father*. New Haven, CT: Yale University Press, 2014.

———. *The Great Awakening: The Roots of Evangelical Christianity in North America*. New Haven, CT: Yale University Press, 2007.

Kidd, Thomas S., and Barry Hankins. *Baptists in America: A History*. New York: Oxford University Press, 2015.

Kling, David W. *A Field of Divine Wonders: The New Divinity and Village Revivals in Northwestern Connecticut, 1792–1822*. University Park: Pennsylvania State University Press, 1993.

———. "The New Divinity and the Origins of the American Board of Commissioners for Foreign Missions." *Church History* 72, no. 4 (2003): 791-819.

———. "The New Divinity and Williams College, 1793–1836." *Religion and American Culture: A Journal of Interpretation* 6, no. 2 (1996): 195-223.

———. "New Divinity Schools of the Prophets, 1750–1825: A Case Study in Ministerial Education." *History of Education Quarterly* 37, no. 2 (1997): 185-206.

Kuklick, Bruce. *Churchmen and Philosophers: From Jonathan Edwards to John Dewey*. New Haven, CT: Yale University Press, 1985.

Kurka, Robert C. "The Role of the Holy Spirit in Conversion: Why Restorationists Appear to Be Out of the Evangelical Mainstream." In *Evangelicalism and the Stone-Campbell Movement*, edited by William R. Baker, 138-51. Downers Grove, IL: InterVarsity Press, 2002.

Lambert, Frank. *Inventing the "Great Awakening."* Princeton, NJ: Princeton University Press, 1999.

Lebeau, Bryan F. *Jonathan Dickinson and the Formative Years of American Presbyterianism*. Lexington: University Press of Kentucky, 1997.

Lovelace, Richard F. *Dynamics of Spiritual Life: An Evangelical Theology of Renewal.* Downers Grove, IL: InterVarsity Press, 1979.

Lumpkin, William L. *Baptist Foundations in the South: Tracing Through the Separates the Influence of the Great Awakening, 1754–1787.* Nashville: Broadman, 1961.

Madueme, Hans, and Michael Reeves, eds. *Adam, the Fall, and Original Sin.* Grand Rapids: Baker Academic, 2014.

Marsden, George M. *The Evangelical Mind and the New School Presbyterian Experience: A Case Study of Thought and Theology in Nineteenth-Century America.* New Haven, CT: Yale University Press, 1970.

———. *Jonathan Edwards: A Life.* New Haven, CT: Yale University Press, 2003.

McBeth, H. Leon. *The Baptist Heritage.* Nashville: Broadman, 1987.

McDermott, Gerald R., and Michael J. McClymond. *The Theology of Jonathan Edwards.* New York: Oxford University Press, 2012.

Noll, Mark A. *America's God: From Jonathan Edwards to Abraham Lincoln.* New York: Oxford University Press, 2002.

———. *The Rise of Evangelicalism: The Age of Edwards, Whitefield and the Wesleys.* Downers Grove, IL: IVP Academic, 2003.

Rack, Henry D. *Reasonable Enthusiast: John Wesley and the Rise of Methodism.* 3rd ed. London: Epworth, 2002.

Ramsey, Paul. "Editor's Introduction." In *Freedom of the Will*, edited by Paul Ramsey, 1-128. WJE 1. New Haven, CT: Yale University Press, 1957.

Rawlyk, G. A. *Ravished by the Spirit: Religious Revivals, Baptists, and Henry Alline.* Kingston, ON: McGill-Queen's University Press, 1984.

Richey, Russell E. *Methodism in the American Forest.* New York: Oxford University Press, 2015.

Rogers, Mark. "Edward Dorr Griffin and the Edwardsian Second Great Awakening." PhD diss., Trinity Evangelical Divinity School, 2012.

Rudisill, Dorus Paul. *The Doctrine of the Atonement in Jonathan Edwards and His Successors.* New York: Poseidon Books, 1971.

Schmidt, Jeanne Miller, Russell E. Richey, and Kenneth E. Rowe. *American Methodism: A Compact History.* Nashville: Abingdon Press, 2012.

Schmidt, Leigh Eric. "'A Second and Glorious Reformation': The New Light Extremism of Andrew Croswell." *The William and Mary Quarterly* 43, no. 2 (1986): 214-44.

Shipton, Clifford Kenyon. "Andrew Croswell." In *Sibley's Harvard Graduates: Biographical Sketches of Those Who Attended Harvard College*, 8:386-407. Cambridge: Massachusetts Historical Society, 1951.

Smith, H. Shelton. *Changing Conceptions of Original Sin: A Study in American Theology Since 1750.* New York: Scribner, 1955.

Smith, John Howard. *The Perfect Rule of the Christian Religion: A History of Sandemanianism in the Eighteenth Century*. Albany: State University Press of New York, 2008.

Snyder, Robert Arthur. "William T. Brantly (1787–1845): A Southern Unionist and the Breakup of the Triennial Convention." PhD diss., The Southern Baptist Theological Seminary, 2005.

Stewart, I. D. *The History of the Freewill Baptists*. 2 vols. Dover, NH: William Burr, 1862.

Sweeney, Douglas A. *Nathaniel Taylor, New Haven Theology, and the Legacy of Jonathan Edwards*. New York: Oxford University Press, 2002.

Sweeney, Douglas A., and Allen C. Guelzo, eds. *The New England Theology: From Jonathan Edwards to Edwards Amasa Park*. Grand Rapids: Baker Academic, 2006.

Tanis, James. *Dutch Calvinistic Pietism in the Middle Colonies: A Study of the Life and Theology of Theodorus Jacobus Frelinghuysen*. The Hague: Martinus Nijhoff, 1967.

Valeri, Mark. *Law and Providence in Joseph Bellamy's New England: The Origins of the New Divinity in Revolutionary America*. New York: Oxford University Press, 1994.

Wigger, John H. *American Saint: Francis Asbury and the Methodists*. New York: Oxford University Press, 2009.

———. *Taking Heaven by Storm: Methodism and the Rise of Popular Christianity in America*. New York: Oxford University Press, 1998.

Wiley, Tatha. *Original Sin: Origins, Developments, Contemporary Meanings*. New York: Paulist Press, 2002.

GENERAL INDEX

SCRIPTURE INDEX